COME–REAP
BIBLICAL STUDIES

VOLUME ONE
OLD TESTAMENT LAW

COME-REAP BIBLICAL STUDIES

VOLUME ONE
OLD TESTAMENT LAW

DR. CURT SCARBOROUGH

gatekeeper press™

Columbus, Ohio

COME-REAP Biblical Studies Volume One Old Testament Law

Published by Gatekeeper Press
2167 Stringtown Rd, Suite 109
Columbus, OH 43123-2989
www.GatekeeperPress.com

The editorial work for this book is entirely the product of the author. Gatekeeper Press did not participate in and is not responsible for any aspect of this elements.

Library of Congress Control Number: t/k

ISBN (paperback):
eISBN:

DEDICATION

To My Father
Curtis Clinton Scarborough
1909 – 1953
and to My Mother
Olive Keith Scarborough
1912 – 1998

Our Parents Gave
to My Sister, Marilyn Sue,
and to Me
Life's Greatest Legacy:
A Christian Home

Table of Contents

Volume One – Old Testament Law

Course #1 – Genesis

Course #2 – Exodus-Leviticus

Course #3 – Numbers-Deuteronomy

COME-REAP Biblical Study Methodology Course

Instructor: Dr. Curt Scarborough   Credit hours: Undergraduate -2; Graduate - 1

Course goals: To give students the rationale of the COME-REAP methodology and to give them the ability to analyze and outline any verse or verses in the Bible, including receiving revelation from the Holy Spirit and making applications for their own lives.

(Note: Students are not permitted to consult Bible commentaries or other references.)

Course Objectives: At the conclusion of this course, the student should be able to:

1. Study selected portions of Scripture to gain intellectual KNOWLEDGE (facts and information, truths and concepts). Write four full sentences stating what the selected Bible verses say.

2. Think about the intellectual knowledge learned in Step #1 to gain UNDERSTANDING (comprehension of the information, facts, truths, and ideas discovered through observation and experience). Meditate on the selected Scripture verses, and write four full sentences stating in their own words the truths that come to mind from this Scripture.

3. Pray to receive enlightenment from the Holy Spirit for intuitive DISCERNMENT (perception of godly principles and values that are related to Step #2). Ask for illumination to perceive revealed spiritual implications based on these Scripture-based truths and ideas. Be open to the Spirit's guidance to other related Bible verses to support these divine revelations. Write four complete sentences stating these revelations, along with citing any related Scripture references.

4. Apply spiritual WISDOM (here defined as KNOWLEDGE plus UNDERSTANDING plus DISCERNMENT . . . Steps #1, #2, and #3 above) to the personal circumstances and practical challenges of your life. From your written notes (above) write four full sentences applying the Meditations and Revelations to your own life by completing the sentence: "As a Christian, I need to . . ."

Class Requirements: See Assignments

Required Textbooks:
1. Holy Bible (Dr. Curt Scarborough's notes use the NKJV.)
2. COME-REAP Methodology Textbooks by Dr. Curt Scarborough

Method of Evaluation:
1. Satisfactory completion of the four written assignments on Genesis 12:1-3, Psalm 23:2-3, John 3:16, and Hebrews 12:1-2.
2. Mastery of the Guidelines for COME-REAP Teaching Outlines.
   (See Guidelines)
3. Final exam: Four complete outlines on Scripture verses: two selected by the instructor; two selected by the student.
4. Course grade will be awarded according to this schedule:
   20% for class participation
   20% for completion of the 4 practice outlines listed above
   60% for the final four outlines written under proctor's supervision

Rationale of the COME-REAP Methodology

CONCENTRATION PRODUCES KNOWLEDGE

Study selected portions of the Scripture to gain intellectual KNOWLEDGE (facts and information, truths and concepts). Write four full sentences stating what the selected Bible verses say. The student may either quote portions of the selected verses or paraphrase them.

MEDITATION BRINGS UNDERSTANDING

Think about the intellectual knowledge learned in step #1 to gain UNDERSTANDING (comprehension of the information, facts, truths, and ideas discovered through observation and experience). Meditate on the selected Scripture verses, and write four full sentences stating in your own words the truths that come to mind from this Scripture.

REVELATION INVOLVES DISCERNMENT

Pray to receive enlightenment from the Holy Spirit for intuitive DISCERNMENT (perception of godly principles and values that are related to step #2.) Ask for illumination to reveal some spiritual implications based on these Scripture-based truths and ideas. Be open to the Spirit's guidance to other related Bible verses to support these revelations. Write four complete sentences stating these divine revelations, along with citing any related Scripture references.

APPLICATION UTILIZES WISDOM

Apply spiritual WISDOM (defined here as knowledge plus understanding plus discernment . . . steps #1, #2, and #3) to the personal circumstances and practical solutions of your life. From your written notes (above) write four full sentences applying the Meditations and the Revelations to your own life by completing the sentence: "As a Christian, I need to . . ."

"COME-REAP"

(Ezekiel 40:4)

I. Concentration: on what the "Man" said to the prophet Ezekiel

1. "Son of man, look with your eyes, and hear with your ears," v. 4a.
2. "Fix your mind on everything I show you," v. 4b.
3. "You were brought here that I might show them to you," v. 4c.
4. "Declare to the house of Israel everything you see," v. 4d.

II. Meditation: on the basic steps of in-depth Bible study outlined here

1. Concentration: look and listen to the truths within the selected Scripture passages.
2. Meditation: set your heart on discerning the deeper spiritual meaning seen here.
3. Revelation: allow God's spirit to reveal insights and implications of truth.
4. Application: relate the truths and revelations to personal life and ministry.

III. Revelation: on the spiritual implications of Ezekiel 40:4

1. God speaks to His people: sometimes audibly, but usually through His word, II Tim. 3:16-17.
2. When God has a word for us, we must concentrate and meditate (look, hear, fix mind, and set heart) on understanding His message, II Tim. 2:15.
3. God wants to show (reveal) His will and way to those who diligently seek Him, Jas. 1:5.
4. God's purpose in revealing truth is more than personal edification and application (as beneficial as that may be) . . . He wants His people to share His revealed truths with others, II Tim. 2:2.

IV. Applications: as a Christian teacher, I need to . . .

1. Concentrate my mind on the word of God, diligently studying it every day.
2. Meditate on the deep truths of the Scripture passages that I read.
3. Receive the revelations from the Holy Spirit as I open to His anointed teaching.
4. Apply the revealed truths to my own life first; then teach others what I have learned and applied.

Observations: on the "COME-REAP" Bible study methodology

1. I have been using this simple method of Bible study for more than 50 years.
2. Originally the headings (Concentration, Meditation, Revelation, Applications) were chosen because they rhymed . . . as I asked and answered these questions:
   (1) What does the Bible say?
   (2) What does it mean?
   (3) What does it imply (under the Spirit's enlightenment)?
   (4) How do these truths apply to my own life and ministry?
3. The foundation verse for this method (Ezek. 40:4) came as I was experiencing a dramatic (444) breakthrough in my spiritual life on 6 February 1986.
4. The methodology name came in a 2-word "flash revelation" on 15 August 2011, upon which occasion the Lord showed me that the first two letters of the four main headings formed the words "COME-REAP" - Dr. Curt Scarborough

Guidelines for COME-REAP Teaching Outlines

<u>Give a title to each outline</u>

Title in 24 pts. Underlined, centered . . . all other copy in 12 pts.

Select a verse or verses to be studied, and write 4 full sentences stating what the passage says; you may quote portions of the Scripture selected or paraphrase it.

<u>**I. Concentration: on (the selected Scripture passage) . . . what does it say?**</u>

    1.

    2.

    3.

    4.

Then meditate on the selected Scripture verse(s), and write 4 full sentences stating the truths that come to mind from this Scripture, using the following structure:

<u>**II. Meditation: on the basic truths seen in these verses . . . what does it mean?**</u>

    1.

    2.

    3.

    4.

Pray for the Holy Spirit's illumination to reveal some spiritual implications based on these Scripture-based truths, and write 4 full sentences stating those revelations, using the following structure:

<u>**III. Revelation: on the spiritual implications seen in these verses**</u>

    1.

    2.

    3.

    4.

From your written notes above, write 4 full sentences applying the meditation and/or the revelations to your own life, using the following structure:

<u>**IV. Applications: as a Christian, I need to . . .**</u>

    1.

    2.

    3.

    4.

COME-REAP Assignments

Assignment One: Concentration

* *Study: The rationale on how the COME-REAP method works.*
* *Study: The COME-REAP teaching outline on Ezek. 40:4.*
* Write a main title for the study (24 pt. underlined) on <u>each</u> of these Scriptures.
    1. Genesis 12:1-3
    2. Psalm 23:2-3
    3. John 3:16
    4. Hebrews 12:1-2
* All other headings and sub-points in the teaching outlines are to be 12 pt.
* Write an underlined explanatory phrase stating the focus (<u>I. Concentration: on . . .</u>)
* Write 4 Concentration sub-points on <u>each</u> of the Scriptures listed above.
* Two possible methods are acceptable here (<u>What does it say?</u>):
    1. <u>Quote</u> parts of the selected Scripture verses (see sample: Matt. 1:20-121)
    2. <u>Paraphrase</u> parts of the selected Scripture verses (see sample: Lk. 2:46-47)
* E-mail the completed assignment to: drcurt@aiccs.org

Assignment Two: Meditation (on Gen. 12:1-3; Psa. 23:2-3; Jn. 3:16; Heb. 12:1-2)

* Write an explanatory phrase stating the focus of each study (<u>II. Meditation: on . . .</u>)
* Using the Concentration points in Assignment One above, write 4 Meditation
    sub-points on <u>each</u> of the assigned Scriptures (<u>What does it mean?</u>)
* Each Meditation sub-point (1, 2, 3, 4) must be connected with the same number of the
    Concentration sub-point above.
* E-mail the assignment to the: drcurt@aiccs.org

Assignment Three: Revelation (on Gen. 12:1-3; Psa. 23:2-3; Jn. 3:16; Heb. 12:1-2)

* Write an explanatory phrase stating the focus of each study (<u>III. Revelation: on . . .</u>)
* Using the Concentration and Meditation sub-points of Assignments One and Two, (and praying
    for enlightenment from the Holy Spirit), write 4 Revelation
    sub-points on <u>each</u> of the assigned Scriptures above (<u>What does it imply?</u>)
* Each Revelation sub-point (1, 2, 3, 4) must be connected to the corresponding number of the
    Concentration and Meditation sub-point above.
* On each Revelation sub-point, give an additional Scripture verse reference to support   the
    spiritual truth (see samples: Matt. 1:20-21 and Lk. 2:46-47).
* E-mail the assignment to: drcurt@aiccs.org

Assignment Four: Applications (on Gen. 12:1-3; Psa. 23:2-3; Jn. 3:16; Heb. 12:1-2)

* Using the Concentration, Meditation, and Revelation sub-points of Assignments One, Two,
    and Three, write 4 Application sub-points on each of the assigned Scriptures above (<u>How
    does it apply?</u>)
* Each sub-point should complete the sentence: "<u>IV. Applications: As a Christian, I need to . . .</u>"
* Each Application sub-point (1, 2, 3, 4) must be connected to the corresponding number of the
    Concentration, Meditation, and Revelation above.
* E-mail the assignment to: drcurt@aiccs.org

Note: Each sub-point must be a complete sentence, punctuated and spelled correctly.
*   All teaching outlines submitted must be one page only; no exceptions. (See samples.)*

The Birth of Jesus

(Matthew 1:20-21)

I. Concentration: on what the angel told Joseph

1. "Do not be afraid to take Mary as your wife," v. 20.
2. "That which is conceived in her is of the Holy Spirit," v. 20.
3. "She shall bring forth a Son and you shall call His name Jesus," v. 21.
4. "He will save His people from their sins," v. 21.

II. Meditation: on the meaning of the angel's message

1. The angel told Joseph not to put away (divorce) Mary but to marry her.
2. The angel explained Mary's pregnancy: that although she was a virgin, she was expecting a child because of the miraculous working of the Holy Spirit.
3. The child was a male, and His name (Jesus) was chosen by His Father in heaven.
4. The Child's mission (as indicated in His name) was to be the Savior of His people f r o m their sins.

III. Revelation: on the spiritual implications seen here

1. God speaks to His servants, giving them commands which should be obeyed, even though the orders sometimes may seem strange or foolish, Matt. 7:24.
2. The virgin birth, prophesied in Isa. 7:14, was necessary so that the sacrifice for our sins would be acceptable to God.
3. The Father sent His only Son to be the Savior of the world because He loves people, Jn. 3:16.
4. The Son's sacrificial death on the cross was purposed even before the creation of t h e world, Rev. 13:8.

IV. Applications: as a Christian, I need to . . .

1. Listen to God's word, and obey His commands.
2. Know that God still performs miracles today.
3. Receive Jesus as my personal Savior, and proclaim the Gospel to others.
4. Seek to know and follow God's plan for my life . . . which He mapped out for me b e f o r e my birth.

Jesus, the Student

(Luke 2:46-47)

I. Concentration: on Jesus in the temple-class at the age of 12 years

1. Jesus sat and listened to the Bible teachers in the temple, v. 46.
2. He asked the teachers insightful questions about their statements, v. 46.
3. He gained knowledge leading to spiritual understanding, v. 47.
4. He answered the teachers' questions, demonstrating His wisdom regarding Scriptural concepts, v. 47.

II. Meditation: on Jesus' spiritual growth process

1. He sat in the midst of His teachers, observing their conduct, absorbing their methods, respecting their positions of authority, and evaluating their ideas and interpretations of Scripture.
2. He probed His teachers' doctrines by asking questions to clarify their teachings and to explain the implications of their concepts.
3. He meditated on the lessons under consideration, receiving revelations from the Father which resulted in His deeper understanding of God's heart and will for His life.
4. He entered into discussion with His teachers, answering their questions and revealing His amazing grasp of spiritual truths and biblical concepts at an early age.

III. Revelation: on the implications of these truths

1. Jesus sat and listened to His teachers, demonstrating the twin traits of humility and submission, Jn. 14:10.
2. He was an active listener, involving Himself in the teaching-learning process, rather than merely being a passive hearer, Jas. 1:22.
3. He combined His intellectual knowledge with heaven-sent spiritual insights to continue growing in wisdom and understanding, Lk. 2:52.
4. He communicated the God-given concepts that were revealed to Him, which amazed His teachers, His parents, and, later, the multitudes who heard Him teach, Lk. 2:48; Matt. 7:28; 13:54.

IV. Applications: as a Christian, I need to . . .

1. Be open to other Bible teachers, listening with a spirit of humility and submission.
2. Be an active listener, diligently exploring the truths that God has revealed to His servant-teachers.
3. Receive revelation knowledge from the Holy Spirit, enabling me to grow daily in grace and wisdom.
4. Share (by speaking and writing) the spiritual truths received from the Father, teaching others the concepts and ideas which have benefitted my life and ministry.

Biblical Studies Degrees

To earn an Associate of Biblical Studies degree (optional title: AMin) (60 credit hours)
- Read the entire Bible (66 books; 1,189 chapters)
- Study 20 textbooks, each covering every chapter within a book (or books) of the Bible and having an average of about 60 chapters each: New Testament (5 courses), Old Testament Law (3 courses), Old Testament History (4 courses), Old Testament Poetry (4 courses), and Old Testament Prophecy (4 courses)
- Successfully pass a 50-question comprehensive examination in each course
- Pay all required fees and tuition
- Each course earns 3 credit hours X 20 courses = 60 credit hours (ABS degree)

To earn a Bachelor of Biblical Studies degree (optional title: BMin) (120 credit hours)
- Read the entire Bible (66 books; 1,189 chapters)
- Study 20 textbooks, as above
- Successfully pass twenty 50-question comprehensive exams, as above
- Successfully complete COME-REAP Methodology course – 2 credit hours
- Write 9 teaching outlines on chosen chapters within each course, using the
- COME-REAP methodology (submit 180-page term paper: 20 courses X 9 pages)
- Pay all required fees and tuition
- Each course earns a total of 6 credit hours (3 for the examination plus 3 for the teaching outlines); 20 courses X 6 = 120 credit hours (BBS degree)

To earn a Master's or Doctor's degree in Biblical Studies (30 graduate credit hours each)
- Read the assigned books in the Bible (201-260 chapters per track)
- Successfully complete COME-REAP Methodology course – 1 credit hour
- Write a teaching outline on each chapter of the assigned Bible books, using the COME-REAP methodology
- Participate in monthly tutoring sessions, including informal oral examinations
- Bind and submit all corrected teaching outlines to be preserved in school library
- Pay all required fees and tuition
- Biblical Studies Graduate-level Tracks: (Cumulative & Sequential)   Credit Hours

	Credit Hours
MMin - New Testament (optional title: MBS) (260-page thesis)	Bachelor + 30
ThM - Old Testament Law plus Job (optional title: MCEd) (229-page thesis) . . . 60 cumulative graduate credits	+ 30 = 60
MDiv - Old Testament History (optional title: CMA) (249-page thesis) . . . 92 cumulative graduate credits	+ 30 = 90
DMin - Old Testament Poetry (optional title: DBS) (201-page dissertation and oral examination) . . . 123 cumulative credits	+ 30 = 120
ThD - Old Testament Prophecy (Optional title: DCEd) (250-page dissertation and oral examination) . . . 155 cumulative credits	+ 30 = 150

Course #1

Created in the Image of God

(Genesis 1:26-27; 2:7)

I. Concentration: on the meaning of "image"

1. Human beings are a special creation of God, purposefully produced to fulfill a pre-ordained role in His world . . . dominion, Gen. 1:26.
2. In creation, God endowed persons with a spiritual aspect of life . . . man did not "receive" a soul, he "became" a soul through God's "breath."
3. Each person is an original, unique creation of God . . . made to be a rational, loving, responsible, moral creature.
4. Human beings are endowed with <u>some</u> of the characteristics of God . . . there is a "likeness" but not a "sameness."

(References: Rom. 8:29; I Cor. 15:49; II Cor. 3:18; 4:4; Col. 1:15; 3:10.)

II. Meditation: on God's nature and man's nature

1. God is spiritual . . . so are humans, which makes possible communication and communion with God, now and throughout all eternity Jn. 4:24.
2. God is an individual "person": a self-functioning entity with values, inclinations, and responsibilities . . . so are men and women.
3. God is holy, just, and righteous . . . persons have a spiritual intuition (inner call) to make free choices to obey their highest instincts in moral, obedient living (rather than to follow their "animal urges" by sin and rebellion against the Creator).
4. God has an eternal purpose for His creation . . . so also, human beings have an instinctive need to be something and to do something . . . this includes the freedom to choose a spiritual relationship with God.

III. Revelation: on "soul" and "spirit" I Thes. 5:23

1. "Soul" includes:
   1) A mind with which to think,
   2) A heart (emotions) with which to love, and
   3) A will with which to choose one's own destiny.
2. "Spirit" includes:
   1) Intuition - immediate and instinctive perception of a truth; direct understanding without reasoning; knowing beyond thinking.
   2) Conscience - inner ability by which a person knows right from wrong; usually through a disturbing awareness of the wrong.
   3) Communion - the need for, and the ability to have, an intimate spiritual relationship and fellowship with God.

IV. Applications: as a Christian, I need to . . .

1. See myself as a unique person, created in God's image.
2. Cultivate my "spirit" by trusting in the Lord to develop the spiritual characteristics which make me more like Him.
3. Deliberately choose each day to obey God's pattern for moral, rational, loving, responsible living.
4. Find and follow God's eternal purpose (destiny) for my life.

Why God Created Eve

(Genesis 2:18-24)

I. Concentration: on why God created Eve (v. 18)

1. Because God desires "good" for His creatures . . . what is right, proper, suitable, and adequate.
2. Because God's plan includes relationship and fellowship between human beings . . . not being "alone" . . . not solitary, single, by oneself.
3. Because every person needs someone to be a helper . . . one who assists, encourages, and supports.
4. Because only another human being would be appropriate (comparable; like; of equal regard or value) to be Adam's companion.

II. Meditation: on the basic truths of this passage

1. Adam and Eve were two actual, historical, created persons, according to Jesus, Mt. 19:4; Mk. 10:6.
2. Before Eve was created, Adam exercised full dominion over God's creation on earth, vv. 19-20.
3. God took a rib (from near Adam's heart) and made a woman ("taken out of man"), vv. 21-23; I Cor. 15:45-49.
4. This Divine creating and joining together of Adam and Eve revealed God's plan for establishing society: the home and family, v. 24.

III. Revelation: on the spiritual implications of this passage

1. God made each human being to serve Him, giving each person an assignment and responsibility, plus the necessary authority.
2. For every specific need which man has, God uses His creative power to meet that need or to fill that lack or void, Phil. 4:19.
3. God uses believers (His "new creation," II Cor. 5:17) to help birth or bring forth other spiritual "children."
4. The ideal "made in heaven" marriage is the spiritual picture of Christ as the bridegroom and the church as His bride, Eph. 5:22-23.

IV. Applications: as a Christian, I need to . . .

1. Know that God always is working things out for my good, Rom. 8:28.
2. Realize that "no man is an island" . . . that we need others for assistance, encouragement, and support, Rom. 14:7.
3. Understand that God gives me not only the responsibility and duty to carry out His will, but He also gives me the authority (dominion and power) to accomplish His purpose.
4. Faithfully witness to unbelievers, bringing them to Jesus Christ where they can be "born again" as children of God.

God's Probing Questions to Adam & Eve

(Genesis 3:1-13)

I. Concentration: on God's inquiries into the sins of Adam and Eve

    1. *"Where are you?"* (v. 9) Adam and Eve were engaged in an impossible attempt to hide from God.

    2. *"Who told you that you were naked?"* (v. 11) Adam and Eve, through their sin of disobedience, had lost their state of perfect innocence, changing the focus of their lives from the spiritual to the physical.

    3. *"Have you eaten from the tree of which I commanded you that you should not eat?"* (v. 11) God confronts His people with the specific sins of which they are guilty, Jn. 8:7-9.

    4. *"What is this you have done?"* (v. 13) Sinners must come to the realization that their sins are against God . . . only God, Psa. 51:4, and that they now stand condemned before the Judge of the universe, Jn. 3:18.

II. Meditation: on the unresponsive answers from Adam and Eve

    1. Where are you? "I heard Your voice and I was afraid," v. 10.

    2. Who told you? (No answer; it was their quickened conscience.)

    3. Have you disobeyed? "The woman gave me the fruit and I ate . . . but this never would have happened if You (God) had not made her!" (v. 12).

    4. What have you done? Eve answered: "The serpent deceived me and I ate . . . but it's partly God's fault, because He made the serpent!" (v. 13).

III. Revelation: on the spiritual implications in this passage

    1. God sees us and He knows exactly where we are and what we are doing, Psa. 139:7-12.

    2. In fact, God even knows all our thoughts and emotions, Psa. 69:5; 139:1-4; Jn. 2:24; 16:30.

    3. God requires us to confess our sins to Him specifically, Psa. 51:3; I Jn. 1:9.

    4. God's heart is broken by man's deliberate rebellion and disobedience because sin always brings its own fearful consequences of judgment and death, Ezek. 18:31; 33:11; Rom. 6:23.

IV. Applications: as a Christian, I need to . . .

    1. Know how much my heavenly Father loves me and how much my disobedience grieves His heart . . . because I have deliberately shifted my focus from fellowship and communion with Him to a focus upon earthly, physical things.

    2. Take full responsibility for my sins, without shifting the blame to others or even hinting that "I couldn't help it because God made me this way."

    3. Live my life with the constant awareness that God is always with me . . . knowing my thoughts, hearing my words, and watching my deeds.

    4. Immediately respond to the conviction of the Holy Spirit whenever I sin . . . repent, confess, forsake my sin, and receive Christ's forgiveness, cleansing, and restoration to spiritual fellowship with Him.

Am I My Brother's Keeper?

(Genesis 4:1-10)

I. Concentration: on these two brothers

1. Cain was the firstborn son of Adam and Eve, v. 1.
2. Cain was a farmer; Abel, his younger brother, was a shepherd, v. 2.
3. Apparently, these boys had been taught about spiritual things (the Garden of Eden events) because both Cain and Abel brought offerings to worship the Lord, vv. 3-4.
4. The Lord respected (esteemed; honored) Abel and his sacrifice, but the Lord did not respect Cain and his offering, vv. 4-5.

II. Meditation: on why God accepted Abel but rejected Cain

1. Perhaps it was because Abel brought a blood sacrifice (for sin), while Cain brought a grain offering (for thanksgiving) . . . although these religious rituals were not established until centuries later, Heb. 12:24.
2. According to Jesus, Abel was "righteous," Mt. 23:35; Lk. 11:51.
3. Abel had faith as he offered his excellent sacrifice to God; Cain did not have such a living faith, Heb. 11:4.
4. Cain "was of the wicked (evil) one" (Satan), I Jn. 3:12; Jude 1:11.

III. Revelation: on God's questions to the murderer, Cain

1. *"Why are you angry? Why has your countenance fallen?"* (v. 6) Cain's anger had grown out of jealousy and envy of his brother, Abel, and Cain's hateful, malicious attitude manifested itself on his face.
2. *"If you do well, will you not be accepted?"* (v. 7) God here extended to Cain the possibility of Divine forgiveness and acceptance if he would repent of his sins and in faith "do well" . . . obey.
3. *"Where is Abel your brother?"* (v. 9) God saw Cain murder Abel and called for his confession, but Cain side-stepped the question, just as his parents had done in Eden. Cain asked: "Am I my brother's keeper?" The answer to Cain's question is "Yes!"
4. *"What have you done?" (v. 10)* This is the same question which God asked Adam and Eve in the Garden of Eden (Gen. 3:13). Sinners must admit their sins before they are in a position to ask God's forgiveness.

IV. Applications: on following the examples given by Abel ("the first man to . . .")

1. Abel was the first man to worship God correctly; I, also, must worship the Lord in righteousness, I Chron. 16:29.
2. Abel was the first man to demonstrate faith accurately; I, also, must demonstrate my faith through my obedient works, Jas. 2:18.
3. Abel was the first man to please God fully; I, also, must walk "fully pleasing" before God . . . spiritually fruitful, increasingly perceptive, and empowered by the Holy Spirit, Col. 1:10-12.
4. Abel was the first man to die physically; I, also, must someday experience death, but through faith in the Lord Jesus, I shall be resurrected, Heb. 9:27; Jn. 11:25-26; I Thes. 4:16-17.

Enoch Walked with God

(Genesis 5:18-24)

I. Concentration: on the man named Enoch

1. Enoch (meaning "dedicated") perhaps was named after his great-uncle Cain's son, for whom a city also had been named, Gen. 4:17.
2. Enoch was the seventh generation from Adam (Gen. 5):
   1) Adam
   2) Seth
   3) Enosh
   4) Cainan
   5) Mahalalel
   6) Jared
   7) Enoch
   8) Methuselah
   9) Lamech
   10) Noah
3. Enoch, therefore, was the great-grandfather of Noah.
4. Enoch lived and walked in such close fellowship with God that he was translated into the presence of God in heaven without dying, v. 24.

II. Meditation: on Enoch's character and accomplishments

1. Enoch lived 365 years by faith before being taken away, Heb. 11:5.
2. Enoch had this good testimony: that he pleased God, Heb. 11:5.
3. Enoch was privileged to be listed as an ancestor of God's Messiah, Lk. 3:37.
4. Enoch prophesied about the Lord's coming to earth in judgment, Jude 1:14-15.

III. Revelation: on Enoch's prophetic spiritual knowledge

1. Enoch "saw" that God would come to the earth in judgment, because the Lord reveals His will to those who walk close to Him, Amos 3:7.
2. Enoch believed that God exists and rewards those who diligently seek Him, Heb. 11:5-6.
3. Enoch's prophecy of judgment was fulfilled when God sent the flood upon the earth in Noah's day.
4. Enoch's prophecy also forecasts another day of judgment: when the Lord comes with His saints to execute punishment upon the "ungodly" . . . a word used four times in Jude 1:15.

IV. As a Christian, I need to . . .

1. Be like Enoch . . . "dedicated" unto the Lord.
2. Walk by faith in intimate spiritual relationship and fellowship with God.
3. Live a godly life which produces a God-pleasing testimony and witness.
4. Hear and speak God's word to my own generation, and to the generations yet unborn.

Noah Found Grace in God's Eyes

(Genesis 6:1-18)

I. Concentration: on the man Noah, whose name means "Comfort" or "Rest"

1. He found grace (God's unmerited gift or favor) in God's eyes, v. 8.
2. He was just . . . fair, true, and honest, v. 9.
3. He was perfect . . . blameless, having maturity and integrity, v. 9.
4. He, like his great-grandfather Enoch, walked with God, v. 9.

II. Meditation: on the sinful world in which Noah lived

1. Satanism. "Nephilim" translated "Sons of God" refers to the fallen, dark angels of Satan, who cohabited with humans, v. 2.
2. Wickedness. People had "twisted" (a related root word) good into evil and vice verse . . . were addicted to depravity, not discerning right from wrong, v. 5.
3. Total corruption of society. "Every intent . . . only evil continually . . . all flesh had corrupted their way," vv. 5, 12.
4. Full of violence. Noah's day was notorious for its cruelty and disregard for human life, v. 12.

III. Revelation: on God's spoken words to Noah

1. "My Spirit shall not strive (struggle; contend) with man forever . . . yet his days shall be one hundred twenty years," v. 3. *At the flood, God reduced the life span of humans from about 900 years to a maximum of 120 years.*
2. "I will destroy them (the Satanic, wicked, corrupt, violent persons) with the earth," v. 13. *This cleansing of the earth by water would destroy the half-human, half-demon giant monsters which intimidated the people of that era, v. 4.*
3. "Make yourself an ark of gopher wood . . . I am bringing floodwaters . . . everything that is on the earth shall die," vv. 14, 17.
4. "I will establish My covenant with you," (and your family), v. 18.

IV. Applications: as a Christian, I need to . . .

1. Live a just, perfect life of integrity by receiving God's grace and by walking daily with Him.
2. Keep my life pure and blameless in the midst of a Satanic, wicked, corrupt, violent . . . crooked and perverse generation, Phil. 2:15-16.
3. Hear and faithfully proclaim God's coming judgment, regardless of the small number of persons who heed my warning over a period of up to 100 years, Gen. 5:32 and Gen. 7:6 . . . for indeed, these are "the days of Noah" which Jesus mentioned in Mt. 24:37-39.
4. Obey God's instructions in order to receive His deliverance . . . His way of; His "ark of safety," Jesus Christ . . . Who saves us from impending doom, Heb. 11:7.

Forty Days and Forty Nights

(Genesis 7:1-24)

I. Concentration: on the Lord's words to Noah

1. "Come into the ark, you and all your household, because I have seen that you are righteous before Me in this generation," v. 1.
2. "You shall take with you seven each of every clean animal . . . also seven each of the birds of the air," vv. 2-3.
3. "Two each of animals that are unclean (inedible)," v. 2.
4. "I will cause it to rain on the earth 40 days and 40 nights, and I will destroy from the face of the earth all living things that I have made," v. 4. (*The flood was a world-wide event; Jesus said so in Mt. 24:37-39 and Lk. 17:27.*)

II. Meditation: on these meaningful words from the Lord

1. God provides an ark of safety for His people who, through obedient faith, have received His righteousness, II Cor. 5:21.
2. God provides His people with all the material possessions they need to use in making an offering when they come to worship Him, Gen. 8:20-21.
3. God cares about all of the creatures He has made, and His plan includes the preservation of each species, v. 3.
4. God always sends judgment upon sinners, Num. 32:23; Gal. 6:7.

III. Revelation: on the truths and implications of the flood

1. Noah obeyed God, gathered the animals, and entered the safety of the ark with his wife, his three sons, and their wives, vv. 7, 13; I Pet. 3:20.
2. God, Himself, shut the door of the ark, v. 16 . . . <u>sealing in</u> all the occupants to preserve them from the flood waters, and <u>sealing out</u> all those who rejected Noah's righteous preaching, II Pet. 2:5.
3. God demonstrated His justice and His omnipotent power . . . "the fountains of the great deep (oceans) were broken up, and the windows (sluice-gates) of heaven were opened . . . all the high hills (mountains) under the whole heaven were covered," vv. 11, 17-20.
4. God eliminated all ungodly persons through the world-wide flood, and He gave mankind a second chance in a new environment, vv. 21-24.

IV. Applications: as a Christian, I need to . . .

1. Trust completely in the mercy and grace of the Lord, and influence my family to do likewise, Josh. 24:15.
2. Rest in the blessed assurance that God will preserve my soul through the "floods" of my life, Isa. 59:19.
3. Warn lost persons that God's final judgment is coming, II Cor. 5:10-11.
4. Know that the Lord is preparing a perfect place (heaven) for His "saved" people, Jn. 14:2-3; Rev. 21:4.

Three Doves and a Raven

(Genesis 8:1-22)

I. Concentration: on the rising and falling of the flood waters

1. God saw and remembered Noah and every living thing in the ark, v. 1.
2. God made a wind pass over the earth and the waters subsided, v. 1.
3. The fountains of the deep and the windows of heaven were stopped, v. 2.
4. The entire flood episode lasted for more than a year, Gen. 7:11; 8:14.

II. Meditation: on the chronology of these events

1. Noah was 500 years old when God told him to build the ark, Gen. 5:32; he spent 100 years building it and preaching, Gen. 6:6; II Pet. 2:5.
2. When Noah was 600 years old, in the second month on the 17th day, the flood began, Gen. 7:11.
3. The flood lasted 150 days at its peak (second month, 17th day until seventh month, 17th day) including the 40 days of rain, before the ark came to rest on Mt. Ararat, Gen. 8:3-4.
4. Another 75 days passed before the tops of other mountains became visible (tenth month, 1st day), Gen. 8:5.
5. Forty days later (eleventh month, 10th day), Noah sent out a raven and a dove, Gen. 8:6.
6. One week later (eleventh month, 17th day), Noah sent out a dove which returned with an olive leaf, Gen. 8:10.
7. In another seven days (eleventh month, 24th day), Noah sent out another dove which did not return, Gen. 8:12 . . . another 40 days passed.
8. In Noah's 601st year, on the 1st day of the first month, the land had become completely dry, and Noah opened the ark, Gen. 8:13.
9. On the second month, 27th day, Noah and his family exited from the ark and offered a sacrifice in worship to God, Gen. 8:14.
10. The Lord received Noah's worship and promised that He would not ever destroy the inhabitants of earth by water again, Gen. 8:21-22.

III. Revelation and Applications: from this account of the flood

1. In His mercy and patience, God gives mankind abundant time to repent of his sins, (He is long-suffering) Psa. 86:15; I Pet. 3:20; II Pet. 3:9, 15; and God has a definite timetable for His purposes to be worked out in us as we fulfill His destiny, Psa. 139:16.
2. The flood waters covered the earth when God opened the windows of heaven; so also God will open the windows of heaven to flood His obedient people with overwhelming blessings, Mal. 3:10.
3. God uses unlikely sources to reveal His will to us: the raven and the three doves brought Noah progress reports on the receding flood waters.
4. Noah worshipped the Lord for His deliverance; today we Christians should worship and thank Jesus for His great salvation, Titus 2:11-14.

Rainbow Blessings and Family Curses

(Genesis 9:1-29)

I. Concentration: on the major themes mentioned in this chapter

1. Sanctity of human life, vv. 1-7.
2. God's covenant of mercy, vv. 8-17.
3. Drunkenness leading to sin, vv. 18-23.
4. Causing a family curse, vv. 24-29.

II. Meditation: on the Scriptural foundations of these themes in Genesis 9

1. "Whoever sheds man's blood, by man his blood shall be shed; for in the image of God He made man," v. 6.
2. "I set My rainbow in the cloud, and it shall be for the sign of the covenant between Me and the earth," v. 13.
3. "Then he (Noah) drank of the wine and was drunk, and became uncovered in his tent," v. 21.
4. "Cursed be Canaan; a servant of servants he shall be to his brethren," vv. 25-27.

III. Revelation: on the implications of these basic Biblical ideas

1. Capital punishment is mandated here as a way of magnifying the importance of the "image of God" life of the victim, whose life was taken away. *According to God's system of justice, the penalty must fit the crime, and no other penalty, except execution, adequately pays the just price for murder.*
2. The rainbow in the sky is a sign of God's covenant of mercy and grace with mankind. *The rainbow is a periodic reminder of God's judgment in days past, and a constant warning of God's future judgment upon the earth . . . not by water, but by fire, II Pet. 3:10, 12.*
3. The fermented juice of grapes contained alcohol, a drug which produces drunkenness. *Drunkenness not only <u>leads</u> to sin, but <u>drunkenness is a sin</u>, Prov. 23:29-35; Gal. 5:19-21.*
4. The influence of a person's sin can adversely affect generations to come. *The curse of Noah's sin (drunkenness and immodesty) plus the curse of the sin of his son, Ham (breaking sexual standards of decency and gossiping about his father's failure) were visited upon the seemingly innocent grandson, Canaan, Ex. 20:5; Num. 14:18.*

IV. Applications: as a Christian, I need to . . .

1. Stand firmly for the sanctity of human life . . . opposing abortion and euthanasia, while also favoring capital punishment as God's just and authorized punishment for pre-meditated murder.
2. Rejoice in my new covenant relationship with Christ, I Cor. 11:25, Whose appearance is associated with a rainbow, Ezek. 1:28; Rev. 4:3; 10:1.
3. Advocate abstinence from alcohol as a Christian virtue, Eph. 5:18.
4. Recognize the importance of my influence over family members and others; live a God-honoring life of spiritual integrity.

Noah's Sons: Shem, Ham, and Japheth

(Genesis 10:1-32)

I. Concentration: on Noah's three sons

1. Noah was around 500 years old when these sons were born . . . about the same time when God told Noah to start building the ark, Gen. 5:32.
2. The three sons were 100 years old and married (but without children) when the flood came, Gen. 7:6-7.
3. Ham sinned against his father, Noah, and his descendants were cursed, but the descendants of Shem and Japheth were blessed,   Gen. 9:25-27.
4. All nations and peoples on the earth today are descended from one of these three brothers, Gen. 10:32.

II. Meditation: on where the descendants of Shem, Ham, and Japheth settled

1. Japheth and his descendants formed the northern nations . . . becoming the Caucasians of Europe and western Asia, vv. 2-5.
2. Ham and his descendants formed the southern nations . . . becoming the Negroes of Africa, vv. 6-20.
3. Shem and his descendants formed the central nations . . . becoming the Jews, Arabs and other Oriental peoples of the middle east, vv. 21-31.
4. "He (God) has made from one blood every nation of men who dwell on all the face of the earth, and has determined their preappointed times and the boundaries of their dwelling," Acts 17:26.

III. Revelation: on the chronological listings in Genesis 5, 10, and 11

1. From Adam to the flood   1,656 years (Gen. 5)
   From the flood to Abraham's call   427 years (Gen. 11)
   Total from Adam to Abraham   2,083 years
2. Adam's life overlapped Methuselah's by 243 years; Methuselah's life overlapped Noah's by 600 years and Shem's by 98 years.
3. Between Adam's death and Noah's birth were 126 years; Shem lived from 98 years before the flood until 75 years after Abraham's call.
4. If Abraham's date was approximately 2000 B.C., then Adam's date was approximately 4000 B.C.

IV. Applications: as a Christian, I need to . . .

1. Accept by faith that the first eleven chapters of Genesis are historically true and correct, not merely mythical poetry.
2. Understand that men lived longer before the flood (1) because sin had only begun its malignant influence on the human race, which had descended from a nature originally intended to be immortal, and (2) because many environmental changes occurred during the flood which shortened mankind's life span.
3. Realize that God keeps a detailed record of all our families . . . including births, important events, and deaths.
4. Reject all racial prejudices because on this earth there are not three races (Caucasian, Negro, and Oriental); there is only one: the human race.

The Tower of Babel

(Genesis 11:1-9)

I. Concentration: on the location and identification of Babel

1. It was in the vicinity of the mountain range of Arafat, where Noah's ark landed (Turkey, southern Russia, or northwest Iran), Gen. 8:6.
2. It probably was in the valley between the Tigris and Euphrates rivers, possibly identified with Abraham's birthplace, Ur, Gen. 11:28, 31.
3. "Babel" means "mixed up" or "confused," vv. 7, 9 . . . later the site became known as "the gate of the god."
4. Babel later became Babylon, the capital of the Babylonian empire, located about 50 miles south of modern Baghdad, Iraq. *It was from this area that Noah's sons "divided" the earth, settling generally in the northern, central, and southern continents of Europe, Asia, and Africa.*

II. Meditation: on some other interesting details about this passage

1. The separation (dividing) of nations caused by the confusion of languages occurred about the time of Peleg's birth, Gen. 10:25.
2. This was 101 years after the flood and 326 years before the call of Abraham, Gen. 11:10-32.
3. "Shinar," v. 2, probably is Mesopotamia, Gen. 10:10.
4. "Eber," v. 4, is the man from whom the Hebrews got their name.

III. Revelation: on the events of the tower of Babel account

1. The people decided to build a tower for these reasons: (v. 4)
   1) To establish themselves as a people within the safety of a city,
   2) To approach God's presence (heaven) through their own works,
   3) To enhance their prideful reputation . . . "make a name," and
   4) To keep from being scattered and separated over the earth.
2. The Lord came down to see, spoke His will, and confused their language so that they were scattered throughout the earth, vv. 5-9.
3. This tower of Babel incident was God's method of defeating false worship.
4. This incident also was God's method for dispersing the human race to subdue the earth, Gen. 1:28. (*Compare with Acts 8:1.*)

IV. Applications: as a Christian, I need to . . .

1. Recognize the power of people with a unified tongue . . . "nothing that they propose to do will be withheld from them," v. 6.
2. Avoid sinning against God by self-preservation, fleshly "good works," pride, and disobedience.
3. Realize that the Lord sees and knows what is happening on earth . . . and that He is actively involved in our lives today.
4. Know that whether or not we cooperate, God certainly shall accomplish His will and purpose on the earth.

God's Call to Abram

(Genesis 12:1-9)

I. Concentration: on God's commands and promises

1. Commands: (1) Get out of your country, (2) from your family, (3) from your father's house, (4) to a land that I will show you, v. 1.

2. Promises: (1) I will make you a great nation, (2) I will bless you . . . and I will bless those who bless you, (3) I will make your name great, and (4) you shall be a blessing to all families of the earth, vv. 2-3.

II. Meditation: on Abram's responses to God's call

1. At age 75, Abram departed, taking his wife, Sarai, and his brother's son, Lot, along with their possessions, vv. 4-5.

2. Abram traveled into the Promised Land (Canaan) to Shechem, where the Lord appeared and reaffirmed His original promises, vv. 6-7.

3. Abram built an altar there to the Lord, v. 7.

4. Abram moved his tent to a site between Bethel and Ai, where he built another altar and called on the name of the Lord before going south . . . outside of the land which God had promised him, vv. 8-9.

III. Revelation: on the relationship between God and Abram's family

1. Abraham could have known Noah's son (Shem) . . . according to the genealogy in Gen. 11. *(Could Shem be Melchizedek in Gen. 14:18?)*

2. Noah's father (Lamech) knew Adam, Gen. 11.

3. Both these genealogical lists (Adam to Noah, and Shem to Abraham) include ten generations, but Adam lived 930 years while Abraham lived a relatively short life span of 175 years, Gen. 25:7.

4. In these early chapters of the Bible, God spoke with Adam and Noah and Abraham (not including Enoch, who was translated); God's intimate communication with men did not overlap . . . a generation passed after Adam and before Noah, and after Noah and before Abraham.

IV. Applications: as a Christian, I need to know that . . .

1. Whenever I obey God's commands, His conditional promises become unconditional promises. *(God told Abram to go . . . and I will bless; Abram obeyed by faith and God affirmed by saying: "I will!" vv. 2, 7.)*

2. Just as Noah heard the Garden of Eden story from his father (Lamech) who got it directly from Adam; and just as Abraham heard the story of the flood from Noah's son (Shem) who was on the ark . . . even so, I stand in a long line of spiritual family members who receive God's words and acts, and pass them along from generation to generation.

3. God's plan is to reveal Himself to individuals who are available to hear His voice, and His purpose is to use their influence for good all the days of their lives and into future generations.

4. In my personal life's journey, I "camp" between Bethel ("House of God") and Ai ("ruin") . . . and my personal choice determines my destiny.

Material Prosperity & Family Disruption

(Genesis 13:1-18)

I. Concentration: on Abram's journey into Egypt . . . into sin (Gen. 12:9-13)

    1. <u>Straying:</u> Abram sinned by moving his family to a place outside of God's promised land . . . out from under the Lord's canopy of blessing, v. 9.

    2. <u>Doubting:</u> Abram moved "in the flesh" to seek a place where he could avoid famine, rather than trusting in God's providence, v. 10.

    3. <u>Lying:</u> Abram conspired with Sarai, and lied to the Egyptian Pharaoh about his husband-wife relationship with her . . . as a means of self-preservation, vv. 11-13.

    4. <u>Stealing:</u> Abram received Pharaoh's rich gifts under false pretenses, with the implication that he was accepting a dowry . . . for which deception he was strongly reprimanded and exiled, vv. 14-20.

II. Meditation: on Abram's return from Egypt (Gen. 13:1-9)

    1. Abram returned to Canaan from Egypt with abundant wealth, vv. 1-2.

    2. Abram came "back to Bethel" where he had built an altar (Gen. 12:8), and there he called on the name of the Lord, vv. 3-4.

    3. Material prosperity caused family disruption, vv. 5-7.

    4. Abram, the head of the family, deferred to his nephew, Lot, giving him the first choice of the land, vv. 8-9.

III. Revelation: on results of the choices made by Lot and Abram (Gen. 13:10-18)

    1. Lot chose the well-watered, fertile plain of Jordan, which included the cities of Sodom and Gomorrah, vv. 10, 12.

    2. Lot associated himself with the men of Sodom, who were exceedingly wicked and sinful against the Lord, vv. 12-13.

    3. Abram dwelt in Canaan . . . and, at God's word, walked through the length and width of the entire "Promised Land," vv. 12, 17.

    4. Abram received God's promises of blessing:

        1) Land as far as the eye can see in all directions, vv. 14-15,

        2) Descendants as numerous as all the dust particles on earth, v. 16.

IV. Applications: as a Christian, I need to . . .

    1. Repent of my sins away from God "in Egypt" and by faith return to Bethel (God's house) for forgiveness, cleansing, renewal of spiritual relationship and revival of intimate fellowship with God.

    2. Build altars for me and my family, where together we can worship, praise, and thank the Lord.

    3. Realize that material possessions often can cause family dissension, and know that as a genuine Christian <u>I am not to demand my own rights</u>, Mt. 5:39-44; Lk. 12:13-14; Rom. 12:10; Eph. 5:21.

    4. Make all my important decisions with an eye on the revealed, spiritual purposes of the Lord . . . for His plan is my roadway of blessings.

The Kings of Sodom and Salem

(Genesis 14:1-24)

I. Concentration: on Abram as a warrior in battle (vv. 1-16)

    1. Abraham enlisted 318 servant-warriors; they attacked and defeated a coalition of four hostile kings who had raided Lot's city.

    2. Abram rescued his nephew, Lot, and other hostages; taking much loot from the defeated army.

    Then *Abram met two strikingly contrasted kings.*

    3. The King of Sodom is a perfect depiction of Satan, the king of hell. "Sodom" literally means "burnt" or "scorched." This king was the leader of a hell-bent city, destined to be destroyed by divine judgment.

    4. The King of Salem (Melchizedek) ruled over the ancient city of Salem (Jerusalem). He is a type of Christ, and his name means "Prince of Peace," Heb. 7:1-10; Isa. 9:6.

II. Meditation: on Abram's dealings with the King of Sodom (vv. 17, 21-24)

    1. Abram was confronted by Satan's representative, the King of Sodom.

    2. Often after winning a great victory, God's people face a new choice in their spiritual priorities, a real and practical temptation to sin.

    3. Such times of testing reveal true priorities; for God's people, no degree of attainment bypasses the need for godly faithfulness in the basics.

    4. The subtlety of the King of Sodom's approach was demonic. He said, "You can have all the plunder, just give me the people." *That's Satan's way: "I'll give you anything, just let me control the souls."*

III. Revelation: on Abram's dealing with the King of Salem (vv. 18-20)

    1. Abram established his relationship with the King of Salem, who gave him bread and wine. v. 18. *(The Hebrews identify Melchizedek with Shem.)*

    2. Melchizedek's actions 2,000 years before Christ foreshadowed the priestly ministry of Christ.

    3. Melchizedek used the same elements Christ used in the Lord's Supper.

    4. Abram worshipped God . . . and he offered tithes.

IV. Applications: as a Christian, I need to . . .

    1. Resist Satan. Abram confronted the King of Sodom with the words, "I have raised my hand (sworn allegiance) to the Lord God Most High, the possesser of heaven and earth," v. 22.

    2. Reject sin. Abram rejected Sodom's proposal, saying (in essence), "I don't want anything that has the smell of your scorched life on it. I don't want you to be able to brag that you made Abram rich."

    3. Put God first. Abram's priority was clear: everything is God's. The tithe showed that he is God's, with no relationship or obligation to Satan.

    4. Hear God's voice. The next chapter (Gen. 15) begins with these words: "After these things the word of the Lord came to Abram in a vision, saying, 'Do not be afraid, Abram, I am your shield, your exceedingly great reward.'"

Cutting the Covenant of Blood

(Genesis 15:1-21)

I. Concentration: on the Lord's personal relationship with Abram

    1. The Lord appeared in a vision to Abram, assuring him that He was his vision, comfort, protection, and reward, v. 1.

    2. Abram asked God to clarify His promise about a son, vv. 2-3. *Would his son come through His servant, Eliezer?*

    3. The Lord told Abram that his son would come directly from him, and that his descendants would be as innumerable as the stars, vv. 4-5.

    4. Abram "believed in the Lord, and He accounted it to him for righteousness," v. 6; Rom. 4:3, 9-22.

II. Meditation: on "cutting" the covenant ("covenant" means "cutting")

    1. God began by repeating His inheritance promises, but Abram asked, "How can I know for sure?" vv. 7-8.

    2. The Lord established a blood covenant with Abram, which included:

        1) Animals sacrificed by being cut in half, vv. 9-10,

        2) Placing the pieces of the dead animals a distance apart, v. 10,

        3) Swearing of a blood-oath between the two parties, vv. 13-16.

        4) Walking between the sacrificed animals as a sign of the surety of the promises made . . . under penalty of death, v. 17.

    3. God did all the work of establishing this covenant; all Abram did was to sacrifice the animals as God commanded him.

    4. "A smoking oven and a burning torch," v. 17, was God's manifestation of Himself walking into the covenant relationship with Abram.

III. Revelation: on the great spiritual truths in this chapter

    1. Humans cannot even begin to count God's blessings . . . they are numberless, like the sand, dust, and stars.

    2. Salvation is by faith, and faith alone, v. 6; Eph. 2:8-9.

    3. The "vultures of Satan" (v. 11) always gather where God and man are doing spiritual business (cutting a covenant); these demonic distractions must be driven away.

    4. The manifestations of God's presence are terrifying to human beings, which, perhaps, accounts for the Lord's appearing to many individuals in dreams or visions . . . as He did when a deep sleep fell on Abram, v. 12.

IV. Applications: as a Christian, I need to . . .

    1. Trust in God for His salvation of me.

    2. Trust in God for His blood-covenant relationship with me.

    3. Trust in God for His fulfilled promises to me.

    4. Trust in God for His vision of destiny for me.

A Triangle of Domestic Disruption

(Genesis 16:1-16)

I. Concentraion: on the characters in this chapter

1. Sarai - Abram's wife who was barren . . . could not bear him children, v. 1.
2. Abram - God's "man of faith" who had these glaring weaknesses:
   1) Committed a cluster of sins on his trip into Egypt (Gen. 12),
   2) Mistakenly thought his servant, Eliezer, would produce him an heir (Gen. 15:2-3),
   3) Allowed his wife, Sarai, to exercise leadership and authority in his home, vv. 2, 5-6,
   4) Violated God's plan by using Sarai's maid, Hagar, as a surrogate mother, v. 3.
3. Hagar - Sarai's Egyptian maid, who was given to Abram (like a piece of property) and became pregnant by him, v. 4.
4. Ishmael - son of Abram and Hagar, v. 15.

II. Meditation: on the victimized life of Hagar

1. Hagar was born an Egyptian; became a slave, v. 1.
2. Hagar was given to Abram; became pregnant, vv. 2-4.
3. Hagar became the center of a domestic "triangle of trouble;" she was despised and probably beaten by the wife, Sarai, vv. 4-6.
4. Hagar became so desperate that she ran away, v. 6.

III. Revelation: on the angel's words to Hagar (vv. 7-10)

1. "Where have you come from?"
   Reflect on your past history.
2. "Where are you going?"
   Consider your future destiny.
3. "Return" and "submit."
   In humble obedience, trust God for protection and provision.
4. "I will multiply your children."
   Receive by faith God's promised blessings.

IV. Applications: on how God deals with me (as He dealt with Hagar)

1. God gives His promises of blessing, vv. 11-12.
2. God reveals Himself: "The-God-Who-Lives-and-Sees-Me," vv. 13-14.
3. God demands obedient submission to His will, v. 15.
4. God fulfills His word; "Ishmael" means "God hears," v. 16.

Circumcision: God's Covenant Sign

(Genesis 17:1-27)

I. Concentration: on the drastic changes initiated by God in this chapter

1. God changed Abram (Father is exalted) to Abraham (Father of a multitude") v. 5. *Sarai was changed to Sarah (Princess), v. 15.*
2. God re-established His everlasting covenant with Abraham, vv. 2, 6-9.
3. The Lord put into place the covenant sign: circumcision, vv. 10-14, 23-27.
4. The Lord named the coming son of promise Isaac ("Laughter"), vv. 17-21.

II. Meditation: on the spiritual significance of these events

1. Both Abram and Sarai underwent a spiritual change by the power of God...characterized by an "h" being added to their original names (Abraham and Sarah). *The "h" sound in Hebrew represents the wind or breath of God, so perhaps these name changes signified the entry of the Holy Spirit into their beings?)*
2. God's continual repetition and expansion of His covenant promises to Abraham (Genesis 12, 13, 15, and 17) signified the Lord's determination to encourage Abraham's faith and hope that His promises surely would be fulfilled.
3. Circumcision became the sign of God's covenant with Abraham's descendants; Abraham and his family all were circumcised on the same day, vv. 24-27.
4. Isaac, Abraham's second son, was chosen to receive God's covenant blessings, rather than his first son, Ishmael. *(See Gal. 4:22-31.)*

III. Revelation: on the lessons of circumcision

1. It involves shedding of blood - a ceremony of initiation into the Hebrew nation, sealed with blood . . . the life of the flesh, Lev. 17:11.
2. It involves cutting away flesh - signifying the removal of a physical part to allow the magnification of the spiritual part of man.
3. It involves pain and suffering - the rite always includes a sacrifice through which a person can move into a healing, joyful relationship with God.
4. It involves the reproductive organ - the act of surgically removing the foreskin of the male genital organ is connected to the process of human procreation. *Note this spiritual picture: Abraham was circumcised (entered God's community of faith)* <u>*before*</u> *he fathered Isaac, vv. 21, 26. Spiritual relationship precedes productivity!*

IV. Applications: as a Christian, I need to . . .

1. Allow God's indwelling Spirit to totally transform my life, II Cor. 5:17.
2. Conform to God's sovereign plan, not insisting on my own will and way.
3. Base my faith and hope of the sure foundation of God's word.
4. Identify the Old Testament covenant sign (circumcision) with the New Testament covenant sign (baptism) . . . being spiritually "circumcised" in ears, eyes, lips, and heart, Dt. 10:16; Ex. 6:12; Jer. 4:4; 6:10; Rom. 2:27-28; I Pet. 3:21.

Is Anything Too Hard for the Lord?

(Genesis 18:1-33)

I. Concentration: on the highlights of this chapter

1. Abraham and Sarah entertained three travelers, vv. 1-8.
2. The Lord promised that Sarah would bear a son, but she laughed scornfully and was rebuked by Him, vv. 9-15.
3. The Lord told Abraham of the pending destruction of Sodom and Gomorrah, vv. 16-21.
4. Abraham "bargained," asking God to have mercy on these wicked cities, for the sake of those few citizens who were righteous, vv. 22-33.

II. Meditation: on the truths revealed through these events

1. The three travelers were the *Lord (a pre-incarnation appearance of Jesus Christ)* and two angels, 18:1; 13, 17-23; 19:1, 16.
2. Sarah's laugh was made in derision and faithlessness, and the Lord said: "Is anything too hard? . . . At the appointed time (you) shall bear a son," v. 14. *Earlier Abraham's laugh (Gen. 17:17) was an expression of amazement and joy of the good news of God's promised heir.*
3. The Lord always reveals what He is about to bring to pass, to at least one of His faithful, spiritually perceptive people, v. 17; Amos 3:7.
4. Continuing intercessory prayer for the lives of endangered persons is patiently heard by the Lord, Who is willing to extend His mercy and grace for the sake of only a few believers.

III. Revelation: on the spiritual implications of these events

1. The Lord appears to, and has intimate fellowship with, those persons who invite Him into their lives and homes, Rev. 3:20.
2. God knows our hearts; we cannot deceive Him with our lies or half-truths . . . He sternly confronts us about our sins!
3. God wants His people to know what He is doing and why . . . so He reveals His will and purpose to His faithful messengers (prophets).
4. The Lord is willing to remove or delay His punishment upon a city full of wicked persons, on the basis of a few righteous ones, and in response to the intercessory prayer of only one concerned, compassionate soul.

IV. Applications: as a Christian, I need to . . .

1. Daily and continuously welcome the Spirit of the Lord Jesus Christ into my life, in sweet communion and intimate fellowship.
2. Believe God's promises to me personally; with integrity, rejoice in His almighty power.
3. Listen for God's revelation to my heart and mind, to my soul and spirit; receive His enlightening word with discerning faith.
4. Engage in intercessory prayer, asking God's mercy and grace upon my city, as well as upon my state, nation, and the world.

Fire and Brimstone

(Genesis 19:1-38)

I. Concentration: on the sins of Sodom which deserved divine punishment

1. The two angels were sent to confirm the wickedness of Sodom, which the Lord already had seen, Gen. 18:20-22; 19:1.
2. The angels stayed overnight at Lot's house and were attacked by the homosexual men of the city, who were stricken blind, vv. 1-11.
3. The angels told Lot to gather his family to flee the doomed city, but his two sons-in-law thought Lot was joking, vv. 12-16.
4. Lot continued to delay, and succeeded in bringing about a compromise: rather than fleeing into the mountains, they were permitted to go into a little city named Zoar, vv. 17-23.

II. Meditation: on God's law of cause and effect

1. Sodom's wickedness ("Sodomy" = sexual intercourse between male human beings or with animals) brought the burning fires of hell falling from heaven, vv. 24-25.
2. Lot's compromise with the citizens of Sodom cost him his influence with his family . . . both sons-in-law scornfully laughed at him and refused to leave the city with their wives. *(See II Pet. 2:6-8.)*
3. Lot's wife "looked back" . . . (held back and/or turned back), and was overtaken and covered by the burning pitch and sulfur, v. 26; Lot's wife actually lived, according to Jesus, Lk. 17:28-29, 32.
4. Lot's daughters, who had grown up in a notorious sex-crazed society, got their father drunk, had incestuous relations with him, and bore illegitimate children . . . whose descendants (Moab and Ammon) were enemies of Israel for many centuries.

III. Revelation: on God's mercy and grace

1. The two angels could have annihilated the attacking Sodomites, but they only blinded them, v. 11.
2. In response to Abraham's intercession (Gen. 18:23-33), God had determined not to send punishment on "righteous" Lot, v. 22.
3. The Lord continued to withhold sending judgment upon Sodom while Lot and his family delayed their departure . . . finally the two angels had to literally drag Lot, his wife, and their two daughters to safety, v. 16.
4. God allowed Lot to flee for safety to a small city, which probably had been originally marked for destruction, vv. 21-22.

IV. Applications: as a Christian, I need to . . .

1. Avoid compromising my Christian convictions for the sake of economic gain, political power, or worldly prestige.
2. Realize that God will surely bring about "payday someday."
3. Know that intercessory prayer does bring God's mercy and grace.
4. Advocate abstinence from alcohol . . . this is the second incident of a family-damaging sin caused by drunkenness (Gen. 9:21; 19:32-35).

Abraham Back-slides Again!

(Genesis 20:1-18)

I. Concentration: on the heathen king, Abimelech

    1. Abimelech was king of the Philistines in Gerar, vv. 1-2; Gen. 26:1.

    2. Abimelech lusted after and sent for Sarah, Abraham's wife, v. 2.

    3. Abimelech was warned by the Lord in a dream not to take another man's wife, v. 3.

    4. Abimelech pled his innocence and integrity, on the basis of his ignorance of the fact that Abraham and Sarah were married, vv. 4-6.

II. Meditation: on God's dealings with Abimelech

    1. In obedience to the Lord's revelation and warning, Abimelech returned Sarah to Abraham, vv. 7-14.

    2. In effect, Abimelech spoke for the Lord when he strongly rebuked Abraham for his sin of deceit, asking him, "What did you have in view, that you did this thing?" vv. 9-10.

    3. Abimelech exhibited a God-like, generous, forgiving spirit, vv. 14-16.

    4. God, through Abraham's intercessory prayers, healed Abimelech's wife and female servants, so that they were able to bear children, vv. 17-18.

III. Revelation: on the spiritual implications of this chapter

    1. Wandering off into heathen territory (Egypt, Gen. 12 and Gerar, Gen. 20) often leads to sin and to the loss of integrity and credibility.

    2. The Lord sometimes reveals His will to unlikely persons, occasionally using those "unworthy" individuals to proclaim spiritual truths to His chosen leaders.

    3. One evidence of a person's spiritual interaction with the Lord is an inner transformation: a change from a selfish to a generous heart, from a vindictive to a forgiving spirit.

    4. Intercessory prayer is used by the Lord to bring life, healing, and productivity out of death, illness, and barrenness.

IV. Applications: as a Christian, I need to . . .

    1. Deliberately choose to live my life within the center of God's will . . . not wandering away like a careless, straying sheep, Isa. 53:6.

    2. Be alert, humble, and teachable . . . receiving the Lord's rebukes and instructions from whatever sources He chooses to use.

    3. Daily spend quality time in the presence of the Lord, so that my life starts to exhibit His Godly characteristics . . . so that I start being conformed to the image of God's son, Rom. 12:1-2; II Cor. 3:18.

    4. Pray for God's love, mercy, and grace on specific persons and situations, even as I acknowledge that my own personal sins may have been a contributing factor to the problem.

The Continuing Story of Hagar

(Genesis 21:1-21)

I. Concentration: on Sarah's maid, Hagar (first introduced in Genesis 16)

    1. Upon Sarah's suggestion, Hagar bore Abraham a son, whom they named Ishmael, Gen. 16.

    2. Fourteen years later, Sarah finally bore Abraham the son of promise, whom they named Isaac, Gen. 21:3.

    3. The teenager, Ishmael, made fun of the infant, Isaac, which caused Sarah to demand that Abraham send Hagar and Ishmael away into the desert where, without water, they faced certain death, vv. 9-14.

    4. Hagar and Ishmael took some provisions and wandered into the Wilderness of Beersheba, v. 14.

II. Meditation: on the dilemma Abraham faced

    1. Abraham loved his first son, Ishmael, and did not want him to come to harm, as Sarah planned, vv. 10-11.

    2. The Lord gave Abraham encouragement, promising him that Ishmael would survive and become a nation, vv. 12-13.

    3. Abraham wanted to maintain domestic peace, so he yielded to Sarah's demands to expel Hagar and Ishmael, v. 14.

    4. Abraham gave Hagar some provisions (bread and water) before sending her and the boy away, v. 14.

III. Revelation: on God's dealings with Hagar

    1. Hagar used up their meager provisions, then put Ishmael in the shade and withdrew a distance because she did not want to see him suffer and die of thirst; both she and the boy cried out in despair, vv. 15-17.

    2. Hagar earlier had an experience with the "God-Who-Sees" (Gen. 16:13); now God hears her cries and sends an angel to aid her and her son, Ishmael, v. 17. (*"Ishmael" means "God hears."*)

    3. The angel comforted and encouraged her . . . "Fear not . . . God has heard" . . . promising that her son would survive and become a great nation, vv. 17-18, 20-21. *(Ishmael became the father of the present-day Arabic nations, which trace their lineage back to Abraham.)*

    4. God opened Hagar's eyes; she saw a well of waters, v. 19. *(It was Hagar, not Sarah, who personally encountered God . . . twice!)*

IV. Applications: as a Christian, I need to know that . . .

    1. God sees my troubles, hears my cries, and sends help . . . because He is loving and merciful.

    2. God gives His people a message of cheer, comfort, and encouragement . . . just when they need it.

    3. God honors parents' concern about their children's welfare, and fulfills His promises to give them hope for the future.

    4. God opens the eyes of hurting persons, allowing them to see His abundant provision for them and His purposed destiny for their lives.

Jehovah-Jireh: The Lord Will Provide

(Genesis 22:1-19)

I. Concentration: on God's test (mid-term examination) of Abraham

    1. It was a test of his spiritual <u>discernment</u> . . . Did he really hear what he thought he heard the Lord say? vv. 1-2.

    2. It was a test of his <u>obedience</u> . . . Abraham obediently rose early next morning to make preparations for the trip, vv. 3, 18.

    3. It was a test of his spiritual <u>perception</u> . . . He "lifted his eyes and saw the place afar off," v. 4 . . . God's place of sacrifice on Mt. Moriah was the future site of the Temple in Jerusalem purchased by David and built by Solomon, I Chron. 21:21-26; II Chron. 3:1; 7:1-3.

    4. It was a test of his <u>faith</u> . . . He believed God's word so completely that even though he actually might sacrifice his son, both of them would return to the camp, v. 5; Abraham believed in the Lord's resurrection power, Heb. 11:17-19.

II. Meditation: on the events occurring on Mount Moriah

    1. Isaac was called Abraham's "only son" in spite of Abraham's first-born son, Ishmael, v. 2. *(Isaac was Abraham's only true covenant son.)*

    2. Isaac asked his father to explain the details of the up-coming sacrifice, v. 7.

    3. Abraham laid his submissive son, Isaac, on the wood, secured him there, and began the act of execution, vv. 9-10.

    4. The Angel of the Lord (Pre-incarnate Christ) stopped Abraham from   killing Isaac and substituted a ram; Abraham called the place, "Jehovah-Jireh" . . . The Lord will provide, vv. 11-14.

III. Revelation: on the Messianic pictures seen here

    1. Jesus Christ is God's only begotten Son, Jn. 1:14; 3:16.

    2. Jesus was totally submissive to the Father's will; yet from the cross he asked the Father, "Why . . .?" Mt. 27:46.

    3. Jesus was nailed (bound) to a wooden cross on the same Mount Moriah where Abraham had offered Isaac . . . the New Testament's cross is the Old Testament's altar, Heb. 13:10.

    4. God substituted the "Lamb of God" to die in our place . . . Jesus Christ became the sacrifice to pay for our sins, Jn. 1:29. *Jehovah-Jireh!*

IV. Applications: as a Christian, I need to . . .

    1. Hear, see, believe, and obey God's personal words to me.

    2. Willingly offer as a sacrifice to the Lord all that I am, all that I have, and all that I can be . . . my dreams, my hopes, my aspirations, my future: all must die, Jn. 12:24.

    3. Receive by faith, with thanksgiving, God's continuing salvation provided by the crucifixion of the Son of God, the Lamb slain from the foundation of the world, Rev. 13:8.

    4. Celebrate God's abundant blessings upon me and my family; rejoice that He is using me to bless other persons on the earth, vv. 15-19.

Abraham Purchases a Burial Plot

(Genesis 23:1-20)

I. Concentration: on the death of Sarah

1. After separating from his nephew, Lot, Abraham settled near Hebron (Mamre), Gen. 13:18, a major city in the hill country of Judah about 19 miles south of Jerusalem and 15 miles west of the Dead Sea.
2. Sarah, Abraham's wife, died in Hebron at the age of 127 years, vv. 1-2.
3. At this time, her son, Isaac, was 37 years old, Gen. 17:17.
4. Since Abraham was a nomad, he had no land of his own, but he needed a permanent place to bury and memorialize his dead wife, vv. 3-4.

II. Meditation: on the burial cave purchased by Abraham

1. After some interesting negotiations (vv. 5-17), Abraham paid Ephron 400 shekels of silver for a field, a cave, and the surrounding trees . . . to be used as a family cemetery plot.
2. Abraham and Sarah were buried there, Gen. 23:19; 25:9.
3. Isaac and Rebekah were buried there, Gen. 35:29; 49:31.
4. Jacob and Leah were buried there, Gen. 49:31; 50:13.

III. Revelation: on the spiritual implications of this chapter

1. All human beings shall die, and it is entirely appropriate to honor their lives with a memorial at their burial site.
2. Abraham insisted on paying Ephron's full asking-price for the land, although it probably was not worth 400 shekels, and he could have received it as a gift. *The true value of a spiritual act is determined by its cost . . . the price paid, II Sam. 24:24.*
3. Abraham officially and legally purchased the land, receiving a permanent "title-deed," vv. 16-18. (*We, also, have a certain inheritance*).
4. Thus, Abraham came into possession of the first part of the land of Canaan, which God had promised to him and his family, vv. 19-20.

IV. Applications: as a Christian, I need to . . .

1. Accept God's ideal of a marriage: through good and bad (for richer or poorer; in sickness and health) . . . it is "until death do us part."
2. Be absolutely fair and scrupulously honest in all my business dealings, refusing to take unfair advantage of another person.
3. Know that, although this world is not my home . . . I am only a pilgrim here . . . my (temporary) ownership/stewardship of private property is fitting and proper in the eyes of God.
4. Realize that the joyful fulfillment of God's promises to me often is accompanied by a season of testing, grief, and sorrow. (*Abraham got part of the Promised Land, but it was connected to the death of Sarah.*)

Four Women at the Well

(Genesis 24:1-67)

I. Concentration: on Abraham's plan to secure a wife for Isaac

    1. Abraham assigned his servant Eliezer the task of traveling back to his original homeland to find a bride for Isaac, vv. 1-4.

    2. Abraham forbade Isaac from returning there personally because Abraham wanted Isaac to remain in the "Promised Land," vv. 5-9.

    3. Eliezer prayed to God for guidance to know which woman the Lord had chosen to marry Isaac, vv. 10-12.

    4. Eliezer asked God for a definite sign . . . that the chosen woman would offer water to him and to his animals, vv. 13-14.

II. Meditation: on Rebekah, who was to become Isaac's wife

    1. Rebekah, a beautiful young woman, was Abraham's great-niece and a second cousin of Isaac, Gen. 22:20-23.

    2. Rebekah fulfilled exactly the signs established by Eliezer, confirming to him that Rebekah was the chosen woman . . . and Eliezer worshipped and thanked the Lord, vv. 15-27.

    3. Rebekah's brother, Laban, and her father, Bethuel, negotiated the nuptial arrangements and received the dowry sent by Abraham, vv. 28-53.

    4. After a brief delay, Eliezer brought Rebekah to Isaac, who was in a field meditating when she arrived, vv. 54-67.

(Note the types of the Trinity here: according to the Father's will, the Holy Spirit brought the bride to the Son.)

III. Revelation: on how God supplies our needs (illustrated by women at the well)

    1. <u>Rebekah</u> (Isaac's bride, Gen. 24) - Sometimes, under the Lord's guidance, we must ask help from a person whom God sends with the "water." <u>Rachel</u> (Jacob's bride, Gen. 29) - Sometimes we must take the initiative and try innovative, non-traditional methods to secure the "water" we need . . . to be shared with others.

    2. <u>Zipporah</u> (Moses' bride, Ex. 2) - Sometimes we must battle enemies in cooperation with others to attain our needed "water."

    3. <u>Samaritan Woman</u> (who met Jesus at Jacob's well in Sychar, Jn. 4) -

    4. <u>Not sometimes, but always</u>, when we ask the Lord for the "living water," He miraculously gives us His "fountain of water springing up into everlasting life," Jn. 4:10, 14.

IV. Applications: as a Christian, I need to . . .

    1. Pray for God's specific guidance ("wisdom") in ascertaining His will in the tasks assigned to me, Jas. 1:5.

    2. Understand that as a thirsty soul, I need a drink of God's water, Mt. 5:6.

    3. Note that God's chosen mates for Isaac, Jacob, and Moses all were found at an oasis. *(The best place to find God's mate is at an oasis: church.)*

    4. Follow the Samaritan woman's example of bringing others to the source of living water, Jesus the Messiah, Jn. 4:28-30.

Twin Sons Born to Isaac and Rebekah

(Genesis 25:19-34)

I. Concentration: on the parents, Isaac and Rebekah

1. Isaac was 40 years old when he married Rebekah, vv. 19-20.
2. Isaac pleaded for many years for the Lord to give Rebekah children, v. 21.
3. In answer to Isaac's prayers, God allowed Rebekah to become pregnant, twenty years after their marriage, vv. 21, 26.
4. Rebekah had a troublesome pregnancy (because she was bearing twins), and she inquired of the Lord, "If all is well, why am I like this?" v0. 22.

II. Meditation: on the twin boys, Esau and Jacob

1. The Lord answered Rebekah, prophesying that (v. 23):
   1) Fraternal, not identical, twins would be born,
   2) The twins would produce two nations,
   3) One twin's people would be stronger than the other, and
   4) The older twin would serve the younger.
2. The twins were born and named Esau (hairy) and Jacob (supplanter or heel-catcher), vv. 24-26.
3. Esau was a physically-endowed outdoorsman, a skillful hunter, v. 27.
4. Jacob was a spiritually-minded "mild man," in sharp contrast to his brother, Esau, v. 27.

III. Revelation: on dysfunctional relationships in this family

1. Isaac loved the more "masculine" Esau because he enjoyed eating the game he provided, v. 28.
2. Rebekah loved the more "feminine" Jacob because he was more gentle and sensitive, v. 28.
3. Jacob took unfair advantage of a weakened Esau, getting him to sell his birthright for some stew, vv. 29-34. *(This caused a "blood" feud.)*
4. Esau "despised" (scorned; held in contempt) his birthright (a double portion of his father's inheritance, plus all the spiritual blessings associated with God's covenant with Abraham), v. 34 . . . Esau was a fornicator and a profane person, according to Heb. 12:16.

IV. Applications: as a Christian, I need to . . .

1. Ask the Lord for enlightenment when the circumstances of my life are in turmoil, or when I am suffering physically.
2. Listen for the words from the Lord, giving me spiritual perception (and occasionally prophetic insight) into God's planned destiny for me.
3. Avoid parental favoritism, which can be the source of severe and long-term family disruption.
4. Magnify the spiritual things of God while avoiding "profanity" . . . irreverent, blasphemous, vulgar words and deeds.

Isaac, the Patient Well-digger

(Genesis 26:12-25)

I. Concentration: on Isaac's digging the wells of water

1. Isaac, whom God had caused "to prosper, to continue prospering, and to become very prosperous" (vv. 12-13), dug again the wells of water which his father Abraham had dug, but which his envious enemies had stopped up, vv. 14-18.
2. Isaac called the unstopped wells by the same names which his father Abraham originally had called them, v. 18.
3. Isaac dug new wells, which aroused opposition from his neighbors; the new wells were appropriately named: "Quarrel" and "Enmity," vv. 19-21.
4. Finally Isaac dug another well which he named "Rehoboth" meaning spaciousness or roominess, and implying frutifulness, v. 22. *Isaac prophesied: "For now the Lord has made <u>room</u> for us, and we shall be <u>fruitful</u> in the land," v. 22.*

II. Meditation: on the Lord's appearance to Isaac (v. 24)

1. Personal - <u>I AM</u> the God of Abraham (Abraham is alive!), Mt. 22:32.
2. Peace - Do not be afraid . . . "<u>Fear not!</u>" (God offers mercy amd grace.)
3. Presence - I AM <u>with</u> you, Mt. 28:20; Heb. 13:5-6.
4. Promise - I will <u>bless</u> you and your family for Abraham's sake!

III. Revelation: on Isaac's responses to God's appearance and promises (v. 25)

1. Isaac built an altar there, marking and memorializing the place where God spoke to him.
2. Isaac called on God's name in worship, praise, thanksgiving, and intercessory prayer.
3. Isaac pitched his tent there . . . settled down; lived there: where God was.
4. Isaac's servants dug another well, providing water for his family and for the generations to come.

IV. Applications: as a Christian, I need to . . .

1. Unstop the sources of blessings which were utilized by my spiritual forefathers . . . resolving to serve the present, with an eye on the future, while respecting the past.
2. Exhibit a quiet, non-violent, humble, submissive spirit in the face of opposition . . . because God will provide and protect.
3. Be open to receive a revelation "word" from the Lord . . . when He speaks, remember His "rhema" word to me, worship Him, live under the covenant blessing, and faithfully serve Him and others.
4. Recognize that, on the day I establish peace in my heart with those who persucute and abuse me, the Lord will give me a new well of spiritual refreshment through the Holy Spirit, v. 32.

Isaac Blesses His Sons

(Genesis 27:1-46)

I. Concentration: on Isaac's plan and Rebekah's counter-scheme

    1. Blind Isaac, sensing his imminent death, asked Esau to hunt game and prepare his favorite meal before receiving his father's blessing, vv. 1-4.

    2. Rebekah overheard Isaac's plan and schemed with her favorite son, Jacob, to deceive the father, Isaac, and to receive the blessing (inheritance) intended for Esau, vv. 5-10.

    3. Rebekah took full responsibility for the deception . . . perhaps believing that she was accomplishing God's will, vv. 11-17.

    4. Isaac was suspicious that the son who brought his food was Jacob rather than Esau, but he proceeded with the Esau blessing, vv. 18-29.

II. Meditation: on how Old Testament blessings worked

    1. Blessings were to be pronounced by faith, as Isaac did, Heb. 11:20.

    2. Once spoken, blessings (or curses) could not be recalled . . . the words took on a permanent life of their own, vv. 33-37.

    3. Traditionally, the elder son received a double portion of the father's inheritance and became the head of the family . . . including assuming the office of the spiritual leader (priest) of the family.

    4. Genuine blessings must proceed from a spiritually perceptive person; although Isaac was old and blind, he was not insensitive to the spiritual conditions of Jacob and Esau . . . his blessings revealed that he knew their true character.

III. Revelation: on the blessings which Isaac intended for each son to receive

    1. Isaac's original blessing to Esau (Jacob in disguise) was entirely involved with the physical realm: material prosperity and earthly dominion over the family and other nations, vv. 27-29.

    2. Isaac's later blessing to Esau included some material prosperity, yet with a prediction of a life of violence, oppression, and rebellion, vv. 39-40.

    3. In neither of Isaac's blessings (in Genesis 27) did he mention the spiritual blessing of Abraham . . . because he knew that Esau was a profane person (Heb. 12:16) and that Jacob was the one through whom the spiritual blessings would flow to benefit all the earth.

    4. Only when Isaac was absolutely sure that he was talking to Jacob did he give the spiritual blessing of the Abrahamic covenant, Gen. 28:1-4.

IV. Applications: as a Christian, I need to . . .

    1. Realize that God will accomplish His will without my deceitful schemes.

    2. Be careful of the words I speak, for they can never be retracted, Mt. 12:36;

    3. Num. 23:11-12, 25-26.

    4. Pronounce blessings upon my children . . . the only act of faith for which Isaac was commended in Hebrews 11.

Jacob's Ladder

(Genesis 28:1-22)

I. Concentration: on Jacob's flight from his home

1. Jacob left home because his brother, Esau, was plotting to kill him in revenge for Jacob's stealing of his birthright, Gen. 27:41.
2. Jacob also left home because his mother, Rebekah, told him to go live awhile with her brother, Laban, Gen. 27:42-45.
3. As soon as Isaac had pronounced the Abrahamic blessing upon Jacob, he sent the young man away to another country to find himself a bride, vv. 1-5 . . . in sharp contrast to what Abraham had instructed Eliezer about finding a bride for Isaac, Gen. 24:6-7.
4. Meanwhile, Esau deliberately rebelled and disobeyed his father's wishes by marrying a daughter of Ishmael and other heathen wives, which had been forbidden to both Jacob and Esau, vv. 6-9.

II. Meditation: on Jacob's dream of a ladder reaching into heaven

1. On his first night away from home, Jacob slept with his head on a stone, and he dreamed about a ladder between earth and heaven, with angels ascending and descending upon it, v. 12.
2. The Lord God stood above the ladder, identified Himself, and reaffirmed the Abrahamic covenant, vv. 13-14.
3. God promised Jacob that He always would be with him, v. 15.
4. God assured Jacob that someday He would bring him back home, v. 15.

III. Revelation: on Jacob's reactions to this heavenly dream

1. Jacob perceived the dream had been a genuine spiritual experience, v. 16.
2. Jacob was afraid of the awesome presence of Almighty God in the place . . . of which he had not been aware originally, vv. 16-17.
3. Jacob used his "pillow" (stone) to construct an altar where he offered a sacrifice to God; he named the place "Bethel," meaning "House of God," vv. 18-19.
4. Jacob made a vow to give God a tithe (one-tenth), if the Lord would bless him as He had promised, vv. 20-22. *(Tithing preceded the Law.)*

IV. Applications: as a Christian, I need to . . .

1. Avoid serious family bickering, malice, confrontation, and violence by leaving the dangerous environment whenever possible.
2. Be open and sensitive to God's revelations of Himself and of His will and purpose for my life . . . recognize true spiritual experiences, and discern their meanings through the Holy Spirit's enlightenment.
3. "Camp" every day and every night at Bethel . . . the house of God (where Abraham earlier had met God, Gen. 12:8); worship the Lord with offerings and vows of faithful service.
4. Know that Jesus Christ is "Jacob's ladder" (Jn. 1:51) . . . upon which   man's prayers ascend to heaven and upon which God's blessings descend to earth, I Tim. 2:5; Phil. 4:19.

We Can't Do That, Because . . .

(Genesis 29:1-35)

I. Concentration: on Jacob's quest for a wife

1. Jacob journeyed east, back toward where his grandfather Abraham had lived many years before, v. 1.
2. Jacob came into the area where his mother, Rebekah, had told him to look for his uncle Laban, Gen. 28:2, 5; 29:5.
3. Jacob met some shepherds from the city where his grandfather Abraham had lived in the years between Ur and Canaan, v. 4; Gen. 11:31.
4. Jacob experienced "love at first sight" when he spotted his cousin Rachel, who arrived at the well to water her sheep, vv. 6, 9.

II. Meditation: on the shepherds' excuses for not watering Rachel's sheep

1. We can't do it, because . . . it's not customary; it's non-traditional, v. 3. *(We've never done it that way before!)*
2. We can't do it, because . . . it's the wrong time, v. 7. *(It may be a good idea, but not now!)*
3. We can't do it, because . . . we won't start a job until we can see that we are well able to complete it, v. 8. *(We're not going to do a partial job . . . if we can't do everything, we won't do anything!)*
4. We can't do it, because . . . it's too difficult without adequate manpower; if someone else will start and do the hardest part (removing the stone from the well), then we'll join in and do our part. *(Let George do it!)*

III. Revelation: on the proper answers to these flimsy excuses

1. The "new" is not necessarily wrong or bad.
2. When the need is perceived as acute, the time is right to take immediate, decisive action.
3. Do not wait until you can be sure of doing all that is needed before you begin . . . or you may never start.
4. Take the Godly risk; by faith, jump in although the task seems too big to be accomplished alone . . . God will give divine strength to finish any task which He calls you to do.

IV. Applications: as a Christian, I need to . . .

1. Seek, find, and follow God's will, ignoring all reasons (excuses) why "It can't be done!" *In this story, Jacob (with no help from the others) watered Rachel's flock, v. 10.*
2. Be passionate in service for my Master, motivated by love . . . Jacob served Laban faithfully for seven years for the hand of his daughter Rachel, and "They seemed only a few days to him because of the love he had for her," v. 20.
3. Remain faithful to my assignment, keeping a steady eye on my God-given objective, in spite of delays, disappointments, and deceit, vv. 21-28.
4. Know that God will reward such faithfulness with abundant prosperity and productivity, vv. 29-35.

Out-foxing the Fox

(Genesis 30:1-43)

I. Concentration: on the continuing battle of wits between Laban and Jacob

    1. Laban tricked Jacob into marrying Leah rather than Rachel, then "black-mailed" him into seven more years of service to get the woman he loved, Gen. 29:16-20.

    2. Laban and Jacob agreed to divide the flock, with Laban taking the solid-colored sheep and goats and Jacob taking the speckled ones, vv. 31-34.

    3. Laban secretly removed all the speckled animals to a far away pasture, vv. 35-36.

    4. Jacob erected speckled rods near the watering troughs so that the animals would be looking at them as they conceived, vv. 37-43. *(There is no scientific credibility to the old wives' tale that things seen by a pregnant mother "mark" her unborn child . . . but, in this case, God used this method to miraculously accomplish His purpose of prospering Jacob, Gen. 31:11-12; Psa. 18:25-26.)*

II. Meditation: on Jacob's wives and children (The Twelve Tribes of Israel)

    1. <u>Leah</u> - bore (1) Reuben, (2) Simeon, (3) Levi, (4) Judah, then later . . . (9) Isacchar, and (10) Zebulun (plus a daughter, Dinah).

    2. <u>Bilhah</u> (Rachel's maid) - bore (5) Dan and (6) Naphtali.

    3. <u>Zilpah</u> (Leah's maid) - bore (7) Gad and (8) Asher.

    4. <u>Rachel</u> - bore (11) Joseph and (12) Benjamin.

III. Revelation: on Laban's earnest request to Jacob (v. 27)

    1. "Please stay" - Laban did not want Jacob to return to Canaan with his daughters and grandchildren . . . and especially with his large flock of sheep and goats.

    2. "If I have found favor in your eyes" - Laban appealed to Jacob to do this as a favor . . . to repay the "generosity" of his father-in-law/uncle.

    3. "For I have learned by experience" - Laban realized that his trickiest schemes would not work against God or God's chosen person.

    4. "The Lord has blessed me for your sake" - The influence of the presence of God's people in a region is a spiritual and material blessing for the entire society . . . they're salt and light, Mt. 5:13-16.

IV. Applications: as a Christian, I need to . . .

    1. Always deal with others in unfailing integrity, complete honesty, and scrupulous fairness.

    2. Praise the Lord, Who is able to bring good (the 12 tribes) out of a bad situation (polygamy), Rom. 8:28.

    3. Choose to associate with and develop friendships with persons who intimately know the Lord and who faithfully serve Him.

    4. Guard my influence, so that persons truly may say of me: "The Lord has blessed me through you."

Mizpah

(Genesis 31:44-55)

I. Concentration: on the parting of Jacob and Laban

1. Jacob's prosperity made him an object of jealousy and envy by Laban's sons, v. 1.
2. Laban's attitude toward Jacob had changed . . . his countenance "was not favorable toward him as before," v. 2.
3. The Lord told Jacob to return to Canaan, and he conferred with his wives about the move, vv. 3-13.
4. Rachel and Leah advised Jacob to take their inheritance and leave the country secretly, vv. 14-21.

II. Meditation: on the final confrontation between Jacob and Laban

1. After three days, Laban heard of Jacob's departure, and he pursued and overtook him within a week, vv. 22-25.
2. Laban asked "Why?" . . . alleging that he would have given them a nice "going-away" party, vv. 26-28.
3. Laban had been told by the Lord not to harm Jacob, v. 29.
4. Laban accused someone in Jacob's party of stealing his household idols; in fact, Rachel had done so, but was not caught, vv. 30-35

III. Revelation: on the resolution of this conflict

1. Jacob angrily rebuked Laban for what he believed to be his false accusation about stealing household gods, vv. 36-37.
2. Jacob also rebuked Laban for the unfair treatment he had given during 20 years of service: "You have changed my wages ten times," vv. 38-41.
3. Jacob asserted that Laban would have sent him away empty-handed, except for God's intervention, v. 42.
4. Laban and Jacob made a covenant and erected a stone pillar ("Mizpah" meaning a "heap of witness") to mark the line between the two men, which they swore never to cross, vv. 43-55.

IV. Applications: as a Christian, I need to . . .

1. Listen with spiritual discernment to receive the Lord's direction for my life and family; wait for a word of confirmation from others who are personally involved.
2. Discuss all major decisions with other members of the family . . . seeking their insight and advice.
3. Deal immediately with inter-personal problems and disagreements; communicate . . . rather than storing up frustrations for twenty years and then exploding with anger!
4. Realize that God indeed does watch over his people while they are absent one from another . . . "Mizpah," v. 49.

God Changes Jacob into Israel

(Genesis 32:1-32)

I. Concentration: on the historical setting of this chapter

    1. Jacob and Laban had erected Mizpah ("Watch"), and Jacob offered a sacrifice before departing, Gen. 31:48-55.

    2. Angels of God met Jacob and he said, "This is God's camp," naming the place Mahanaim ("Double Camp"), vv. 1-2.

    3. Jacob, the manipulator, sent messengers and gifts to pacify his brother Esau, in an attempt to protect his family, vv. 3-8, 13-23.

    4. Jacob was greatly afraid and distressed, and he prayed, vv. 7, 9-12.

II. Meditation: on Jacob's prayer unto the Lord

    1. He identifies himself with Abraham and Isaac, reminding God of His promise at Bethel (Gen. 28:12-22) to bring him back safely into Canaan, v. 9.

    2. He expressed deep humility before God: "I am not worthy," v. 10.

    3. He thanked God for His mercies and blessings, v. 10.

    4. He asked God for protection and deliverance from Esau, vv. 11-12.

III. Revelation: on Jacob's personal encounter with the Lord

    1. Jacob was alone in a quiet place, where he spent several hours with a "Man," v. 24 . . . "Man" is the Angel of the Lord (Hos. 12:4) . . . the Pre-incarnate Christ.

    2. Jacob "wrestled" (spiritually struggled, contended, grappled, strove with) the "Man," and the struggle was so intense that it produced physical injury and pain, v. 25; Lk. 22:44.

    3. Jacob persisted in asking for a blessing, v. 26.

    4. The Lord heard and changed his name from Jacob ("Heel-catcher") to Israel ("Prince with God") . . . the name change symbolized the inner transformation of Jacob's life.

IV. Applications: on my personal walk after I have encountered God

    1. More than ever, I deeply will desire to come to know the Lord better . . . "Tell me Your name, I pray." v. 29.

    2. In humility and thanksgiving, I will memorialize the place of my spiritual experience with God, v. 30 . . . Jacob called the place "Peniel," meaning "Face of God."

    3. Since I had my life-changing experience with God, I now will walk differently; Jacob "limped," v. 31 . . . my spiritual steps also should testify of my up-close-and-personal encounter with the Lord.

    4. I need to fulfill my vows unto the Lord; Jacob pledged to tithe God's blessings when he returned to his homeland, Gen. 28:22. *(To whom did Jacob give the tithe? He probably did not sacrifice to the Lord one out of every ten animals he owned, but possibly Jacob gave that portion to his brother, Esau, vv. 13-15. Our gifts to others may be seen as gifts to the Lord, Mt. 25:40.)*

Old Habits Are Hard to Break!

(Genesis 33:1-20)

I. Concentration: on Jacob's meeting with Esau after 20 years

1. Jacob sent his least favored wives and children ahead to meet the potentially dangerous Esau, vv. 1-2.
2. Jacob bowed himself to the ground before Esau seven times, v. 3.
3. Esau cordially met Jacob's family with embraces and kisses, vv. 4-7.
4. Esau asked his brother why he had sent all the gifts, v. 8.

II. Meditation: on Jacob's continuing attempts to manipulate Esau

1. Jacob flattered Esau: "I have seen your face as if I had seen the face of God," v. 10.
2. Jacob urged a gift (bribe) upon Esau, to assure his family's safety, v. 11.
3. Jacob made lame excuses to get away from Esau's presence, vv. 12-15.
4. Jacob lied about his destination, telling Esau he would join him in Seir (Edom), but journeying instead to Canaan and permanently settling there, vv. 16-18.

III. Revelation: on Jacob's settling his family in the Promised Land

1. Jacob stopped temporarily east of the Jordan River at Succoth ("Booths"), so named for the shelters (booths) he made for his livestock; there he built himself a house, v. 17.
2. Later, he crossed the Jordan River into Canaan and settled near Shechem, sometimes identified with Sychar (Jacob's Well), v. 18; Jn. 4:5-6.
3. He bought a parcel of land from the children of Hamor, Shechem's father, for 100 pieces of money. *(Here the bones of Joseph, Jacob's son, were transported from Egypt and buried centuries later, Josh. 24:32.)*
4. He erected an altar there, and worshipped "El Elohe Israel" . . . "God, the God of Israel," v. 20.

IV. Applications: as a Christian, I need to . . .

1. Exercise wise caution in caring and providing for my family, but ultimately trust them into the safe hands of the Lord.
2. Avoid trying to manipulate people by flattery, gifts, deceitful excuses, and deliberate lies . . . such actions reveal a lack of faith in God.
3. Realize that although I have encountered God and He is in the process of changing me into the image of His Son, there still is a lot of "Jacob" in me which needs to be transformed into the character of a true member of God's royal family: "Israel" . . . "Prince with God."
4. Settle down in the "promised land" which God has given to me; "Bloom where I am planted!" . . . here erecting an altar and worshipping Him.

Massacre at Shechem

(Genesis 34:1-31)

I. Concentration: on the characters involved in this tragic episode

    1. Dinah, v. 1 - daughter of Leah, Gen. 30:21.

    2. Jacob, v. 1 - father of Dinah.

    3. Hamor, v. 2 - ruler of the territory; father of Shechem.

    4. Shechem, v. 2 - son of Hamor; his father's capital city was named for him.

    5. Simeon and Levi - Dinah's brothers, v. 25; Gen. 29:32-33; 30:21.

II. Meditation: on the events in this chapter

    1. Shechem raped Dinah; then asked his father, Hamor, to get her for his wife, vv. 2-4, 8-12.

    2. Jacob and his sons were grieved and angry; they plotted revenge, vv. 5-7.

    3. Jacob's sons agreed to allow Dinah to marry Shechem, who was not a Jew, if all the males in the city would be circumcised, vv. 13-24.

    4. On the third day after surgery, while the men were still in pain, Simeon and Levi killed all the males of Shechem, rescued Dinah, plundered the city, and took their wives and children captive, vv. 25-29.

III. Revelation: on the spiritual principles seen here

    1. Association with ungodly persons easily can lead to wickedness and tragedy: "Dinah . . . went out to see the daughters of the land," v. 1.

    2. Sexual attraction, "true love," and tender feelings are not grounds enough to bring God's approval upon a marriage between a believer and an unbeliever, v. 3; II Cor. 6:14.

    3. "The love of money is a root of all kinds of evil," I Tim. 6:10 . . . the men of Shechem agreed to circumcision motivated by a desire for economic gain, vv. 20-23.

    4. Sin always brings judgment and punishment . . . the men of Shechem were killed by Simeon and Levi; later, Simeon and Levi were cursed by their father, Jacob, because of their cruelty, vv. 30-31; Gen. 49:5-7.

IV. Applications: as a Christian, I need to . . .

    1. Choose my friends and close associates (if possible) from among the people who know and serve the Lord . . . fellow Christians.

    2. Avoid sexual immorality by marrying a spouse who shares my Christian commitment, I Cor. 7:2, 9.

    3. Know that spiritual considerations and Godly principles are the real "bottom line" . . . not monetary profits!

    4. Live in peace with my enemies (Mt. 6:44), realizing that vengeance belongs to the Lord, Rom. 12:19-21.

Back to Bethel

(Genesis 35:1-29)

I. Concentration: on the main events in this chapter

1. God told Jacob (Israel) to return to Bethel, vv. 1-15.
2. Rachel, Jacob's wife, died giving birth to Benjamin, vv. 16-20.
3. Reubin, Jacob's eldest son (by Leah) had illicit sexual relations with Bilhah, his father's concubine (Rachel's maid), vv. 21-26. *This act caused Jacob to curse Reubin in Gen. 49:3-4.*
4. Isaac died at the age of 180 years, and was buried by his sons, Jacob and Esau, vv. 27-29; Gen. 49:29-32.

(Note: verse 8 tells of the death and burial of Deborah, Rebekah's nurse. She is mentioned only once in Scripture, but she probably was important to Jacob because she had been his nanny.)

II. Meditation: on "Bethel" . . . the House of God

1. Bethel was the place where Abraham first settled, built an altar, and called on the name of the Lord, Gen. 12:8; later Abraham returned "Back to Bethel" following his journey into Egypt, Gen. 13:3.
2. Bethel was the place where Jacob saw the vision of the angels ascending and descending on a ladder between earth and heaven, Gen. 28:10-19.
3. Bethel was the place to which the Lord commanded Jacob to return from his wanderings in a foreign land with his uncle, Laban, Gen. 31:13.
4. Bethel was the place which God chose to become the temporary place of worship for the nation, before Jerusalem became the site of the temple in the days of David and Solomon, Gen. 35:1-8, 15-16; I Sam. 10:3.

III. Revelation: on the spiritual meanings of going "Back to Bethel"

1. Reconstruction of broken-down, unused altars, vv. 6-7.
2. Revival of spiritual fellowship with the Lord, v. 9.
3. Restoration of God's covenants with His chosen family, vv. 10-12.
4. Renewal of communion with God and sacrifice to Him, v. 14.

IV. Applications: as a Christian, I need to . . .

1. Hear the Lord's call to return (literally or in my thoughts) to the holy place where I first met Him.
2. Prepare myself for this return to the Lord by renouncing all idols, purifying myself through repentance and confession, putting on the righteous robes of Christ, and arising and moving toward Bethel . . . God's house, vv. 2-3.
3. Testify to my family members, and others, about my spiritual experiences of encountering Almighty God, vv. 3-7.
4. Revisit my old altars of worship, reaffirming my sacred vows to the Lord, and pouring out my life before Him as a sacrificial offering, v. 14; Phil. 2:17; II Tim. 4:6.

Who on Earth Was Anah?

(Genesis 36:1, 5, 14, 24)

I. Concentration: on the family of Esau

1. Abraham . . . Isaac . . . Jacob and Esau: Jacob (renamed Israel) was a sneaky, devious, deceptive type of person, while Esau was a vulgar, profane, rebellious type of individual.
2. Esau, much to the grief of his parents Isaac and Rebekah, married not one but three Canaanite (heathen) women, vv. 2-3.
3. Genesis 36 records the genealogy of Esau, which includes one of his wives, Aholibamah, who was the daughter of Anah, v. 2, 5, 14.
4. Anah, the focus of this study, was Esau's father-in-law.

II. Meditation: on verse 24

"This was the Anah who found water in the wilderness (hot springs in the desert) as he pastured the donkeys of his father Zibeon," Gen. 36:24.

III. Revelation: on what is known about Anah, v. 24

1. Anah labored in a desolate, God-forsaken place.
2. Anah tended a herd of donkeys.
3. Anah faithfully served his father, Zibeon.
4. Anah did one significant thing in his life (made one important discovery) which benefited people for many generations to come . . . he found water in the wilderness . . . hot springs in the desert.

IV. Applications: as a Christian, I need to learn these lessons . . .

1. God may assign me to work in an obscure, out-of-the-way place.
2. I may be given a task as difficult as taking care of stubborn donkeys.
3. Even in a desert place doing a difficult, unsung task, I must faithfully serve my Father.
4. Occasionally . . . but at least once in each lifetime . . . I will have an opportunity to accomplish something significant to benefit generations yet unborn; I don't want to miss that chance!

How will I be remembered? "This is the Curt Scarborough who . . ."

Joseph's Dream of Destiny

(Genesis 37:1-36)

I. Concentration: on why Joseph was hated by his brothers

1. Because he brought a bad report about them to their father, Jacob . . . *whether Joseph merely was obeying his father's orders or being a "tattle-tale" is not clear from this Scripture, vv. 1-2.*
2. Because he was their father's favorite son of his favorite wife, Rachel, Joseph became the object of criticism and envy, vv. 3-5, 11.
3. Because his father favored him with obvious preferential treatment by giving him a distinctive tunic of many colors, v. 3.
4. Because he told his brothers about his two prophetic dreams, vv. 5-11.

II. Meditation: on Joseph's dreams of destiny

1. Dream One: While binding sheaves in the field, Joseph's sheaf arose and stood upright, but the brothers' sheaves bowed down to his, vv. 6-7.
2. Interpretation: Joseph would reign in dominion over his brothers, v. 8.
3. Dream Two: The sun, moon, and stars all bowed down to Joseph, v. 9.
4. Interpretation: Joseph's father (sun), his mother (moon), and his brothers (stars) all would bow down before him, v. 10.

III. Revelation: on the spiritual principles taught in this chapter

1. It is usually unwise to share God's personal vision or revelation with others . . . especially with unbelievers, I Cor. 2:14.
2. Joseph's brothers sold him into slavery and many years passed . . . between God's vision and its fulfillment, there always is a time of testing of a person's faith.
3. God is able to overcome all malice, betrayal, and lies . . . He can bring good out of bad, Rom. 8:28.
4. "What goes around, comes around" or "Chickens always will come home to roost" . . . just as Jacob deceived his father, Isaac, to obtain Esau's blessing, so also Jacob's sons deceived their father about the violent "death" of Joseph, vv. 12-36; Num. 32:23.

IV. Applications: as a Christian, I need to . . .

1. Be open to see God's spiritual vision and to hear God's prophetic word about my personal destiny in life.
2. Expect a long and tedious period of delay between God's promises to me and their fulfillment, II Pet. 3:8-9.
3. With living and growing faith, trust in the Lord to accomplish His will for me, in me, and through me.
4. Be absolutely sure that God knows my sinful nature, and that He will repay my deeds with His righteous (poetic) justice . . . my only hope is Christ's mercy and grace, Rom. 6:23.

Tamar Outsmarts Judah

(Genesis 38:1-30)

I. Concentration: on the Canaanite woman named Tamar

1. "Tamar" means "date palm."
2. This Tamar is listed as a part of the lineage of Jesus Christ, Matt. 1:3.
3. This Tamar is <u>not</u> David's daughter listed in II Samuel 13.
4. This Tamar was cited as part of the blessing which the elders pronounced when Ruth married Boaz, Ruth 4:12.

II. Meditation: on Tamar's ill treatment by Judah (one of the 12 sons of Jacob)

1. Tamar was the wife of Judah's eldest son, Er, a wicked man who died without producing a son, vv. 6-7.
2. Judah gave Tamar his second son, Onan, for the purpose of producing a son in the name of the dead man, Er, vv. 7-8.
3. Onan refused to impregnate Tamar, so God took his life, vv. 9-10.
4. Judah refused to allow his third son, Shelah, to become Tamar's husband because he feared for Shelah's life . . . Judah believed that Tamar was "bad luck" on husbands, vv. 11, 14.

III. Revelation: on God's use of Tamar's scheme to teach Judah a valuable lesson

1. Tamar disguised herself as a prostitute and agreed to have sexual relations with her father-in-law, Judah, vv. 12-15.
2. Judah and Tamar agreed upon a price (one goat), but Tamar asked for Judah's signet (ring), cord, and staff as a pledge, vv. 16-18.
3. Tamar resumed her role as Judah's daughter-in-law; Judah searched but could not find the "harlot" to pay his debt, vv. 19-23.
4. Three months later, when it became obvious that Tamar was pregnant, Judah wanted to have her burned as a harlot . . . but she produced his signet ring, cord, and staff to prove that he was the father; twin boys were born: Perez and Zerah, vv. 24-30.

IV. Applications: as a Christian, I need to . . .

1. Live according to God's laws (not attempting to circumvent them or "to find a loop-hole") . . . *The Levirate Law <u>required</u> a dead man's brother to marry his childless widow and father a son who would assume the dead man's name and inherit his portion of the Promised Land, Dt. 25:5-10. (See Ruth 2:20; 3:2, 9-13; 4:1-11; Mt. 22:23-33.)*
2. Realize that Almighty God can and will accomplish His perfect will, sometimes even using unworthy people and sinful actions to bring about His ultimate good, Rom. 8:28.
3. Refrain from making any hasty judgments, condemning a person who "obviously" is guilty of a gross sin, Mt. 7:1-5. *Remember that pride goes before a fall, Prov. 16:18.*
4. Confess my own guilt and sin before the Lord, recognizing that I am a dirty (but forgiven) sinner myself. *Judah was right when he said, "She has been more righteous than I," v. 26.*

Joseph "Framed" by Potiphar's Wife

(Genesis 39:1-23)

I. Concentration: on the events of Joseph's life in this chapter

Joseph had been sold by his brothers to Ishmaelites (children of Abraham by Hagar), Gen. 37:25-28; 39:1, also identified with the Midianites (children of Abraham by his second wife, Keturah), Gen. 25:1-2. These two clans probably had inter-married, becoming known by both names.

1. Potiphar, captain of the Egyptian Pharaoh's guard, purchased Joseph from the Ishmaelites, v. 1.
2. The Lord prospered all Joseph put his hand to, and he was given total authority over Potiphar's household, vv. 2-6.
3. Potiphar's wife tried unsuccessfully several times to seduce Joseph; then "framed" him for attempted rape, vv. 7-18.
4. Joseph was thrown into jail, where soon the keeper gave him authority over the entire prison system, vv. 19-23.

II. Meditation: on why Joseph was so successful in his responsibilities

1. Because the Lord was with him, vv. 2-3, 21-23.
2. Because Joseph had strong moral character, vv. 6-8, 10-13.
3. Because Joseph realized that adultery (and all other sins) are "against God," v. 9; Psa. 51:4.
4. Because the Lord showed mercy toward Joseph, preserving his life for His destined purpose . . . to save God's chosen people, v. 21.

III. Revelation: on the spiritual implications found here

1. The Lord will never forsake those whom He has chosen, Heb. 13:5-6.
2. God's people are to be holy (pure), just as God is holy, Lev. 11:44-45; I Pet. 1:16.
3. At the root, all sins are rebellion against the Creator's will.
4. God's mercy allows Him to use imperfect human beings to accomplish His heavenly purposes.

IV. Applications: as a Christian, I need to . . .

1. Walk by faith, trusting in the Lord, Who will be with me "always, even unto the end of the age," Mt. 28:20.
2. Keep my life pure . . . by repenting of my sins and receiving God's forgiveness and cleansing, I Jn. 1:9; 3:2-3.
3. Surrender my will completely to the Father, praying as Jesus did, "Your will be done," Mt. 26:42.
4. Claim God's mercy and grace as I seek to fulfill the destined purpose He has mapped out for my life, Phil. 3:13-14.

The Butler and the Baker

(Genesis 40:1-23)

I. Concentration: on Joseph's relationship with his fellow inmates

1. Joseph, as a "trustee," administered the royal prison, Gen. 39:21-23.
2. He was given charge over two of Pharaoh's imprisoned servants: the chief butler and the chief baker, vv. 1-4.
3. He noticed their sad and dejected faces and expressed genuine concern, asking, "Why do you look so sad today?" vv. 5-7.
4. The two prisoners said, "We each have had a dream, and there is no interpreter of it," v. 8.

II. Meditation: on the dreams and Joseph's interpretations

1. The butler's dream concerned a vine with three branches from which he pressed grape juice into Pharaoh's cup, vv. 9-11.
2. Joseph's interpretation: Within three days Pharaoh will release you from prison and restore you to your position, vv. 12-13.
3. The baker's dream showed him carrying on his head three baskets of baked goods for Pharaoh, which the birds came and ate, vv. 16-17.
4. Joseph's interpretation: Within three days, Pharaoh will execute you and the birds will eat your flesh, vv. 18-19.

III. Revelation: on the key events in this chapter

1. Joseph gave God all the credit . . . because God is the only One Who is able to interpret dreams, v. 8.
2. Joseph asked the butler to return his favor and kindness by mentioning to Pharaoh that an innocent man was being held in prison and should be released, vv. 14-15.
3. All the events which God had revealed to Joseph came to pass . . . the butler was restored and the baker was executed, vv. 20-22.
4. The chief butler failed to remember to speak to Pharaoh about Joseph, for two whole years, Gen. 40:23; 41:1.

IV. Applications: as a Christian, I need to . . .

1. Give God all the glory for the things which He does.
2. With humility, make requests for needed help from other persons to whom I have ministered and given assistance, Gal. 6:2.
3. Realize that God is faithful to bring to pass all those prophesied things which He has promised.
4. Recognize that men generally are unreliable; only the Lord is faithful to always keep His word.

Fat Cows and Skinny Cows

(Genesis 41:1-57)

I. Concentration: on the main events in this chapter

    1. Pharaoh had two dreams: of seven fat and seven skinny cows, and of seven plump heads of grain and seven thin heads, vv. 1-7, 17-24.

    2. None of Pharaoh's astrologers or wise men could interpret his dreams.

    3. Finally, the chief butler remembered Joseph and recommended him to the Pharaoh, vv. 9-13.

    4. Joseph was summoned from the dungeon and cleaned up; he gave God the glory for interpreting dreams; he told Pharaoh what his two dreams meant, vv. 14-16, 25-32.

II. Meditation: on Joseph's God-given interpretation

    1. Both dreams are pictures of the same coming events, vv. 25-26.

    2. There will be seven years of great, plentiful harvest in Egypt, v. 29.

    3. These "fat" years will be followed by seven "lean" years of severe famine, vv. 27, 30-31.

    4. "The dream was repeated to Pharaoh twice because the thing is established by God, and God will shortly bring it to pass," v. 32.

III. Revelation: on how God works to accomplish His purpose

    1. First, God shows one of His servants what He is about to do (Amos 3:7) . . . here Joseph passed God's word along to Pharaoh, v. 28.

    2. Next, God looks for a spiritually discerning person to appoint over his work, v. 33; then God gives His chosen leader specific plans to accomplish His divine purpose, vv. 34-37.

    3. God anoints His chosen leader with the Holy Spirit, empowering him for service and exhibiting God's presence in his life, v. 38.

    4. God gives His chosen, anointed leader the authority necessary to accomplish every duty and responsibility He assigns; here Pharaoh gave Joseph virtually total authority in Egypt, signified by his signet ring, royal garments, gold chain, and a chariot of honor, v. 39-44.

IV. Applications: as a Christian, I need to . . .

    1. Wait patiently, through adversity, knowing that the Lord has a destiny and purpose for me to fulfill during my life on earth.

    2. Faithfully carry out the details of the plan which God has revealed to me, vv. 44, 47-49, 53-54.

    3. Receive with thanksgiving the manifold blessings from the Lord, including my children. *Joseph's sons were named Manasseh (Forgetful) . . . God made Joseph forget his troubles, and Ephraim (Fruitful) . . . God made him fruitful in Egypt, vv. 50-52. (See also Gen. 48:20.)*

    4. *Observe with reverence and praise the life-preserving deliverance that Almighty God brings about through my humble service, vv. 53-57.*

Joseph's Brothers Journey to Egypt

(Genesis 42:1-38)

I. Concentration: on the main events in this chapter

1. Because of the famine, Jacob sent his ten oldest sons to Egypt to buy grain, vv. 1-5.
2. Joseph, the governor of Egypt, recognized them (although they did not recognize him); he accused them of being spies and threw them into prison for three days, vv. 6-17.
3. Joseph agreed to sell them grain, but kept Simeon as a hostage until the brothers returned from Canaan with their youngest brother, Benjamin, vv. 18-24.
4. The nine brothers returned to their father, Jacob, with the sacks of grain which also contained the money that Joseph had secretly restored to them, vv. 25-35.

II. Meditation: on Joseph's dealings with his brothers

1. Joseph's brothers bowed down before him, fulfilling his first dream, v. 6; Gen. 37:5-7.
2. Joseph tasted their hearts to see if they valued the life of one brother over the benefits they could gain by betrayal. *Would they abandon the hostage, Simeon, or return to Egypt with Benjamin?*
3. The brothers connected Joseph's harsh treatment with their selling their brother into slavery . . . their consciences began to disturb them, and their discussion was overheard and understood by Joseph.
4. Joseph tested their honesty and integrity by secretly returning the money they paid for the grain . . . the brothers also connected this event with the punishment of God for their earlier cruelty and greed.

III. Revelation: on God's master plan for His chosen people

1. The land of Canaan was promised to Abraham, Isaac, Jacob, and 12 sons.
2. God sent Joseph to Egypt to save his people when the famine came.
3. Eventually Jacob's entire family moved to Egypt, where they lived 400 years, first as honored guests, later as slaves.
4. During these four centuries, the Hebrews multiplied from about 70 persons to about two million at the Exodus . . . they had grown from a small family into a nation of people who, through God's help, could conquer and occupy the Promised Land.

IV. Applications: as a Christian, I need to know that . . .

1. God understands my extreme grief and sorrow over the loss of a loved one, vv. 36-38, and that He provides comfort and peace.
2. The Lord always fulfills His promises . . . the dreams of destiny He gives.
3. God provides a Savior to deliver His chosen people.
4. God uses adverse circumstances to test my heart, to prick my conscience, and to evaluate my faithfulness and integrity.

Joseph's Heart Yearned!

(Genesis 43:1-34)

I. Concentration: on the background of the events in this chapter

    1. The famine continued, and the family of Jacob (Israel) needed more grain from Egypt, but they couldn't return without Benjamin, vv. 1-5.

    2. Jacob didn't want to place Benjamin in jeopardy, but he had no choice if he wanted his family to survive, v. 7.

    3. Judah (son #4) pledged his life as a surety that Benjamin would return to his father from Egypt, vv. 8-9.

    4. Jacob sent all ten of his remaining sons back to Egypt with gifts and the money which had been returned from the previous trip, vv. 10-13.

II. Meditation: on the emotional upheaval of Israel's heart

    1. Jacob scolded the brothers for even mentioning Benjamin, but they only had answered Joseph's direct interrogation . . . to prove that they were not "spies" since it would be very unlikely that a band of spies all would be brothers, v. 6.

    2. Israel was upset in the past: he thought Joseph was dead; he was upset in the present: Simeon was in an Egyptian prison; he was upset about the future: Benjamin would be in danger if he left home; . . . and the whole family was in danger of dying of starvation!

    3. Israel lifted a prayer that God Almighty would prompt the Egyptian governor (Joseph) to have mercy on them, v. 14.

    4. Jacob surrendered himself to the inevitable, almost without hope: "If I am bereaved, I am bereaved!" v. 14.

III. Revelation: on Joseph's second meeting with his brothers

    1. Joseph invited them to his house for a meal, and the brothers were mortally afraid to be brought into his house, vv. 15-18.

    2. Joseph's servant reassured them, calmed their fears, released Simeon, and took care of their needs, vv. 19-24.

    3. When Joseph arrived, he asked about his father, and was secretly overcome with emotion when he saw his brother, Benjamin, vv. 25-31.

    4. Joseph continued the masquerade as an Egyptian, but he showed extreme favoritism to Benjamin . . . continuing to test the sincerity and integrity of the brother's hearts, vv. 32-34.

IV. Applications: as a Christian, I need to realize that . . .

    1. God controls all the circumstances of my life, and that my only hope is to surrender myself to the mercy of Almighty God.

    2. The Lord speaks peace to my heart, calms my fears, releases me from bondage, and supplies all my needs, Phil. 4:19.

    3. The Ruler of the universe continually tests my heart for integrity and faithfulness.

    4. The heart of the Lord is tender and long-suffering, and He yearns passionately to reveal Himself to me and to bless me abundantly.

The Final Examination

(Genesis 44:1-34)

I. Concentration: on Joseph's final test of his brothers

1. Joseph told his steward to secretly put the governor's silver cup into Benjamin's sack of grain, vv. 1-2.
2. Joseph then sent officials to arrest the brothers soon after they started home for Canaan, vv. 3-6.
3. The brothers pled innocence saying, "With whomever of your servants it is found, let him die, and we also will be my lord's slaves," vv. 7-9.
4. The silver cup was found in Benjamin's sack, and, according to Joseph's decree, Benjamin was arrested but the others were found blameless and released, vv. 10-12.

II. Meditation: on Judah's reactions to Benjamin's arrest

1. The brothers tore their clothes (a sign of grief and repentance), and they all returned to the Egyptian city, v. 13.
2. Judah (Jacob's 4th son) spoke for the entire group, pleading their case before Joseph, vv. 14-17.
3. Judah begged for mercy so that his father, Jacob, would not die from the shock of the loss of his favorite son, Benjamin, vv. 18-31.
4. Judah offered himself as a substitute to stay in Egypt as a slave in the place of his brother, Benjamin, vv. 32-34.

III. Revelation: on the poignant questions asked in this chapter

1. "Why have you repaid evil with good?" v. 4. *This applied not only to the "theft" of Joseph's cup, but also to the brothers' treatment of Joseph.*
2. What deed is this you have done?" v. 15. *Confession of sin is necessary!*
3. "What shall we speak . . . God has found out the iniquity of your servants." v. 16. *God's Spirit continues to convict us of our sins.*
4. "How shall I go up to my father if the lad is not with me?" v. 34. *Yes, I am my brother's keeper!*

IV. Applications: as a Christian, I need to . . .

1. Recognize that God sees all my deeds and knows all my thoughts and motivations. *The Lord is omniscient!*
2. Repent of my evil deeds; confess and ask for forgiveness. *The question Joseph asked his brothers ("What deed is this you have done?" v. 15) was the same one God asked Adam (Gen. 3:13) and Cain (Gen. 4:10).*
3. Remember that there always are consequences to all my choices and actions. *The brothers connected their present troubles in Egypt with the selling of their brother into slavery years earlier . . . "God has found out our iniquity!"*
4. Realize that a true brother (or friend) is willing to lay down his life for another person, Prov. 18:24; Jn. 15:13. *Judah <u>demonstrated</u> his love for his father, Jacob, and for his brother, Benjamin.*

Joseph Reveals His True Identity

(Genesis 45:1-28)

I. Concentration: on the emotional high points of this chapter

1. Joseph wept aloud as he revealed himself to his brothers, vv. 1-3.
2. The brothers were dismayed and frightened in Joseph's presence, v. 3.
3. Joseph fell on his brother Benjamin's neck and wept, and he kissed and embraced all his brothers, vv. 14-15.
4. With Pharaoh's blessing, the brothers returned to Canaan to report to their father, Jacob, that his son, Joseph was alive. *Jacob's heart stood still, because he did not believe them; but his spirit soon revived and he determined to travel into Egypt to see Joseph, vv. 25-28.*

II. Meditation: on Pharaoh's blessings upon Joseph's family

1. Pharaoh rejoiced over Joseph's reunion with his family, and he gave gifts for the brothers to take back into Canaan, vv. 16-17.
2. Pharaoh told them to bring their father, Jacob, and the whole family to live in the best land of Egypt, vv. 18-20.
3. Pharaoh (through Joseph) provided them transportation, clothing, money, and food . . . with extra gifts for Benjamin, vv. 21-24.
4. Pharaoh did all these kind deeds to the family because of his respect and admiration for his Prime Minister, Joseph.

III. Revelation: on Joseph's wise words of spiritual insight

1. Do not be grieved or angry with yourselves . . . What's past is past; just let by-gone's be by-gone's, v. 5.
2. God (not you brothers) sent me to Egypt to preserve the lives of you and your families, vv. 5-8.
3. As his dream had forecast, Joseph had become "Lord of all Egypt," (v. 9) and through him, God's chosen people would be preserved through five more years of famine, vv. 10-11.
4. Joseph cautioned his brothers as they departed for Canaan, "See that you do not become troubled along the way," v. 24 . . . that they do not become fearful or suspicious, and that they avoid self-recrimination, deceitful intrigue, family conflict, and human scheming.

IV. Applications: as a Christian, I need to . . .

1. Exhibit a genuine loving, forgiving, Christ-like spirit toward others who have hurt me.
2. Recognize that Almighty God controls all the circumstances and situations of my life . . . and that He brings good out of bad, Rom. 8:28.
3. Realize that God's purposed destiny shall be fulfilled through a person who yields to His sovereign will . . . and decide to be such a person.
4. In dealing with my fellow human beings under God's guidance, shun fearful doubt and skepticism, while also avoiding envy and deceit.

Israel's Family Moves into Egypt

(Genesis 46:1-34)

I. Concentration: on Israel's (Jacob's) new vision from God

    1. Israel came south to Beersheba (where Abraham had worshipped God, Gen. 21:31-34), and he there offered sacrifices to the Lord, v. 1.

    2. God spoke to Israel in a night vision, as the Lord had done many years before, v. 2; Gen. 28:12-15.

    3. God commanded Israel to take his family into Egypt, where He promised they would grow into a great nation, v. 3.

    4. God assured Israel that he would see Joseph, and that his favorite son would "put his hand on your eyes" . . . that Joseph would close Israel's eyes when he died, v. 4.

II. Meditation: on Israel's family members who went into Egypt

    1. The sons of Leah: Reubin, Simeon, Levi, Judah, Issachar, Zebulun, and a daughter, Dinah - 31 sons and grandsons plus a daughter (two sons already had died before this journey into Egypt), vv. 8-15.

    2. The sons of Zilpah (Leah's maid): Gad and Asher - 16 sons and grandsons, vv. 16-18.

    3. The sons of Rachel: Joseph and Benjamin - 14 sons and grandsons, but Joseph and his two sons already were living in Egypt, vv. 19-22.

    4. The sons of Bilhah (Rachel's maid) - Dan and Naphtali - 7 sons and grandsons, vv. 23-25.

III. Revelation: on the Israelites occupying the land of Goshen

    1. Sixty-six sons and grandsons accompanied Israel into Egypt (not counting their wives), v. 26, and these 66 plus Israel, himself, and Joseph and his two sons brought the total to 70 persons, v. 27.

    2. "Goshen" meaning "inundated land" was the fertile area of the Nile Delta suitable for both farming and grazing animals; Pharaoh gave this "best of the land" to Joseph's family, vv. 6, 11.

    3. In a joyful meeting, Israel and Joseph were re-united, vv. 29-30.

    4. The Pharaoh "Rameses" (v. 11), along with the advice of Joseph for his family to state their occupation as "cattlemen" rather than as "shepherds," helps to establish the date of this event. *The despised Hyksos (foreign, non-Egyptian rulers, sometimes translated "Shepherd Kings") ruled for a period of years over a large portion of the nation.*

IV. Applications: as a Christian, I need to . . .

    1. Return to the spiritual landmarks and altars established by my forefathers in the faith.

    2. Seek a new spiritual encounter and a fresh vision from the Lord.

    3. Obey God's directions, and influence my family to do likewise.

    4. According to God's will, depend upon Him to prolong my life and to bring me into His heavenly kingdom through a peaceful death in the presence of my loved ones.

"My Son, the Prime Minister"

(Genesis 47:1-31)

I. Concentration: on the events of this chapter

1. Joseph presented five of his brothers to Pharaoh, who officially gave them Goshen and employed some of them as chief herdsmen over his own livestock, vv. 1-6.
2. Joseph presented his father to Pharaoh, and Israel blessed this Egyptian ruler, vv. 7-10.
3. As the Prime Minister of Egypt, Joseph supplied the people with food during the famine in exchange for their freedoms ... the Egyptian population (except for the religious leaders) agreed to become slaves of Pharaoh, and their land and possessions became property of the state; essentially, they became share-croppers, paying 20% of their crops to Pharaoh, vv. 13-26.
4. At age 130, Israel entered Egypt, and 17 years later he sensed that his death was near, so he asked Joseph to bury him back in Canaan, not in Egypt, vv. 27-31.

II. Meditation and Revelation: on the spiritual implications of these events

1. Which brothers did Joseph present to Pharaoh? *We do not know, but possibly they were the four oldest (Reubin, Simeon, Levi, and Judah) and the youngest (Benjamin).*
2. Israel humbly answered Pharaoh's question about his age, saying that his "few and evil" years had not attained those of his grandfather, Abraham (175) and his father, Isaac (180), vv. 8-10. *Yet, Israel's "mere" 130 years put him in the position to bless the younger Pharaoh.*
3. Here we observe an example of government taxation and of religious exemption to such taxation, an arrangement which has been a part of the structure of many societies in many nations over the centuries.
4. It was important to Israel that he be buried in the Promised Land, rather than on foreign soil ... *"There's no place like home!"*

III. Applications: as a Christian, I need to ...

1. Honor others in my human family, recognizing that regardless of their degree of prominence or economic position, each of us stands equal before Almighty God, Who created us all.
2. Show proper respect for my local, state, and national government leaders by praying for and blessing them daily, Rom. 14:1-8; I Tim. 2:1-2.
3. Realize that whether I live in a democracy or a dictatorship, it is proper for citizens to pay taxes to provide needed services, and it also is proper for the government to recognize the important contribution made by organized religion to the moral, ethical, and spiritual fiber of society by allowing certain charitable tax exemptions, Mt. 22:17-21.
4. Recognize that my life on earth is very brief, and that my true citizenship is not here but in heaven, Psa. 90:10, 12; Heb. 11:13-16.

Israel Blesses Joseph's Sons

(Genesis 48:1-22)

I. Concentration: on Israel's testimony about his spiritual pilgrimage

1. Israel, on his death bed, gathered his strength to speak with Joseph and his two sons, Manasseh and Ephraim, vv. 1-2.
2. Israel told them how God had appeared to him in a vision at Luz (Bethel), v. 3; Gen. 28:12-19.
3. Israel reviewed God's covenant promises to him and to them, v. 4.
4. Israel recounted the death of Joseph's mother (Rachel) and her burial . . . at the future site of Messiah's birthplace Ephrath (Bethlehem), v. 7; Micah 5:2.

II. Meditation: on Israel's blessings upon Joseph and his sons

1. Israel worshipped God, giving thanks for His mercy in allowing him to "see" his son and grandsons, vv. 8-12.
2. Going against Joseph's wishes and ancient tradition, Israel, under God's guidance, deliberately gave the "right hand (greater) blessing" to Joseph's second son, Ephraim, and the "left hand (lesser) blessing" to his first son, Manasseh, vv. 13-14, 17-20.
3. Israel blessed Joseph and his sons with the formal "Abraham and Isaac" family blessing, giving these two grandsons equal shares of the inheritance in the Promised Land . . . essentially giving Joseph the "eldest son's double share" of his father's estate, vv. 15-16, 21-22.
4. Israel (Jacob) pronounced these blessings <u>by faith</u>, believing that God would bring to pass the words he spoke, Heb. 11:21.

III. Revelation: on the spiritual implications of these events

1. It is beneficial to the family for the patriarch (oldest member) to review God's providential care and divine guidance over the years.
2. God's will and purpose often goes against human wisdom and tradition.
3. Christians are heirs to the promised blessings contained in God's covenant with Abraham, Gal. 3:7-9, 13-14, 26-29.
4. The key to Godly living is faith in the Lord, for without faith, it is impossible to please Him, Heb. 11:6.

IV. Applications: as a Christian, I need to . . .

1. Speak regularly to my family about God's spiritual dealings with me over all the years of my life.
2. Realize that the Lord is not bound by human wisdom or tradition, but that He delights in doing a "new thing" to accomplish His divine will and purpose, Isa. 43:18-19.
3. Rejoice that I have received the blessing of "Abraham's Seed" (Gal. 3:16) . . . that the Lord Jesus Christ is my personal Savior.
4. Cultivate a living faith and a growing confidence in my Lord, the Almighty "mountain-moving" God, Mt. 21:21-22.

Israel's Last Will and Testament

(Genesis 49:1-33)

I. Concentration: on the events in this chapter

1. Israel gathered all twelve of his sons together to hear his final prophetic words, vv. 1-2.
2. He systematically listed each son, high-lighted a characteristic, and gave a prophetic word, vv. 3-28.
3. He charged his sons to bury him in the cave in Canaan where his grandparents (Abraham and Sarah), his parents (Isaac and Rebekah), and his first wife (Leah) were buried, vv. 29-32.
4. Jacob finished his words, drew his feet up into the bed, breathed his last, and "was gathered (spiritually) to his people," v. 33.

II. Meditation: on Israel's prophetic words concerning his sons

1. His first three sons were cursed, not blessed:
   1) Reubin, because he had sexual relations with his father's concubine, Bilhah, vv. 3-4; Gen. 35:22.
   2) Simeon and Levi, because of their cruel murders at Shechem, vv. 5-7; Gen. 34:25-29.
2. Judah (son #4) became the leader of the Twelve Tribes, and the one through whom God's promised Messiah would come, vv. 8-12.
3. Joseph (son #11) was given a "double portion" of Israel's Promised Land inheritance through the equal shares received by his sons, Manasseh and Ephraim, vv. 22-26.
4. All the other sons received Israel's brief evaluations and prophesies about their future, vv. 13-21, 27-28.

III. Revelation: on the spiritual implications of these prophecies

1. Breaking the laws of God is sin, and sinning removes persons from the canopy of God's blessings upon their lives.
2. Jesus the Messiah came from the tribe of Judah, and Israel saw Him as
   1) King ("scepter"), 2) Lawgiver, 3) Shiloh (Peace-giver or Rest), and 4) Blood-sacrifice (wine; blood), vv. 10-12.
3. Faithfulness to the Lord through persecution and suffering (as Joseph endured) will be abundantly rewarded, Mt. 25:21.
4. God knows everything about us, including our past deeds, our present attitudes, and our future destiny.

IV. Applications: as a Christian, I need to . . .

1. Avoid committing sin; but when I do break God's laws . . . repent, confess, and ask for forgiveness and cleansing, and ask to be restored to the place of God's favor and blessing, I Jn. 1:7-9.
2. Worship Jesus . . . my Lord, my Judge, my Peace, and my Savior.
3. Serve the Lord faithfully, in spite of all difficulties.
4. Realize that God knows all about me . . . yet He still loves and cares for me.

In a Coffin in Egypt

(Genesis 50:1-26)

I. Concentration: on the events in this chapter

1. Joseph had his father's body embalmed by the Egyptians, and the family journeyed back into Canaan for the burial ceremony, vv. 1-13.
2. Joseph's brothers, out of fear, told him the lie that their father had made a dying request that Joseph forgive his brothers for their treachery against him, vv. 14-18. *(I think Joseph saw through this deception.)*
3. Joseph told them not to be afraid; promised to provide for them; comforted them; and spoke kindly to them, vv. 19-21.
4. Joseph lived to be 110 years of age, and he left instructions for his bones to be returned to Canaan when the Israelites exited from Egypt . . . some 400 years later, vv. 22-26.

II. Meditation: on Joseph's understanding of divine providence

1. Joseph knew that God existed, but that he (Joseph) was not God! v. 19.
2. Joseph knew that God was able to override any evil intent against His chosen person or contrary to His destined will, v. 20.
3. Joseph knew that God could (and did) bring good out of evil . . . that his being sold into slavery was used by the Lord to save his family and the lives of countless other persons, v. 20.
4. Joseph knew that his brothers were untrustworthy, but he treated them with kindness and mercy . . . because he had a forgiving, gracious heart like God's, v. 21; Psa. 103:17.

III. Revelation: on the Scriptural bases of these truths which Joseph knew

1. "As the heavens are higher than the earth, so are My ways higher than your ways, and My thoughts than your thoughts," reads Isa. 55:9.
2. "Our God whom we serve is able to deliver us from the fiery furnace, and He will deliver us," said the three Hebrew men in Dan. 3:17.
3. "All things work together for good to those who love God, to those who are the called according to His purpose," wrote Paul in Rom. 8:28.
4. "Let all bitterness, wrath, anger, clamor, and evil speaking be put away from you, with all malice. And be kind to one another, tenderhearted, forgiving one another, even as God in Christ forgave you," wrote Paul in Eph. 4:31-32.

IV. Applications: as a Christian, I need to . . .

1. Recognize my proper position as a created being serving the Almighty Creator of the universe.
2. Believe that nothing is too difficult for the Lord to accomplish, Jer. 32:17 . . . He is omnipotent!
3. Realize that God is using all the "bad" circumstances of my life to produce His "good" results . . . *usually, however, I am able to see these things in their true perspective only by hindsight.*
4. Always exhibit the forgiving attitude and spirit of Christ, Mt. 6:14-15.

Course #2

The Years Between Joseph and Moses

(Exodus 1:1-22)

I. Concentration: on the period between Genesis and Exodus

    1. The Israelites remained in Egypt for 430 years, Ex. 12:40-41 . . . from I Kgs. 6:1, we learn that the Exodus was 480 years before King Solomon's fourth year as king (957 B.C.), which would date the Exodus at 1,437 B.C. (957 + 480). *Other Bible scholars set the date at 1,270 B.C., 167 years later.*

    2. During these four centuries, the original 70 men grew to an estimated total population of 2 million (603,550 men plus Levites, women and children, Num. 1:45-47), vv. 1-6 . . . *this means that the Israelites' population doubled every generation of 30 years.*

    3. During this period, there was a change in the Egyptian dynasty, and the new Pharaoh did not "know" Joseph . . . failed to respect and abide by the original agreement, v. 8; Gen. 47:6; Acts 7:6 . . . "oppression" (not residency in Egypt) lasted 400 years.

    4. The new Pharaoh placed the Israelites under bondage and forced them to serve as slaves in his building projects, vv. 11-14.

II. Meditation: on Pharaoh's treatment of the Israelites

    1. Pharaoh feared that the rapidly multiplying Israelites might rebel against him and join with his enemies, vv. 7-10.

    2. Pharaoh set taskmasters over the slaves to afflict them, yet the Egyptians continued to live in "dread of the children of Israel," vv. 11-14.

    3. Pharaoh commanded the midwives (Shiphrah and Puah) to kill the male Hebrew newborns, but they disobeyed his command, vv. 15-21.

    4. Pharaoh commanded all the Hebrew parents to throw their infant sons into the Nile River, v. 22.

III. Revelation: on the spiritual implications in this chapter

    1. The world is just one generation away from paganism . . . a Pharaoh who did not know Joseph changed the Israelites from honored guests into oppressed slaves.

    2. Satan hates God's people and seeks to put them under spiritual bondage.

    3. "We ought to obey God rather than men," Acts.5:29.

    4. The Lord rewards those who obey Him . . . the midwives were given "households for them," vv. 20-21; Mark 10:29-30.

IV. Applications: as a Christian, I need to . . .

    1. Be a faithful witness for the Lord every day.

    2. Expect Satan's persecution as I serve God, II Tim. 3:12.

    3. Obey God rather than men, when there is a spiritual conflict.

    4. Know that the Lord rewards those who faithfully serve and obey Him.

Moses: the First Eighty Years

(Exodus 2:1-22)

I. Concentration: on the main events in this chapter

1. Moses' mother placed him in an ark in the Nile River, where he was found and raised by Pharaoh's daughter, vv. 1-10.
2. As a man, Moses killed an Egyptian who was beating a Hebrew, and he had to flee into Midian, vv. 11-15.
3. In Midian, Moses protected seven daughters of Reuel, who were watering their father's flocks, vv. 16-20.
4. Moses was employed by Reuel; married one of the daughters (Zipporah); they had two sons: Gershom (Stranger there) and Eliezer (God is my help), vv. 21-22; Ex. 18:4.

II. Meditation: on Stephen's words about Moses in Acts 7:20-29

1. Moses was "well pleasing to God," v. 20 . . . "beautiful" in v. 23; Ex. 2:2.
2. Moses learned all the wisdom of Egypt, v. 22.
3. Moses was mighty in words and deeds, v. 22. (*Contrast this statement with Moses' evaluation of himself in Ex. 4:10.*)
4. Moses had an early sense of destiny that he would deliver his people from Egyptian bondage, but he had to mature under God's tutoring before he was spiritually qualified to assume that leadership role, v. 25.

III. Revelation: on Moses' faith as seen in Hebrews 11:23-27

1. Moses' faith, no doubt, grew out of (and was shaped by) the faith of his parents and of his sister and brother, Miriam and Aaron, v. 23.
2. Moses refused to be called the son of Pharaoh's daughter, choosing rather to suffer affliction with the people of God than to enjoy the passing pleasures of sin, vv. 24-25.
3. Moses esteemed the reproach of Christ (the hardships of being God's Messiah-Deliverer) to be greater than the treasures in Egypt; for he looked to the (heavenly; spiritual) reward, v. 26.
4. Moses "endured as seeing Him Who is invisible," v. 27.

IV. Applications: as a Christian, I need to . . .

1. Choose to suffer persecution as a faithful believer rather than to compromise my convictions to enjoy the passing pleasures of sin.
2. Value godly, spiritual things above physical, material things.
3. Expect a heavenly reward for my service for the Lord God.
4. See beyond sight: cultivate "heavenly vision" . . . the ability to see God at work in the invisible, spiritual realm.

I Want to Be a Burning Bush

(Exodus 3:1-10)

I. Concentration: on what was so special about that bush

1. It was planted on the mountain of God (Sinai; Horeb); as a "sign" (v. 12), God's liberated people would come back here to worship Him.
2. The Angel of the Lord (Pre-incarnate Christ) was in the midst of the bush, similar to the Son of God appearing in the fiery furnace in Dan. 3:25.
3. The bush burned without burning up! *Moses "marveled" (Acts 7:31) because as a nomad in the wilderness for forty years, he had never seen anything like that!*
4. It produced the results which God purposed: stop, turn aside, draw near, and listen.

II. Meditation: on where I can find holy ground

1. It is the place where I hear God's voice speaking my name personally, v. 4. *God repeated Moses' name, making the call personal and unmistakable.*
2. It is the place where I transact spiritual business with God; "Here I am," v. 4. *I respond to His calling my name, and confirm my commitment to follow His plan and purpose.*
3. It is the place where I discover God's character and His heart; "I AM," vv. 5-9. *God sees, hears, loves, and purposes to save His people.*
4. It is the place where God reveals His purpose and His promise to me, vv. 10-12. *God puts me on the road of fulfilling His destiny in me and through me.*

III. Revelation: on why I should take off my shoes

1. God is clean, pure, and holy, but my shoes are dirty. *It shows my reverence for holy God, and it acknowledges that I have walked in some filthy, impure, unholy places.*
2. This necessary act (repentance) allows Jesus to wash my feet, Jn. 13. *He can't wash my feet until I remove my dirty shoes.*
3. It signifies that someone else besides me is the Redeemer, Ruth 4:6-7. *I can't be the Redeemer; I relinquish all rights to that role.*
4. I am going to walk differently from now on . . . barefoot on the sharp rocks. *On rocky terrain, I must place my feet more slowly, more carefully. (In fact, the Lord will give me a new pair of shoes, Lk. 15:22; Eph. 6:15.)*

IV. Applications: on why I want to be a burning bush

1. I want to be planted on God's mountain . . . where He chooses.
2. I want to be filled with the presence of the Lord Jesus Christ.
3. I want to burn brightly, but not to "burn out."
4. I want to cause people to turn aside, to draw near, and to experience God.

Prayer: *"Lord, plant me, fill me, illuminate me, and use me. Amen."*

The Signs God Gave to Moses

(Exodus 4:1-31)

I. Concentration: on the events in this chapter

1. God gave Moses three miraculous signs, vv. 1-9.
2. God silenced all of Moses' excuses for not wanting to lead the Israelites out of Egypt; God gave him Aaron, his brother, to assist him, vv. 10-17.
3. Moses prepared his family for the trip into Egypt, including reinstating the ancient Hebrew ritual of circumcision, vv. 18-26.
4. Moses and Aaron showed God's signs to the elders of the children of Israel, who believed and worshipped the Lord, vv. 27-31.

II. Meditation: on the four signs which God gave to Moses

1. The burning bush, which was not consumed, Exodus, chapter 3.
2. The rod that turned into a serpent, then back into a rod, Ex. 4:2-5.
3. His hand that became leprous, then was healed, Ex. 4:6-8.
4. The water that changed into blood, Ex. 4:9.

III. Revelation: on the spiritual significance of these signs

1. All three signs in Exodus chapter 4 (serpent, leprosy, and blood) represent death and/or life. *God created life (snake from a rod); God healed (leprosy cleansed); God revealed that life is in the blood, Lev. 17:11.*
2. God's purpose for these three "signs" (miracles) was not only to bolster the faith of the Israelites, but also to "show up" (expose as false) the gods of Egypt, Ex. 12:12. *God's two signs to the Egyptians overcame their serpent god and their Nile River god, Ex. 7:8-25.*
3. Why was the leprosy sign shown only to the Israelites? *God's purpose was to heal His chosen people, but not the Egyptians, Ex. 15:26.*
4. The rod, the healthy hand, and the water all represent the natural abilities which man depends upon, but which God can take away or restore . . . *God can turn a blessing into a curse and vice versa.*

IV. Applications: on how to identify a genuine God-called leader

1. He has had a "burning bush" experience, a personal encounter with God.
2. He obeys the Lord and "casts down his rod" . . . renounces and discards his natural abilities which he has depended on for success. *God changes his human, dead abilities, talents, gifts (rod) into spiritual life (serpent) which is seen by both believers and unbelievers, II Cor. 2:15-16; Phil. 2:17; Col. 1:24.*
3. He has his private leprosy (secret sins) publicly exposed (confessed) to God's people, and cleansed by the Lord, Jas. 5:16. *This is manifested only to those who have "eyes to see" . . . to the Israelites, not to the Egyptians, Ex. 34:29-35; I Cor. 2:9-16; 3:7 - 4:7.*
4. He "pours out" his life in sacrificial service to produce spiritual results in others . . . either life or death, depending upon the responses of those being ministered to, *II Tim. 4:6; Phil. 2:17; II Cor. 2:14-16.*

Moses Confronts Pharaoh

(Exodus 5:1-23)

I. Concentration: on the events in this chapter

1. Moses and Aaron asked Pharaoh to allow the Israelites to go into the wilderness for three days to sacrifice to God; Pharaoh refused, vv. 1-4.
2. Pharaoh intensified the bondage of the Israelites, forcing them not only to make the same quota of bricks, but also to gather the straw, vv. 5-14.
3. The leaders of the Israelites complained about the unfairness of this policy, but Pharaoh said, "You are idle! Idle! Therefore you say, 'Let us go and sacrifice to the Lord,'" vv. 15-19.
4. The Israelites blamed Moses and Aaron for Pharaoh's intensified cruelty; Moses asked God why He had not yet delivered His people as He had promised, vv. 20-23.

II. Meditation: on Pharaoh's responses to Moses' request

1. He said, "Who is the Lord . . . I do not know the Lord," v. 2.
2. He accused Moses and Aaron of causing a work stoppage, of encouraging his slaves to rebel and rest from their labor, vv. 4-5.
3. He made the Israelite's tasks more difficult, so that they would turn against Moses and his message, vv. 6-9.
4. He demanded that the Israelites fulfill their daily quota of bricks, even under almost impossible circumstances, vv. 16-18.

III. Revelation: on the spiritual principles seen here

1. Cruel tyranny and forced slave labor always are connected with national leaders who do not know the Lord God.
2. Despotic dictators do not allow any criticism of their regime, but they take all means within their power to stamp out opposition.
3. Religious persecution often is a policy of a ruler with absolute power . . . because the belief in a God Who loves all persons equally, and Who allows them freedom of choice, is a direct contradiction of the oppressive policies of a godless dictator.
4. Immature children of God often make the mistake of blaming God and His chosen leaders for the troubles which have been inflicted upon them by Satan and his agents.

IV. Applications: as a Christian, I need to . . .

1. Pray for local, state, national, and world political leaders, that they may come to know, love, follow, and serve the Lord.
2. Stand up and speak out against injustice in all its forms.
3. Expect to suffer persecution (subtle and overt), II Tim. 3:12.
4. Cultivate spiritual perception which will enable me to distinguish between good and evil, between God's work and Satan's work.

"I Am the Lord"

(Exodus 6:1-13, 26-30)

I. Concentration: on God's revelation of Himself to Moses

1. "I am the Lord" . . . Who appeared to Abraham, Isaac, and Jacob, and Who established My covenant with them, vv. 2-4.
2. "I am the Lord" . . . Who hears the groanings of the children of Israel, and Who will rescue and redeem them, vv. 5-6.
3. "I am the Lord" . . . Who will claim the Israelites as My own chosen people, and Who will be their God, v. 7.
4. "I am the Lord" . . . Who will bring My people out from Egyptian bondage, and Who will give them the Promised Land as their heritage, v. 8.

II. Meditation: on the reasons for Moses' discouragement

1. Moses felt inadequate to confront Pharaoh, perhaps because he had a   s p e e c h   impediment, vv. 12, 30.
2. The Israelites did not heed Moses because of their "anguish of spirit" . . . acute pain of mind, grief, anxiety, and emotional torment, v. 9.
3. The Israelites did not heed Moses because of their increasing physical pain and suffering . . . "cruel bondage," v. 9.
4. Pharaoh was stubborn and unreasonable, refusing even to consider Moses' request, vv. 12, 30.

III. Revelation: on what "I Am the Lord" can do

1. God empowered Moses' communication skills, and sent his brother, Aaron, for companionship, encouragement, and assistance.
2. God, through the Exodus, delivered His people from their emotional torment into exuberant rejoicing, Ex. 15:1-21.
3. God (Jehovah-Rapha, Ex. 15:26) changed the injuries, pains, and diseases of His people into complete physical healing and continuing wellness, Deut. 7:15.
4. God sent ten plagues upon Egypt, which proved His superiority over all the Egyptian gods, and which finally forced Pharaoh to free the Hebrew slaves, Ex. 12:31-33.

IV. Applications: as a Christian, I need to . . .

1. Remember that the Lord's call to me also includes His strength and power to accomplish His purpose.
2. "Rejoice in the Lord always. Again I say, rejoice!" Phil. 4:4.
3. Realize that God's provision includes physical healing, according to His will and word, Mt. 8:16-17; Isa. 53:4; Mk. 16:18; Jas. 5:13-16.
4. Recognize that God is omnipotent, and that His will and His purpose in this world shall be done.

Pharaoh Hardened His Heart

(Exodus 7:1-25)

I. Concentration: on the major events in this chapter

    1. The Lord reaffirmed His call and purpose to Moses and Aaron, vv. 1-7.

    2. At the Lord's command, Moses and Aaron cast down a rod before Pharaoh and it became a serpent; Pharaoh's sorcerers did likewise, but Aaron's rod (serpent) swallowed up their rods, vv. 8-12.

    3. At God's command, Moses struck the Nile with the rod, and the river and all the ponds and containers of water in Egypt were filled with blood; Pharaoh's magicians duplicated the miracle, vv. 15-22.

    4. As the Lord had said, Pharaoh's heart was hardened, and he refused to heed Moses' signs and free the Israelite slaves, vv. 3-4, 13-14, 23-25.

II. Meditation: on some interesting truths found here

    1. In verse 1, the Lord said to Moses: "See, I have made you as God to Pharaoh, and Aaron your brother shall be your prophet." *This means that God had endowed Moses with awesome divine power (which frightened Pharaoh and deterred him from executing the brothers) and that God had made Aaron the one who spoke God's messages.*

    2. Although God knew that Pharaoh would choose to "harden" his heart, the time would come when God, Himself, would harden Pharaoh's heart. *A person, by repeated rejection of God's will, can "sin away his day of grace," vv. 3, 13, 23.*

    3. God can and does use "senior citizens" to accomplish His purposes; Moses and Aaron (ages 80 and 83) were well beyond "retirement age," v. 7.

    4. Satan's followers can work miracles by "black magic" . . . demonic powers, vv. 11, 22; Mt. 7:21-22.

III. Revelation: on the spiritual implications of these truths

    1. Those whom God calls, He empowers by His Spirit.

    2. It is dangerous to reject God's will, for He "shall not strive with man forever," Gen. 6:3, and "No one can come to Me (Jesus) unless the Father draws him," Jn. 6:44.

    3. As long as God leaves a person on this earth, He has a divine purpose for that individual to fulfill.

    4. Satan's powers are awesome, but they are inferior to God's power . . . the Lord's snake consumed the sorcerer's snakes, v. 12; I Jn. 4:4.

IV. Applications: as a Christian, I need to . . .

    1. Hear God's call to service and receive His power to serve.

    2. Respond immediately to the Holy Spirit's conviction and guidance by repentance and obedience.

    3. Seek, find, love, and fulfill God's divine destiny for my life.

    4. Know that through the Lord's power, I shall be triumphant and victorious over Satan, Rom. 8:37; I Jn. 5:4.

Pharaoh Offers Compromises to Moses

(Exodus 8:1-32)

I. Concentration: on the events in this chapter

    1. Pharaoh's magicians came to the end of their powers and reported to him that, "This is the finger of God," v. 19.

    2. Pharaoh begged Moses to remove the frogs (v. 8) and later the flies (v. 28), but when relief came, he reneged on his promises, vv. 15, 32.

    3. God separated His people from the Egyptians when He sent the plague of flies everywhere in Egypt except in the land of Goshen, vv. 22-23.

    4. Desperate for relief, Pharaoh began offering compromises, v. 28.

II. Meditation: on the state of Pharaoh's heart following each plague

    1. Water into blood - Pharaoh's heart was unmoved, 7:23.

    2. Frogs - Pharaoh hardened his heart, 8:15.

    3. Lice - Pharaoh's heart grew hard, 8:19.

    4. Flies - Pharaoh hardened his heart, 8:32.

    5. Livestock deaths - Pharaoh's heart became hard, 9:7.

    6. Boils - The Lord hardened Pharaoh's heart, 9:12.

    7. Hail - Pharaoh hardened his heart, 9:34.

    8. Locusts - The Lord hardened Pharaoh's heart, 10:20.

    9. Darkness - The Lord hardened Pharaoh's heart, 10:27.

    10. Death of firstborn - The Lord hardened Pharaoh's heart, 14:8.

III. Revelation: on Pharaoh's unacceptable compromising proposals to Moses

    1. At first, Pharaoh flatly refused Moses' demands that he allow the Hebrews to go free, 8:19.

    2. Then Pharaoh, under duress, offered to let them go a short distance into the wilderness (and then return), 8:28.

    3. Next Pharaoh offered to let only the men go, but to leave behind their wives and children (knowing that they would surely return), 10:8-10.

    4. Finally, Pharaoh offered to let all the people go, but to leave their flocks and herds behind (again assuming that they would return), 10:24.

IV. Applications: on how Satan attempts to get God's people to compromise

    1. The devil always and repeatedly lies to God's people, Jn. 8:44.

    2. The devil tempts believers to go only a short distance into sin . . . to sin just "a little bit."

    3. The devil tries to divide the families of God's people . . . "Let the old folks worship God, but leave the young ones to me!"

    4. As a last resort, the devil tries to strip believers of God's promised provisions, Jn. 10:10 . . . to make them dependent upon material things which are under Satanic control.

For This Purpose I Have Raised You Up

(Exodus 9:1-35)

<u>I. Concentration: on God's stated purpose for putting Pharaoh on his throne</u>

"Indeed for this purpose I have raised you up, that I may show My power in you, and that My name may be declared in all the earth," Ex. 9:16.

<u>II. Meditation: on the New Testament teachings about governing authorities</u>

1. "You (Pilate) could have no power at all against Me (Jesus) unless it had been given you from above," Jn. 19:11.
2. "There is no authority except from God, and the authorities that exist are appointed by God," Rom. 13:1.
3. "I exhort first of all that supplications, prayers, intercessions, and giving of thanks be made for all men, for kings and all who are in authority," I Tim. 2:1-2.
4. "Be subject to rulers and authorities," Titus 3:1.

<u>III. Revelation: on the spiritual implications of these truths</u>

1. God has ordained all kinds and types of governments, and He places men in places of authority as He chooses.
2. Persons who attain high positions of government authority are responsible and accountable before God for their stewardship and actions (for good or evil) while they occupy those places of power.
3. God-fearing people of all nations down through the centuries have been expected to pray for their earthly rulers and authorities; this principle would include even praying for:
   1) The Egyptian Pharaohs and the Babylonian Kings,
   2) The Herods of Judea and the Emperors of Rome,
   3) Joseph Stalin and Adolph Hitler,
   4) Richard Nixon and Bill Clinton.
4. Government authority is preferable to anarchy, and believers are to be subject to earthly rulers except when their edicts conflict with the commands of Almighty God, Acts 4:19-20; 5:29.

<u>IV. Applications: as a Christian, I need to . . .</u>

1. Know that God's purpose in raising up government leaders in the United States and everywhere else in the world has not changed (Ex. 9:16):
   1) To exhibit the Lord's power (and will) through the chosen ruler, and
   2) To declare the Lord's glorious name to all nations.
2. Realize that God is the One Who appoints all national leaders, not merely the benevolent or democratic ones.
3. "First of all" . . . prioritize praying for my government officials above and before all other actions, such as mocking and criticizing them.
4. Recognize that in matters of biblical and spiritual principles, I am subject to a higher, heavenly authority.

The Plagues of Egypt: Pictures of Hell

(Exodus 10:1-29)

I Concentration: on the primary purpose for God's sending the plagues upon Egypt

To demonstrate God's superiority over all the pagan gods of Egypt, Ex. 12:12.

1. Water to blood defeated the Egyptian Nile River god, Ex. 7:20.
2. Frogs defeated Egyptian worship of amphibians, Ex. 8:6.
3. Lice defeated Egyptian worship of insects, Ex. 8:17.
4. Flies defeated Egyptian worship of insects, Ex. 8:24.
5. Death of livestock defeated Egyptian worship of a bull, Ex. 9:6.
6. Boils showed that Egyptian sorcerers could not stand before God, Ex. 9:10.
7. Hail defeated the Egyptian gods of the sky: thunder, lightening, Ex. 9:23.
8. Locusts defeated Egyptian worship of insects, 10:14.
9. Darkness defeated Egyptian sun god, 10:22.
10. Death of firstborn defeated Egyptian Pharaoh-worship, Ex. 11:5.

II. Meditation: on the fact that all pagan gods are demons

1. Lev. 17:7 "They shall no more offer their sacrifices to demons."
2. Deut. 32:17 "They sacrificed to demons, not to God."
3. Psa. 106:37-38 "They even sacrificed their sons and their daughters to demons . . . to the idols of Canaan."
4. I Cor. 10:20 "The things which the Gentiles sacrifice, they sacrifice to demons and not to God."

III. Revelation: on a secondary purpose of the plagues upon Egypt

To demonstrate and illustrate hell's punishments and torments, which have been prepared for Satan and the fallen angels (demons), Mt. 25:41.

1. Hell is a place of thirst (putrefied blood to drink).
2. Hell is a place of horror and stench.
3. Hell is a place of perpetual itching.
4. Hell is a place of mind-tormenting buzzing noises.
5. Hell is a place of constant hunger and rottenness.
6. Hell is a place of intense pain over the entire body.
7. Hell is a place of terror and fire.
8. Hell is a place of endlessly being bitten by bugs.
9. Hell is a place of infinite darkness.
10. Hell is a place of separation from loved ones: weeping and sorrow.

IV. Applications: as a Christian, I need to . . .

1. Worship Jehovah, the one and only true and living God.
2. Celebrate Jehovah's victory over Satan and his pagan demons.
3. Recognize that hell is a horrible place of weeping, wailing, and gnashing of teeth, Mt. 8:12; Lk. 13:28.
4. Witness to unbelievers about the merciful God Who freely offers salvation from hell through His crucified, resurrected Son.

The Step-brothers Lose Their Tempers

(Exodus 11:1-10)

I. Concentration: on the increasing tension between Moses and Pharaoh

1. Since Moses had been raised as a son of Pharaoh's daughter, and the present Pharaoh possibly was her son, then probably Moses and Pharaoh had been raised in the palace as step-brothers.
2. Such a relationship in childhood, more than a half-century before, could account for their strange confrontational, yet non-violent relationship.
3. As the close of the preceding chapter, Pharaoh threatened to kill Moses if he ever saw his face again, Ex. 9:27-29.
4. Moses did, however, see Pharaoh one last time to pronounce the final plague (death of the firstborn), but Moses went out from the stubborn, unrepentant Pharaoh with deep frustration and anger, v. 8.

II. Meditation: on the Lord's words to Moses in this chapter

1. The Lord promised that this time Pharaoh not only would let the Israelites go, he would "surely drive you out of here altogether," vv. 1, 8.
2. The Lord told Moses to instruct the Hebrews to ask the Egyptians to give them silver and gold, and the Egyptians did so because they greatly feared and respected Moses, vv. 2-3.
3. The Lord told Moses of the coming of the death angel to kill the firstborn child of every Egyptian family, vv. 4-6.
4. The Lord said that He would treat His people differently . . . not even a dog would bark at them, v. 7.

III. Revelation: on the spiritual implications seen here

1. It is futile to resist and to try to fight against the will of Almighty God, Psa. 33:10-11; Prov. 16:9; Acts 9:5.
2. God provides for His people from the spoils of His enemies, Dt. 10:6-12; Josh. 24:13; Eccl. 2:26.
3. On God's appointed Day, He will send His angels to sweep over the earth in final judgment.
4. Only the persons who have followed God's plan of deliverance through the blood shall be saved.

IV. Applications: as a Christian, I need to . . .

1. Submit my stubborn will to the will of the Lord.
2. Receive God's provisions for all my needs . . . whether by miraculous manna from heaven or by "farewell" gifts from my enemies!
3. Be prepared each and every day for the Lord's appearance.
4. Witness to the lost that a Lamb has been slain to bring them salvation.

The Passover Lamb

(Exodus 12:5-11)

I. Concentration: on the major events in this chapter

    1. The Lord, through Moses and Aaron, gave detailed instructions for observing the Passover, vv. 1-20.

    2. Moses called the elders and gave them the Lord's word to be passed along to the Hebrew people, vv. 21-28.

    3. The Lord struck all the firstborn of the Egyptians, and Pharaoh ordered the Israelites to leave Egypt immediately, vv. 29-38.

    4. The Exodus of 600,000 men occurred after the Hebrews had been in Egypt 430 years, and the Lord commanded them to memorialize this important event throughout all coming generations, vv. 39-51.

II. Meditation: on the Passover lamb (vv. 5-11)

    1. The Passover lamb was to be without blemish, and kept under close observation for four days, vv. 5-6.

    2. The Passover lamb was to be killed and the blood sprinkled on the house as a sign of deliverance from death, vv. 6-7.

    3. The Passover lamb's flesh was to be roasted and eaten with unleavened bread and bitter herbs (to remind them of the unpleasant days of slavery); leftovers were to be completely burned with fire, vv. 8-10.

    4. The Passover lamb was to be eaten in haste by persons dressed and prepared to move out immediately upon the Lord's command, v. 11.

III. Revelation: on "Christ, our Passover," I Cor. 5:7

    1. Jesus Christ is our perfect, sinless Lamb of God, Who was observed in public ministry for almost four years before being sacrificed for our sins, Jn. 1:29; II Cor. 5:21.

    2. Christ's blood (memorialized in the wine of the Lord's Supper) brings deliverance (salvation) from man's sins, Lev. 17:11; Heb. 9:14, 22, 28.

    3. Christ's broken body (memorialized in the unleavened bread of the Lord's Supper) provides spiritual and physical strength to those who believe and partake, I Cor. 11:23-29; Mt. 8:16-17; Isa. 53:4-5.

    4. Persons, who enter into the New Covenant relationship with Christ through His blood, are to move out in His victorious power to conquer the world and to enter into His Promised Land, Mt. 28:18-20.

IV. Applications: as a Christian, I need to . . .

    1. Praise and worship the perfect Lamb of God, Who was slain from before the foundation of the world, Rev. 13:8.

    2. Come daily to Christ in repentance and faith to receive forgiveness and cleansing through His precious blood, I Jn. 1:7, 9.

    3. Receive spiritual strength and physical healing through the broken body of the Lord.

    4. Witness faithfully to those who need to receive Christ as their personal Savior (Passover).

Unleavened Bread

(Exodus 13:1-22)

I. Concentration: on the highlights of this chapter

1. The Lord taught the Israelites to consecrate all the firstborn to Him in remembrance of His deliverance when all the Egyptian firstborn were slain, vv. 1-2, 11-16.
2. The Lord connected the feast of unleavened bread with the Passover, and commanded that they both be kept as a perpetual memorial, vv. 3-11.
3. The Lord led the Hebrews out of Egypt by a pillar of cloud by day and a pillar of fire by night . . . on an indirect route to avoid having to fight the Philistines at this time and possibly becoming discouraged enough to want to return to Egypt, vv. 17-18, 20-22.
4. Moses brought the bones of Joseph with him, as the Israelites had promised 400 years earlier, v. 19; Gen. 50:15-26.

II. Meditation: on the feast of unleavened bread

1. Unleavened bread (without yeast) was used as an object lesson (parable) to teach a number of spiritual lessons, vv. 3, 8; Ex. 12:26.
2. The feast of unleavened bread was a week-long observance immediately following Passover . . . Passover memorialized the deliverance of the Hebrews through the blood and "unleavened bread" memorialized God's provision for them on their journey from Egypt to Canaan.
3. This observance was to be a "sign" of God's covenant relationship with His people . . . impacting all they thought, said, and did: "between your eyes" and "in your mouth" and "on your hand," vv. 9, 16.
4. The lives of Christians are to be "unleavened" . . . without malice and wickedness; with sincerity and truth, I Cor. 5:6-8.

III. Revelation: on the evil influences represented by leaven (yeast)

1. Leaven of Herod, Mk. 8:15 - worldliness and cruelty, Mk. 6:14-28.
2. Leaven of the Sadducees, Mt. 16:6-12 - theological liberalism: non-belief in the miracles of Scripture or in the resurrection, Acts. 23:6-8.
3. Leaven of the Pharisees, Lk. 12:1 - hypocrisy, Mt. 23:13-33.
4. Leaven of the Corinthians, I Cor. 5:1-13 - immorality.
5. Leaven of the Galatians, Gal. 5:1-9 - legalism.

IV. Applications: as a Christian, I need to . . .

1. Recognize that Christ is the true "unleavened" bread of my life, and feed upon Him for spiritual nourishment, Jn. 6:32-58.
2. Make the spiritual connection between God's salvation and His provision
3. . . . He gives me both deliverance through the blood and sustenance through the "bread of life."
4. Cleanse my life of all "leaven" . . . worldliness, unbelief, hypocrisy, immorality, and legalism.
5. Realize that I am to be a consecrated "firstborn" of the Lord through the new birth . . . totally dedicated to His service.

Crossing the Red Sea

(Exodus 14:1-31)

I. Concentration and Meditation: on the participants in this miraculous event

1. God:
   1) The Lord spoke to Moses, v. 1.
   2) The Lord sent the Angel of God . . . the pillar of cloud by day and the pillar of fire by night, vv. 19-20. *Note: God's manifest presence is light to believers but darkness to unbelievers, v. 20.*
   3) The Lord divided the Red Sea, vv. 21-22.
2. Egyptians:
   1) The Egyptian Pharaoh's heart continued to be hardened against the Hebrew slaves, vv. 4-5, 8.
   2) The Egyptian army pursued the Israelites even into the dried out Red Sea, vv. 6-9.
   3) The wheels came off the Egyptian chariots, and the army was trapped and drowned in the Red Sea, vv. 23-28.
3. Moses:
   1) Moses heard the voice of the Lord, vv. 1, 15-18.
   2) Moses encouraged the people to "stand still, and see the salvation of the Lord," vv. 13-14.
   3) Moses obeyed the Lord, stretched out his hand with the rod, and the sea divided, and later returned, vv. 21, 27.
4. Hebrews:
   1) The Hebrews cried out in fear and blamed Moses for taking them out of the "safety" of Egypt into certain death, vv. 10-12.
   2) The Hebrews crossed over the Red Sea on dry ground, vv. 22, 29.
   3) The Hebrews observed God's miracle, feared (reverenced), and believed in Him and in His servant, Moses, vv. 30-31.

II. Revelation and Applications: as a Christian, I need to . . .

1. Be spiritually alert to hear the voice of the Lord giving me His assignments for spiritual service.
2. Encourage persons over whom I have influence to have greater faith in the Lord, Who will fight for us and bring us victory.
3. Obey the Lord by stretching out my hand toward the problem, realizing that it is not by my own ability (hand) nor is it by my method (rod), but that the miracle is done by the power of Almighty God, Zech. 4:6.
4. Cultivate faith in God to overcome my human fears, faithfully supporting the spiritual leaders whom God has placed in authority over me.
5. March forward at the command of the Lord, depending upon Him for solid ground upon which to walk, for light for my path, and for protection from my enemies.
6. Reverence God and worship Him, while also honoring those spiritual leaders who have blessed my life.

Singing of God's Protection and Provision

(Exodus 15:1-27)

I. Concentration: on the main events in this chapter

1. Moses and the Israelites sang a joyful song of God's victory over the army of the Egyptians, vv. 1-19; Miriam, the prophetess (sister of Aaron and Moses), led the women in singing and dancing as part of the celebration, vv. 20-21.
2. The thirsty people complained about the bitter drinking water at Marah, and the Lord showed Moses a tree to cast into the waters, which made the water sweet, vv. 22-25.
3. God promised to maintain the health of the Hebrews and to heal all their diseases . . . "Jehovah-Rapha," v. 26.
4. At an oasis named Elim, they found twelve wells of water and seventy palm trees, v. 27.

II. Meditation: on the song of Moses (See Rev. 15:3-4.)

1. It was a song celebrating victory by God's power, v. 2.
2. It was a song praising God for His mighty works of deliverance and His providential care, v. 11.
3. It was a song magnifying God's character traits: strength, holiness, mercy, redemption, greatness, justice, and truth, v. 13.
4. It was a song prophesying future events and blessings which the Lord would surely bring to pass, v. 18.

III. Revelation: on the marvelous provisions of the Lord

1. The Lord delivers His people from their enemies.
2. The Lord transforms bitterness into sweetness, as He changes bad things into good things for our benefit.
3. The Lord reveals Himself as "Jehovah-Rapha" . . . the God Who heals.
4. The Lord anticipates the particular needs of His people, and He specifically meets those needs . . . at Elim, there was a well for each tribe (12), and a palm tree for each elder (70) who was appointed later in Ex. 18:25; 24:1, 9.

IV. Applications: as a Christian, I need to . . .

1. Praise and worship the Lord for His great salvation, Isa. 12:2.
2. Thank the Lord for His power to transform the bitter into the sweet . . . to bring good out of bad, Rom. 8:28.
3. Depend upon the Lord for my physical strength and healing, Jas. 5:13-16.
4. Trust the Lord to supply each and every one of my needs, Phil. 4:19.

Principles of Providential Provision

(Exodus 16:1-36)

I. Concentration: on the main teachings in this chapter

    1. God knows the needs and answers the prayers of His people, vv. 1-3.

    2. God tests the faith and obedience of His people, v. 4-22.

    3. God established the Sabbath principle: six days of labor and one day of rest, before He give the Ten Commandments, vv. 23-31.

    4. God wants His people to remember His blessings and to worship Him faithfully, vv. 32-36.

II. Meditation: on how God supplies the needs of His people

    1. God does the supplying, but man must do the gathering, v. 16.

    2. God supplies needs according to His plan and timetable:

        1) Gather only enough; do not try to hoard, v. 16.

        2) Gather in the morning because after noon, the provision "melts away," v. 21.

        3) On the sixth day, gather a double portion, v. 22.

        4) NGather daily, except on the Sabbath, v. 26. (*If we will follow God's plan of provision, we will not have to work seven days a week!*)

    3. The provision is miraculous and beyond man's understanding . . . "Manna" means "What is it?" v. 15.

    4. Disobeying God's word (not following exactly His plan) results in want, need, starvation, and death, v. 20.

III. Revelation: on why God deals with His people this way

    1. To test their obedience, v. 4.

    2. To stretch their faith, v. 6 . . . in the evening, they shall "know" by believing God's promises.

    3. To reveal His glory, v. 7 . . . in the morning, they shall "see" by spiritual revelation.

    4. To accomplish His destined purpose for them and through them, v. 35.

IV. Applications: as a Christian, I need to . . .

    1. Obey God's orders, and follow His specific plans to receive His provision.

    2. Reflect and meditate upon the promises of God's word in the "twilight" (times of walking in dim light) . . . trusting Him by faith to guide me into the place of His abundant provision.

    3. Receive the Lord's illumination in the "morning" (times of divine enlightenment) through the spiritual perception given by the revelation of the Holy Spirit.

    4. Follow God's day-by-day plan for my life, through my years of spiritual wilderness wandering into the Promised Land of His fulfilled destiny.

The Lord Is My Victory Banner!

(Exodus 17:1-16)

I. Concentration: on the significant events in this chapter

1. The Hebrews complained again about the lack of water, vv. 1-3.
2. At God's command, Moses struck the rock with his rod, and water gushed forth, vv. 4-7.
3. Amalek (descendants of Esau, Jacob's brother, Gen. 36:12) fought against Joshua and the Israelites while Moses prayed, supported by Aaron and Hur, vv. 8-12.
4. Through the Lord's power, the Israelites won the victory, and Moses built an altar and worshipped at the place he named "Jehovah-Nissi" . . . meaning "The Lord is my (victory) banner," vv. 13-16.

II. Meditation: on the characters mentioned in this chapter

1. Moses - God's chosen man to deliver His people from bondage.
2. Joshua - Moses' assistant: chosen to lead the Hebrew army, to go with Moses part-way up Mt. Sinai, to dwell in the tabernacle, to represent the tribe of Ephraim in spying out the land of Canaan, and eventually to succeed Moses in leading the Israelites into the Promised Land, Ex. 17:9-13; 24:13; 32:17; 33:11; Num. 13:8; Josh. 1:1.
3. Aaron - Moses' older brother (3 years his senior) who was appointed as the first High Priest of the nation of Israel, Ex. 7:7; 28:1.
4. Hur - according to Jewish tradition, Hur was Moses' brother-in-law (husband of Miriam), who served as a trusted advisor, Ex. 17:10-12; 24:14, and who was the grandfather of the gifted young man (Bezalel) who worked on the furnishings of the tabernacle, Ex. 31:2-5.

III. Revelation: on the spiritual implications seen here

1. There is a battle being fought every day between the people of God and the forces of Satan.
2. The real life-and-death war is being waged in the spiritual realm through intercessory prayer.
3. Every warrior in God's arena of battle needs at least three others on the sidelines supporting him in prayer.
4. Intercession is difficult and fatiguing; prayer warriors need others to join with them in "holding up their hands to Almighty God."

IV. Applications: as a Christian, I need to . . .

1. Put on my spiritual armor each day before going into battle, Eph. 6:10-18.
2. Engage in fervent intercessory prayer for God's will to be done.
3. Find at least one other believer to join with me as my prayer partner.
4. In prayer, support my spiritual leader . . . hold up the hands of the pastor of my local home church.

How to Give Advice to In-laws

(Exodus 18:1-27)

I. Concentration: on Jethro, Moses' father-in-law

1. Jethro (also called Reuel and Hobab, Num. 10:31-32), was the priest of Midian (descendants of Abraham through his concubine, Keturah, Gen. 25:2); he had a daughter, Zipporah, who married Moses and bore him two sons, vv. 1-6.
2. Jethro listened to Moses' accounts of divine deliverance from Egyptian bondage and the difficulties encountered by the Israelites; he rejoiced with them over their victories, vv. 7-8.
3. Jethro worshipped God with Moses and the elders, vv. 10-12.
4. Jethro observed Moses' style of leadership: do everything; accept no help from anyone; delegate no responsibility or authority, vv. 13-16.

II. Meditation: on Jethro's advice to Moses

1. Jethro gave advice for the good of the people: so they could receive judicial decisions more quickly, v. 17.
2. Jethro gave advice for Moses' good: to keep him from "burning out" and to help him better fulfill his major duties, v. 18.
3. Jethro's advice: 1) divide the work, 2) designate others to assist you, and 3) delegate authority to them . . . men who are able, God-fearing, truthful, and honest, vv. 19-22.
4. Jethro was not arrogant or "pushy" . . . he made only suggestions, to be checked out by Moses to see if they were God's will, v. 23.

III. Revelation: on involving other family members in a person's ministry

1. Ideally, family members can give valuable advice because they know intimate details of the situation and because they sincerely care about the minister.
2. Family members can help merely by listening to the minister talk about his experiences and problems.
3. Family members can show their sincere interest by observing the minister at work, then by evaluating with sensitive compassion his motives and methods.
4. Family members only should make suggestions; the final decision must by made by the minister as God reveals His will to him.

IV. Applications: as a Christian, I need to . . .

1. Sincerely care about the problems of fellow Christians in need . . . because they are my spiritual "family."
2. Be a good listener, as others share their troubles with me.
3. Observe (objectively gather information and receive insight) before giving any kind of advice . . . spiritual or otherwise.
4. Offer Scripture-based spiritual suggestions with a sweet spirit of humility and submission, trusting the Lord to reveal His will to the person needing practical help.

Enlightenment from an Eagle

(Exodus 19:1-25)

I. Concentration: on the awesome events of this chapter

1. Arriving at Mt. Sinai (where he had seen the burning bush, Ex. 2), Moses again heard God's voice; he spoke the Lord's commands to the people, and they agreed to obey, vv. 1-8.

2. God gave strict instructions to the people through Moses about preparing for the Lord to draw near to them; these commands had to be obeyed under penalty of death, vv. 9-15.

3. The Lord revealed Himself with awesome and terrifying signs: through thunderings, lightnings, thick cloud, smoke, fire, earthquake, and His audible voice from heaven, vv. 16-20.

4. Over Moses' protest that he already had warned the people, God again sent Moses down the mountain to establish boundaries and to urge   the people to consecrate themselves to encounter God, vv. 21-25.

II. Meditation: on Biblical lessons about eagles

1. "I (God) bore you on eagle's wings and brought you to Myself," Ex. 19:4.

2. "As an eagle stirs up its nest, hovers over its young, spreading out its wings, taking them up, carrying them on its wings," (so the Lord alone led him), Dt. 32:11.

3. "Those who wait on the Lord shall renew their strength; they shall mount up with wings like eagles," Isa. 40:31 . . . "Who (God) satisfies your mouth with good things, so that your youth is renewed like the eagle's," Psa. 103:5.

4. "For wherever the carcass is, there the eagles will be gathered together," Mt. 24:28.

III. Revelation: on the spiritual implications of these Scripture passages

1. God carries us to Himself . . . delivering us from the enemy.

2. God "stirs" us out of our comfort zone to produce growth and maturity . . . He forces us to stretch our wings and fly.

3. God strengthens and renews us . . . makes us feel young!

4. God uses us as "signs of the times."

IV. Applications: as a Christian, I need to . . .

1. Allow God to transport me, to bring me to His place of my destiny.

2. Get out of my comfort zone; develop spiritual maturity through service in areas where I have never served before.

3. Depend upon the Lord for my strength and renewal.

4. Spiritually fulfill my purpose, thereby revealing God's plan to others. *Eagles serve like vultures to identify death, decay, and rottenness, and they work to "clean up" the mess caused by the evil works of Satan.*

The Ten Commandments

(Exodus 20:1-17)

I. Concentration: on God's laws of basic morality

1. Trust the Lord God only, vv. 2-3.
2. Worship the Lord God only; no idol worship, vv. 4-6.
3. Use the name of the Lord God only in ways that honor Him, v. 7.
4. Rest on the Sabbath day; meditate about the Lord God, vv. 8-11.
5. Honor your parents, v. 12.
6. Do not murder, v. 13.
7. Be sexually true to your spouse, v. 14.
8. Do not steal or cheat, v. 15.
9. Tell the truth; do not deceive others, v. 16.
10. Be content with what you have; do not be greedy for another person's possessions, v. 17.

II. Meditation: on the "Law"

1. The Law revealed our sins to us and acted as a "tutor" to bring us to Christ for salvation through faith, Gal. 3:24.
2. The Law is a complete unit, a whole; disobeying one of the ten commandments makes a person guilty of breaking the whole Law, Jas. 2:10-11.
3. Jesus summed up the entire Decalog (Ten Commandments) by stating the two great principles of love which are the foundation of God's Law: *"You shall love the Lord your God with all your heart, with all your soul, and with all your mind. This is the first and great commandment. And the second is like it: You shall love your neighbor as yourself. On these two commandments hang all the Law and the Prophets,"* Mt. 22:37-40.
4. Jesus claimed not to have come to destroy the Law, but to fulfill it, Mt. 5:17-20. *He expanded the Law to its ultimate meaning (thus filling it full), emphasizing inward motivation rather than outward observance.*

III. Revelation and Applications: as a Christian, I need to . . .

1. Observe and obey the Ten Commandments because they are God's laws of basic morality; but when I sin (and I do!) I may come to Jesus in repentance and confession, and I shall receive His forgiveness and cleansing, I Jn. 1:7-9.
2. Realize that in God's sight "sin is sin," and that there are no "little white ones and dirty black ones!" *The Lord's list includes every possible transgression from an inward thought (covetousness) to a violent act (murder) to a careless curse word (name in vain).*
3. Love the Lord and love my fellow human beings to fulfill the King's Royal Law, Jas. 2:8.
4. Recognize that inward motivation is much more important in God's sight than outwardly keeping the letter of the law, I Cor. 13:1-3.

Interpretation of Commandments V & VI

(Exodus 21:1-36)

I. Concentration: on God's laws about treatment of parents and other persons

    1. Commandment V - "Honor your father and your mother," Ex. 20:12.

    2. Commandment VI - "You shall not murder," Ex. 20:13.

II. Meditation: on the practical application of these basic laws

    1. Cursing or striking parents was an offense punishable by death, because the proper family relationship is absolutely necessary as the major, fundamental building block of society, vv. 15, 17.

    2. This chapter expands on the statement prohibiting murder by specifying other associated laws regarding interpersonal behavior:

        1) Persons who are purchased as slaves (or who become indentured servants) must be freed after six years, v. 2.

        2) Such persons may <u>voluntarily</u> become permanent "love slaves" if they so choose, vv. 3-6.

        3) Female servants (especially those married by their masters) have additional rights for their own protection, vv. 7-11.

        4) There is a difference between manslaughter and premeditated murder, vv. 12-14.

        5) Kidnapping is a capital offense, v. 16.

        6) Assault and battery carries a penalty to fit the seriousness of the injuries sustained, vv. 18-19.

        7) Corporal punishment of slaves is allowed, but if a servant dies, the master is charged with the death, vv. 20-21.

        8) Violence which injures the unborn child of a pregnant woman will be punished . . . "eye for eye," vv. 22-25.

        9) Servants who are seriously injured while being punished (by losing an eye or a tooth) will be set free, vv. 26-27.

        10) Specific injuries to animals or by animals are to be judged according to the circumstances, vv. 28-36.

III. Revelation and Applications: I need to observe these spiritual principles . . .

    1. God's laws establish guidelines to protect the life and well-being of all persons, including servants, women, unborn children, and the elderly.

    2. God's laws include specific "women's rights," particularly within the marriage relationship.

    3. God's laws recognize the differences between premeditated murders and unpremeditated or accidental killings.

    4. God's laws uphold a high degree of accountability; for example, owners are responsible for the harm caused by their animals which have a previous pattern of violence or destruction, v. 36.

In summary, I must obey God's mandates by treating all persons with kindness, fairness, justice, and integrity.

Interpretation of Commandment VIII

(Exodus 22:1-31)

I. Concentration: on God's law about honesty

"You shall not steal," Ex. 20:15.

II. Meditation: on the practical applications of this basic law

1. Penalties, including making restitution and paying fines, are specified for stealing oxen or sheep, vv. 1, 4.
2. Owners who kill burglars in the dark of night are guiltless, but those who kill thieves in the light of day shall be held accountable, vv. 2-3.
3. Persons responsible for property damage or other loss shall make restitution plus pay fines or penalties, vv. 5-15.
4. A man having sexual relations with an unbetrothed virgin shall pay the bride-price to her father, whether or not he marries her, vv. 16-17.
5. Mistreatment, oppression, and affliction of foreigners, widows, and orphans are forbidden, vv. 21-24.
6. Hebrews who loan money to their fellow Israelites are prohibited from charging them interest, vv. 25-27; Lev. 25:35-37.
7. Hebrews also are commanded to be honest in paying tithes and offerings unto the Lord, vv. 29-31; Mal. 3:8-9.

Also included in this chapter are prohibitions against certain pagan practices (sorcery, bestiality, idolatry, blasphemy, and cursing) under penalty of death, vv. 18-20, 28.

III. Revelation and Applications: I need to observe these spiritual principles . . .

1. Honesty in the sight of the Lord includes never taking anything which is another person's property.
2. Honesty includes not using more force than is absolutely necessary in defending my home and private property.
3. Honesty includes accepting responsibility for property damage or other loss which I have caused, or which I could have prevented.
4. Honesty includes accepting full responsibility for my actions in the realm of interpersonal relationships, such as in courtship and marriage.
5. Honesty includes assisting helpless persons who are in need.
6. Honesty includes not exploiting or taking advantage of persons who need to borrow money or other possessions from me.
7. Honesty also includes acknowledging God's ownership of all that I possess, and presenting to Him tithes and offerings as He has commanded.

The Angel of the Covenant

(Exodus 23:1-33)

I. Concentration: on the main teachings in this chapter

1. The Ninth Commandment ("You shall not bear false witness against your neighbor," Ex. 20:16) is expanded upon and interpreted, vv. 1-9.
2. The Fourth Commandment ("Remember the Sabbath Day, to keep it holy," Ex. 20:8-11) is expanded to include a "Sabbath of years" to allow the land to rest every seventh year, vv. 10-13.
3. Three annual feasts are named, which all Hebrew males are required to attend: (1) Feast of Unleavened Bread (2) Feast of Harvest and (3) Feast of Ingathering, vv. 14-19.
4. God promises to send His Angel to bless His chosen people, vv. 20-23.

II. Meditation: on the "Angel of the Covenant"

God's "Angel" is the pre-incarnate Christ, the Son of God, Who appears several times in the Old Testament, Ex. 3:2-4; Dan. 3:25; Mal. 3:1.

1. This Angel, sent by the Lord, is to be reverenced and obeyed, vv. 20-21.
2. This Angel has authority to forgive sins, for God's name is in Him, v. 21.
3. This Angel will lead God's people into the place prepared for them, v. 20.
4. This Angel will bring victory to God's people over their enemies, vv. 22-24.
5. This Angel will provide the basic necessities of life (bread and water), v.25.
6. This Angel will heal them and give them health and long life, vv. 25-26.
7. This Angel will give them security, assurance, and confidence, vv. 27-28.
8. This Angel will help them to mature and to gain strength, vv. 29-30.
9. This Angel will maximize the bounds of their inheritance, v. 31.
10. This Angel will guide them into proper worship and faithful service of the Lord God, vv. 32-33.

III. Revelation and Applications: as a Christian, I need to . . .

1. Reverence and obey Jesus Christ, Who was sent by God the Father.
2. Receive forgiveness, as I pray in Jesus' name.
3. Follow the Lord Jesus wherever He leads me.
4. Rejoice in the victories won through Jesus' power.
5. Receive provision for all my needs through Jesus, Phil. 4:19.
6. Receive physical healing and spiritual life through Jesus.
7. Receive the comfort of Jesus' abiding presence.
8. Receive daily strength as I grow toward the likeness of Jesus Christ.
9. Experience the full measure of my inheritance as a child of God through Jesus Christ . . . here on earth and in heaven throughout eternity.
10. Faithfully serve and worship the Lord Jesus Christ, the Son of God.

God's Glory on Mount Sinai

(Exodus 24:1-18)

I. Concentration: on the events in this chapter

    1. The Lord God called Moses, Aaron, and other leaders of the nation to a solemn assembly at Mt. Sinai, vv. 1-3.

    2. Moses read the Book of the Covenant to the people, and sealed their agreement by sprinkling the blood of the sacrifice, vv. 4-8.

    3. Moses and the other leaders were allowed to see partially and to commune briefly with the Lord God, vv. 9-11.

    4. Moses took Joshua up into the mountain of God to receive the tablets of stone (Ten Commandments), leaving Aaron and Hur in charge of the people down in the valley; Moses remained on Mt. Sinai for forty days and nights, vv. 12-18.

II. Meditation: on the spiritual implications seen here

    1. God calls His chosen leaders to a closer fellowship with Him than is normally available to the common people.

    2. God reveals Himself and His laws to His people whose response should be, "All that the Lord has said we will do, and be obedient," vv. 3, 7.

    3. God's covenant relationship with mankind is initiated by Him and sealed with a blood sacrifice.

    4. The power and presence of Almighty God is awesome, and His glory is as a consuming fire . . . man only can bow in reverent worship.

III. Revelation: on New Testament illustrations of these truths

    1. The Lord appeared as a blinding light when He called the Apostle Paul, Acts 9.

    2. The Lord's call is to full obedience, Jn. 13:21.

    3. The Lord's blood established our new covenant with God the Father, I Cor. 11:25.

    4. John testified: "When I saw Him, I fell at His feet as dead," Rev. 1:7.

IV. Applications: as a Christian, I need to . . .

    1. Realize that the way into God's presence is wide open to me through the torn veil, Mt. 27:51, and I am encouraged to come boldly to His throne of grace, Heb. 4;16.

    2. Obey the words of the Lord to build my house (establish my life and ministry) upon the Rock, Mt. 7:24.

    3. Know that Jesus, the great Shepherd of the sheep, makes me complete in every good work to do God's will . . . "through the blood of the everlasting covenant," Heb. 13:20-21.

    4. Bow before the One Whom God has highly exalted, before the name which is above every name . . . and confess that Jesus Christ is Lord, to the glory of God the Father, Eph. 2:9-11.

The Tabernacle of God

(Exodus 25:1-40)

I. Concentration: on the main instructions in this chapter

    1. The Lord instructed the people (through Moses) to bring various offerings to be used in building a sanctuary (tabernacle; tent) for worshipping God, vv. 1-9.

    2. The Lord instructed them on building the Ark of the Covenant (a gold-covered wooden box to contain the Ten Commandments), vv. 10-22.

    3. The Lord instructed them about making a table upon which to set the "showbread," vv. 23-30.

    4. The Lord instructed them on how to design a gold lampstand, vv. 31-40.

II. Meditation: on the lessons taught regarding these items

    1. Each person was to make an offering to the Lord with a willing heart; whatever a person possessed (from gold to badger skins) could be used in the Lord's service, vv. 2-3, 5.

    2. God's purpose was to consecrate a place where He could meet and speak with His chosen people, v. 22.

    3. The twelve loaves of showbread on the table inside the tabernacle pictured God's provision for the twelve tribes of Israel, v. 30; Lev. 24:5-9.

    4. The seven-branched lampstand (menorah) symbolized the perfect eternal light of God's presence, guidance, and revelation, v. 37.

III. Revelation: on the New Testament fulfillment of these Old Testament symbols

    1. Christians are first to give themselves (all that they are and all that they possess) unto the Lord, Mk. 10:21; II Cor. 8:3-5.

    2. "The Word (Christ) became flesh and dwelt (tabernacled) among us," Jn. 1:14; "Behold, the tabernacle of God is with men," Rev. 21:3.

    3. "I am the bread of life," Jn. 6:35.

    4. "I am the light of the world," Jn. 8:12.

IV. Applications: as a Christian, I need to . . .

    1. Present my body as a living sacrifice unto the Lord, Rom. 12:1-2.

    2. Joyfully invite and receive Christ's indwelling and abiding presence in my life, Jn. 15:4-7.

    3. Thankfully accept the Lord's abundant provision for all my daily needs, Mt. 6:11; Phil. 4:19.

    4. Walk daily in the illumination of the Lord's presence, with spiritual perception and vision of His destiny and purpose for my life . . . letting the glory of His light shine through me, Mt. 5:16.

The Detailed Pattern of the Tabernacle

(Exodus 26:1-37)

I. Concentration: on the basic materials to be used

1. Fine linen curtains with artistic designs of cherubim (angels) were to be woven out of blue, purple, and scarlet thread to form the interior walls of the tabernacle, vv. 1-6.
2. Goat hair curtains were to be incorporated as part of the walls of the tent, vv. 7-13.
3. Ram skins dyed red and badger skins were to form the protective, weather-proofed outer covering of the tabernacle, vv. 14-15.
4. Boards (frames) and bars (cross-members) of acacia wood, and sockets and fasteners of gold, silver, and bronze were to be made to give the tent (tabernacle) stability, vv. 16-29.

II. Meditation: on the pattern . . . "shown on the mountain," (v. 30)

1. The tabernacle was to be constructed without windows or any cracks through which curious eyes could gaze . . . for God is holy and separate from sinful mankind, vv. 31-32.
2. The interior of the 15 feet by 45 feet tent was fitted with a thick veil forming a "Holy of Holies" room (15' X 15") in which rested the Ark of the Covenant, vv. 33-34.
3. In the outer room ("Holy Place," 15' X 30') were placed the table of showbread, the gold lampstand, and an altar of incense, v. 35.
4. The interior walls, the veil, and the screen for the entrance of the tabernacle were blue, purple, and scarlet . . . perhaps representing God's spiritual, majestic, and eternal qualities, vv. 36-37.

(The sky-blue color could speak of the heavenly realm; the purple could speak of the Almighty King's power to reign; and the scarlet could speak of the blood, which is life, according to Lev. 17:11.)

III. Revelation and Applications

1. God is holy and righteous.
   I should approach Him with humility, awe, and reverence.
2. God has provided a place of sacrifice (Calvary) where His love and grace can be received.
   I am invited to come to His "mercy seat" through the veil of Christ's torn flesh, Heb. 10:19-22.
3. God provides for His people nourishment (showbread), illumination (lampstand), and a way of communion through prayer (incense).
   I may appropriate Christ's blessings into my spiritual life: He is the Bread of life; He is the Light of the world; and He is my access to the Father through prayer, I Tim. 2:5.
4. God deserves man's worship.
   I need to praise Him daily for His righteous character, for His almighty power, and for His gift of eternal life.

The Altar, the Court, and the Oil

(Exodus 27:1-21)

I. Concentration: on additional details about the tabernacle

1. The term "tabernacle" in Scripture sometimes refers specifically to the tent, but in other places it refers to the entire complex, including the curtained courtyard in which the tent stood.
2. The court of the tabernacle was an area 150 feet long and 75 feet wide, enclosed by a wooden and curtained fence seven-and-a-half feet tall, vv. 9-18.
3. Inside this open-air enclosure, the Lord instructed Moses to build a brazen altar of burnt offering (seven-and-a-half feet square and four-and-a-half feet high), vv. 1-8.
4. Aaron and his sons were instructed about preparing the olive oil to be burned in the bowls of the lampstand inside the tabernacle, vv. 20-21.

II. Meditation: on the spiritual significance of these things

1. Although God is an invisible Spirit and He has prohibited the making of any idol to represent His person, He orders the construction of the tabernacle to represent the place of His presence among His chosen people, Ex. 25:8.
2. The careful and minutely detailed instructions given about the construction of the tabernacle and its furnishings was to aid and to instruct the people about the Lord and how to correctly approach and worship Him.
3. The brazen altar where sacrifices and burnt offerings were made included a perpetual fire (Lev. 6:9) that allowed the people to come to the Lord at any time and make atonement for their sins.
4. The olive oil in the lampstand also was to burn continually in the holy   place inside the tabernacle, representing God's eternal enlightenment.

III. Revelation and Applications: I need to know that . . .

1. The Lord God is looking for persons who will worship Him by faith, not by sight, Heb. 11:1, 3, 6, 27.
2. God is Spirit, and true worshippers must worship Him in His way . . . in spirit and in truth, Jn. 4:23-24.
3. The altar of burnt offering pointed to Jesus Christ, Who was the final sacrifice for sin . . . and Who always is available to forgive and cleanse confessing, repentant sinners, I Jn. 1:9.
4. The oil to be burned in the lamps tended by Aaron and his sons was symbolic of the Holy Spirit, Who always works in our behalf and Who always is available to enlighten believers, Jn. 16:7-14; Rom. 8:26.

Urim and Thummim

(Exodus 28:1-43)

I . Concentration: on the garments for the priesthood

1. The priestly garments, to be made by gifted artisans whom God had filled with the spirit of wisdom, included a breastplate, an ephod (an ornamental vest), a robe, a skillfully woven tunic, a turban, and a sash, vv. 1-4.

2. The ephod was to include on the shoulders two stones engraved with the names of the twelve tribes of Israel, vv. 5-14.

3. The breastplate included twelve precious stones, each engraved with the name of one of the sons of Jacob; the breastplate also included two other stones: Urim and Thummim, vv. 15-30.

4. Among the other items of the priestly garments was an engraved signet to be worn on the High Priest's turban which read, "HOLINESS TO THE LORD," vv. 31-43.

II. Meditation: on the Urim and Thummim

1. "Urim" means "lights" and "Thummim" means "perfections" or "completeness," vv. 29-30.

2. When God's people needed a special sense of guidance or discernment (which only God could give, and human wisdom seemed inadequate or undependable), the High Priest would inquire of the Lord by the Urim and Thummim, Num. 27:21; I Sam. 28:6; Ezra 2:63; Neh. 7:65.

3. The breastplate, which represented righteousness (Eph. 6:14), was worn over the heart of the High Priest, v. 29.

4. Although exactly how the device worked is unknown, we do know this:
   1) It provided direction and gave answers through "lights" . . . spiritual enlightenment.
   2) It also gave guidance by affirming the right or correct choice by "perfections" . . . a peaceful confirmation that the perceived message was correctly understood.

Apparently, there was a combination of a supernatural signal blended with an inner sense of God's peace, wholeness, composure, and assurance to the heart of the High Priest.

III. Revelation and Applications: as a Christian, I need to know that . . .

1. The New Testament "Urim and Thummim" is the Holy Spirit, Who dwells within the hearts of believers.

2. The Holy Spirit gives spiritual guidance to those who live clothed in the righteousness of Christ, I Cor. 5:21; Phil. 3:9.

3. The Holy Spirit reveals to us the "light" of God's word . . . opening the eyes of our spiritual understanding, Jn. 16:13; Col. 1:9.

4. The Holy Spirit also signals "right" or "wrong" to us by His inner "ping" . . . giving us perfect peace when we are on the right track, and "checking" us in our spirits when we go astray, Col. 3:15; Phil. 4:17.

The Ordination Ceremony of the Priests

(Exodus 29:1-46)

I. Concentration: on the spiritual aspects of the ordination ceremony

1. "Hallow them for ministry," v. 1, means to make them holy and pure.
2. "You shall anoint them," Ex. 28:41, means to pour oil on the head of the priest representing the empowering by the Holy Spirit.
3. "You shall . . . consecrate them," Ex. 28:41, means to be wholly given over to (or consumed by) the Lord.
4. "You shall . . . sanctify them," Ex. 28:41, means to be set aside entirely for the service of the Lord.

II. Meditation: on the elements of the ceremony

1. The ceremony included washing to represent cleansing from sin.
2. The ceremony included blood sacrifices to bring forgiveness of sin.
3. The ceremony included putting on of special garments to represent the righteousness and holiness required for the priestly office.
4. The ceremony included anointing with oil to represent the Spirit of the Lord coming upon the one being ordained.

III. Revelation: on putting the blood on the right ear, thumb, and big toe (v. 20)

1. "Right" signifies the position of importance, power, and authority.
2. "Ear" represents one's spiritual hearing or divine perception.
3. "Thumb" represents the actions and work of one's hands.
4. "Big toe" represents one's walk . . . where one goes.

IV. Applications: as a Christian, I need to . . .

1. Come to the Lord Jesus Christ for cleansing and forgiveness through His shed blood on Calvary.
2. Receive the divine anointing of the Holy Spirit for power and authority in my service and ministry for the Lord.
3. Dedicate my best, my all, (my right side) to the Lord God.
4. Allow God's touch to affect my spiritual hearing, my deeds of service, and my daily walk with Him, as I open and close each day with gifts of worship unto Him, vv. 38-42.

Significant Symbols Used to Worship God

(Exodus 30:1-38)

I. Concentration: on the worship items described in this chapter

1. The altar of incense was to be constructed of wood covered with gold; its dimensions were 18 inches by 18 inches by 36 inches tall, vv. 1-10.
2. The ransom money (atonement fee) was to be paid by all Hebrew males to help support operating expenses of the tabernacle, vv. 17-22 . . . it later became the temple tax, Mt. 17:24-27.
3. The bronze laver (basin) was to be constructed and set just outside the tabernacle; it was filled with water to be used by the priests to wash their hands and feet, vv. 17-21.
4. A holy anointing oil was to be prepared according to a very specific formula, vv. 22-33.
5. The incense for the incense altar also was to be prepared according to a very specific formula, vv. 34-38.

II. Meditation: on the spiritual significance of these things

1. Fire was taken from the brazen altar, placed on the smaller inner incense altar, and incense was applied, resulting in a sweet smelling aroma; this was a symbol of worship and intercession.
2. The ransom fee was the same amount for rich and poor, because all are equal sinners in the sight of God.
3. Repeatedly the priests were instructed to wash in the laver during the religious ceremonies as a reminder of their continuing need for spiritual cleansing.
4. The holy anointing oil was used to symbolize the "setting apart" of persons and things for special service to God; it was applied to the priests, to the tabernacle, and to all the furnishings and utensils.
5. The incense, representing the prayers ascending unto the Lord, was made of rare and expensive ingredients to symbolize that God is entitled to the best available . . . He is worthy.

III. Revelation and Applications: as a Christian, I need to know that . . .

1. Christ's ministry includes His continual intercession for all believers, Heb. 7:25.
2. God is no respecter of persons; all have sinned and come short of the glory of God, Acts 10:34; Rom. 3:23.
3. In my role as a "priest," I have received the "washing of regeneration and the renewing of the Holy Spirit," Titus 3:5 . . . but my feet, like Peter's, need regular washing, Jn. 13:10.
4. I need to be "anointed" for service . . . continually being filled with the Holy Spirit, Eph. 5:18.
5. God is worthy of my highest praise; I must offer to Him in worship . . . my best, my all, myself as a living sacrifice, Rom. 12:1-2.

Bezalel and Aholiab

(Exodus 31:1-18)

I. Concentration: on the main themes of this chapter

    1. God calls specific persons into His service, vv. 1-6.

    2. God gives them particular tasks to perform, vv. 7-11.

    3. God reveals His character through His redemptive names, such as: "Jehovah-M'Kaddesh" - "The God Who Sanctifies," v. 13. *(See also Lev. 20:8 and Ezek. 20:12.)*

    4. God established the Sabbath as one of the covenant signs between Himself and His people, vv. 13-18.

II. Meditation: on how God deals with the person He calls

    1. God called Bezalel personally, by name; Bezalel was the grandson of Hur, who probably was Moses' brother-in-law, v. 2; Ex. 17:10-12; 24:14.

    2. God filled Bezalel with the Holy Spirit, endowing him with (vv. 3-5):

    1) Wisdom   3) Knowledge

    2) Understanding   4) Creativity (design; workmanship)

    3. God gave Bezalel a qualified associate, Aholiab, v. 6.

    4. God put into Bezalel's heart the ability to teach others, Ex. 35:34.

III. Revelation: on the spiritual implications revealed here

    1. No matter how obscure or unknown we may be, God knows our names.

    2. Those whom God knows and calls are empowered to do His service by the filling of the Holy Spirit.

    3. The ability to serve God effectively is a gift; the ability to teach others how to serve God also is a gift and an additional blessing.

    4. God usually gives us a partner in service, someone to assist with the work and to be an encouragement to us.

IV. Applications: as a Christian, I need to . . .

    1. Cultivate the discipline of listening for God's voice, calling me by name.

    2. Be continually being filled with the Holy Spirit . . . for all the attributes and gifts I need to accomplish God's destiny in my life.

    3. Accept with humility and thanksgiving God's assignment to teach others how to serve Him effectively, Jas. 3:1.

    4. Express my appreciation and gratitude to God for the fellow-laborers whom He gives to assist me in my work.

Aaron, the Weak-willed Wimp

(Exodus 32:1-35)

I. Concentration: on the events in this chapter

1. When Moses delayed upon Mt. Sinai, the people appealed to Aaron to make them gods, v. 1.
2. Aaron told them to bring him golden earrings, which he made into a golden calf for them to worship, vv. 2-4.
3. Aaron built them an altar and proclaimed a day of celebration, v. 5.
4. Aaron encouraged the drunken sex orgy, rather than trying to restrain it, vv. 6, 25.
5. God saw Israel's sin and revealed it to Moses, who prayed for the Lord to have mercy, vv. 7-14.
6. Moses came down from the mountain and, in anger, cast down and broke the stone tablets containing the Ten Commandments, vv. 15-19.
7. Moses punished the people, forcing them to drink the water containing the gold from the idol which had been ground into powder, v. 20.
8. Aaron lied to Moses, shifting the blame to the people and claiming that the golden calf had appeared miraculously from the flame, vv. 21-24.
9. At Moses' command, the tribe of Levi executed 3,000 men (but spared the life of the most guilty person, Aaron), vv. 26-28.
10. Moses prayed earnestly for the Lord to forgive the sins of the people . . . but, if not, to blot him out of God's book also, vv. 29-35.

II. Meditation and Revelation: on the spiritual truths revealed here

1. People always will worship some kind of a god, true or false . . . there is an empty place in man's heart for God.
2. A weak, unprincipled spiritual or national leader can bring disaster upon his followers.
3. Wrong worship (in flesh and falsehood, rather than in spirit and truth) opens the door to all kinds of sin and evil.
4. Sin (and lying about sin) brings punishment and death.

III. Applications: as a Christian, I need to . . .

1. Truly worship the Lord in spirit and in truth, guarding against impatience at His divine timetable.
2. Stand up for what is right, even against public opinion.
3. Repent and confess my guilt, realizing that my sins can and do influence others to sin also.
4. Accept God's discipline for my own good, perceiving the contrast between the law and grace. *(Under the law, 3,000 persons died in Ex. 32:28; but under grace, 3,000 persons were saved in Acts 2:41.)*

"Here Is a Place by Me . . . on the Rock"

(Exodus 33:1-23)

I. Concentration: on the highlights of this chapter

1. The Lord commanded Moses to leave Mount Sinai and lead the Israelites on toward the Promised Land, vv. 1-6.
2. Moses met regularly with the Lord in the tabernacle; the people saw God's presence in the pillar of cloud; the Lord spoke to Moses face to face, as a man speaks to his friend, vv. 7-11.
3. God promised His accompanying Presence because He had extended grace to Moses, vv. 12-17.
4. God showed Moses His glory . . . literally His "weight," that is, the "heavy, worthy" inner reality that makes God Who He is, vv. 18-23.

II. Meditation: on the truths to be learned from this passage of Scripture

1. Although God is able to consume humanity in one moment, He deals with them as He had promised, even though they are a "stiff-necked people," vv. 3, 5.
2. God spoke to Moses directly, up-close-and-personal, intimately as with a friend . . . but although they met "face to face," (v. 13), Moses never actually saw God's face, v. 20.
3. Moses prayed for God to show him His "way," (v. 13) . . . stating that if God's Presence did not go with them, Moses did not want to start the journey, v. 15.
4. Moses prayed for God to show him His "glory," (v. 18), and God revealed His goodness, grace, and compassion . . . as a partial revelation of Himself, vv. 19-20.

III. Revelation: on the spiritual implications of these truths

1. Sinful man's only hope is for God to deal with him in mercy and grace.
2. Through the Lord's loving compassion, an obedient and humble person can have intimate "friendship" with Him, Jn. 15:14.
3. The Presence of the Lord is with His people always, even unto the end of the world, Mt. 28:20; Heb. 13:5.
4. God has prepared for us "a place by Me, and you shall stand on the rock" . . . in the cleft of the rock . . . covered by My hand, vv. 21-22; Mt. 16:18; II Sam. 22:2, 47; Psa. 61:2-4.

IV. Applications: as a Christian, I need to . . .

1. Trust in the Lord's grace and mercy for my salvation, provision, protection, and direction.
2. "Abide" in close connection and fellowship with the Lord, Jn. 15:1-7.
3. Receive the "rest" which God promised (v. 14), and which Jesus Christ offers, Mt. 11:28-30.
4. Realize that my "place" of security here on earth is upon the solid foundation of the words of Christ (Mt. 7:24-25), and that the Lord also is preparing for me a "place" near Him in heaven, Jn. 14:2-3.

God's Radiance Shown on Moses' Face

(Exodus 34:1-35)

I. Concentration: on the events in this chapter

1. At the Lord's command, Moses cut two new stone tablets to replace the ones he had broken (Ex. 32:19); Moses ascended Mount Sinai again to meet with God, vv. 1-9.
2. God offered to renew His covenant agreement with the Israelites, cautioning them to stamp out paganism and avoid idolatry, vv. 10-17.
3. The Lord reviewed His regulations concerning the Sabbath and the other religious feast days, vv. 18-28.
4. Although he was unaware of it at first, Moses' face shined with the radiance of the Lord which had been absorbed during his days spent on Mount Sinai; Moses covered his face with a veil, vv. 29-35.

II. Meditation: on the spiritual principles seen in this chapter

1. The Lord God gave Moses and the Israelites another chance because He is "merciful and gracious, long-suffering, and abounding in goodness and truth . . . forgiving iniquity and transgression and sin," vv. 6-7.
2. The Lord is a holy God, a "jealous" God . . . not willing for His people to love and worship any pagan god or demonic idol.
3. The Sabbath and feasts of the Lord were to be observed "religiously" because they reminded the people of the God they served and of what He had done for them.
4. Spending time in the presence of Almighty God always changes a person's face . . . and his spiritual character and godly influence.

III. Revelation: on God's radiance shining on Moses' face

1. God is light, I Tim. 6:16; I Jn. 1:5; Rev. 21:23.
2. The light of God's divinity shined out from the presence of the Lord Jesus Christ, Mt. 17:2; Acts 9:3-5.
3. Persons who spend time worshipping the Lord absorb the spiritual illumination of His presence, and this radiance can sometimes be seen by perceptive, observant believers.
4. Discontinuing the practice of intimate, daily communion in the Lord's presence causes the spiritual radiance to fade away, according to Paul . . . which is the reason Moses put on the veil, II Cor. 3:7-13.

IV. Applications: as a Christian, I need to . . .

1. Know that God is the source of all light and truth.
2. Recognize that Jesus is God's revelation of His light to us, Jn. 1:9.
3. Spend quality, quiet time every day in the presence of the Lord Jesus Christ, being filled with the Holy Spirit's illumination.
4. Realize that my "radiance" and illumination depends upon the Lord's light . . . I am not the source of the light, only the "reflection" of His presence shining through me to bless others.

Spiritual Principles of Fund-raising

(Exodus 35:4-35)

I. Concentration: on the basic principles taught in this chapter

1. Emphasize that the gift is to be a "freewill offering" to the Lord, vv. 5, 29.
2. Publicize the fact that every person may participate because every type and size of gift is needed, vv. 5-9.
3. Advertise the cause: state that the offerings are needed for . . . and will be used for . . . specific purposes in the work of the Lord, vv. 10-19.
4. Realize how persons respond to appeals for contributions: *"Everyone came whose heart was stirred, and everyone whose spirit was willing, and they brought the Lord's offering," v. 21.*
5. Acknowledge specifically, with thanks, the gift and the giver, vv. 22-29.
6. Assign trustworthy persons to handle the contributions and to accomplish the work as planned, vv. 30-35.
7. Stop soliciting funds for the project when the contributions needed have reached the goal, Ex. 36:5-7.

II. Meditation: on the spiritual implications for a fund-raiser

1. Do not coerce or use high pressure tactics.
2. Truly value everyone's gift, large or small, because all gifts are necessary to achieve the goal. *(See Mark 12:41-44.)*
3. Project a God-given vision . . . a cause in which donors can become vitally involved, a ministry of which contributors can claim ownership.
4. Know how persons make charitable gifts:
    1) They hear about the cause or need (mind thinks).
    2) Their emotions are moved (heart stirred).
    3) Their will decides to act (positive choice).
    4) The contribution is made (deed done).
5. Charitable organizations should immediately say "thank you" to their donors and issue receipts for their contributions.
6. The charity soliciting the gifts must act with honesty and integrity, making sure the money is spent wisely (with good stewardship) to accomplish the ministries as advertised.
7. Godly leaders must not deceive or mislead those who give to support their work; when one project or ministry thrust ends, they must state that fact, while also encouraging supporters to invest in whatever new directions, new causes, new challenges, or new opportunities which God has revealed to them.

III. Revelation and Applications: as a Christian ministry leader, I need to . . .

1. Project God's vision of ministry, and trust Him to raise up the persons He has chosen to support this particular cause.
2. Use only worthy appeals and godly methods in raising funds.
3. Treat all individuals and gifts with equal appreciation and respect.
4. Deal with fund-raising (and all matters of life) with honesty and integrity.

Wood Overlaid with Gold

(Exodus 36:34, 36, 38)

I. Concentration: on the wood and metals used in the tabernacle

1. Acacia - a gum tree with heavy, strong wood, sometimes called mimosa.
2. Bronze - an alloy of copper, tin, and zinc (sometimes translated brass, an alloy of only copper and zinc).
3. Silver - a soft, white precious metal.
4. Gold - a bright, yellow precious metal.

II. Meditation: on Christ as a combination of wood and gold

1. There is a repeated directive in Exodus that the wooden objects and furnishings of the tabernacle should be overlaid with gold, as for example in vv. 34, 36, 38.
2. Since many portraits of the Messiah are seen in the tabernacle, perhaps this could be a beautiful picture of the blend of Christ's humanity and His divinity; "Immanuel" means "God with us," Isa. 7:14; Mt. 1:23.
3. "The Word became flesh and dwelt (tabernacled) among us," Jn. 1:14, may be foreshadowed by the wood (Jesus' vulnerable, ordinary flesh) combined with the gold (His glorious and worthy Divine nature).
4. The Christmas carol, "Hark! The Herald Angels Sing" contains these words: *"Veiled in flesh the God-head see; Hail the incarnate Deity!"*

III. Revelation: on a Christian as "wood overlaid with gold"

1. Christians are building in God's kingdom using valuable and permanent materials (such as gold) or worthless and temporary materials (such as wood), I Cor. 3:12.
2. Christians may become honorable, sanctified, useful, prepared vessels for the Lord (gold) or dishonorable ones (wood), II Tim. 2:20-21.
3. Christians are to put on (be clothed in) Christ's "golden" holiness and righteousness, Eph. 4:24.
4. Christians are to be "overlaid" (covered) with Christ's robe (character), II Cor. 5:21; Lk. 15:22; Rev. 19:8.

IV. Applications: as a Christian, I need to . . .

1. Search the Scriptures for pictures of the Messiah, God's Anointed One.
2. Worship the Lord Jesus Christ, my Immanuel . . . Divine, Almighty, Majestic God in human form and flesh.
3. Realize that the nearer I draw unto God's presence, the more of the weight of His glory I experience. *(In the construction of the tabernacle, the materials got more valuable the closer the worshipper came to the manifest Presence of God . . . from the brazen altar outside the tent to the pure golden "Mercy Seat" within the Holy of Holies.)*
4. Allow Christ, through my repentance and faith, to cloth me with His "golden" robe of holiness and righteousness, Titus 3:5.

Golden Rings and Wooden Poles

(Exodus 37:1-5, 10-15, 25-28)

I. Concentration: on the furnishings of the tabernacle

    1. Ark of the Covenant, Ex. 37:1-9; 25:10-22.

    2. Table for the Showbread, Ex. 37:10-16; 25:23-30.

    3. Gold Lampstand, Ex. 37:17-24; 25:31-40.

    4. Altar of Incense, Ex. 37:25-29; 30:1-10.

    5. Altar of Burnt Offering, Ex. 38:1-7; 27:1-8.

    6. Bronze Laver, Ex. 38:8; 30:17-21.

II. Meditation: on the instructions concerning these holy objects

    1. Bezalel and his associates were instructed to construct the tabernacle and its furnishings precisely according to the directions which God gave to Moses, Ex. 25:9, 40; 26:30; Acts 7:44; Heb. 8:5.

    2. Interestingly, detailed dimensions were given only for the Ark, the Table, and the two Altars.

    3. Bezalel was given instructions for the intricate workmanship of the menorah (lampstand), but he was not given the exact size; he was given no details at all about the size or shape of the laver.

    4. Four of the furnishings were to be carried by <u>wood poles through gold rings</u>, but neither the lampstand nor the laver had such devices for picking up and transporting them.

III. Revelation: on the spiritual implications to be seen here

    1. Most of the time, the Lord gives detailed commands for His people to follow . . . through His holy word.

    2. At other times, He gives general directions to His chosen, gifted, Spirit-filled persons, allowing them to take the initiative and to have some latitude in carrying out His orders.

    3. Sinful persons may not touch the holy things of God directly, under penalty of death (II Sam. 6:6-7); the <u>rings and poles</u> were means by which sinful men could draw near to Almighty God yet live . . . a beautiful picture of how we may "touch" God the Father through the Lord Jesus Christ.

    4. The water in the laver and the light shining from the lampstand represent God's blessings of cleansing and illumination, which are freely available to all believers who will receive them.

IV. Applications; as a Christian, I need to . . .

    1. Obey the Lord's clear commands as revealed in His word.

    2. Be filled with (and guided by) the Holy Spirit to use His gifts of creativity and originality in rendering service unto the Lord.

    3. Draw near unto God through the Lord Jesus Christ, Who is my one and only Mediator, Jas. 4:8; I Tim. 2:5.

    4. Allow the Lord to cleanse my life, I Jn. 1:9, and to shine His light through me, Mt. 5:16.

Shekels and Talents

(Exodus 38:21-31)

I. Concentration: on the Old Testament system of weights (money)

1. A shekel weighed approximately 0.4 ounce.
2. A talent equaled 3,000 shekels, or 75 pounds.
3. A bekah was a half-shekel or 0.2 ounce.
4. The monetary value of a shekel, therefore, would vary depending on whether it was made of gold, silver, or some other metal.

II. Meditation: on the precious metals contributed for the tabernacle

1. The people gave 29 talents and 730 shekels of gold, v. 24; this equaled 87,730 shekels or 35,092 ounces of gold. *At $350 per ounce, this totals over $12 million.*
2. The people gave 100 talents and 1,775 shekels of silver, v. 25; this equaled 301,775 shekels or 120,708 ounces of silver. *At $16 per ounce, this totals over $2 million.*
3. The silver was the atonement or ransom tax, at the rate of one bekah for every Hebrew male 20 years of age and above (603,550 men), v. 26.
4. The people gave 70 talents and 2,400 shekels of bronze, v. 29; this equaled 212,400 shekels or 84,960 ounces of bronze. *(Value unknown.)*

III. Revelation: on the spiritual lessons to be learned from this accounting

1. God keeps an exact census of all His people and He maintains a precise record of our gifts to His service.
2. Whatever our "metal," God values us, needs us, and uses us for His glory.
3. Every person owes the same "ransom" price, because all of us are guilty sinners standing in need of atonement.
4. God's place of worship should reflect His matchless glory and worth.

IV. Applications: as a Christian, I need to . . .

1. Know that God observes all my thoughts, words, and deeds, including how much I give to support His ministries, Mk. 12:41-44.
2. Know that whatever my background, education, or talents, the Lord has need of me . . . and can use my life to accomplish His purposes.
3. Know that no human being deserves God's grace and mercy; we all need a Savior . . . the Lord Jesus Christ, Acts 4:12.
4. Know that church buildings and grounds, whatever their monetary value, should reflect the Lord's beauty and worth, and reveal the members' honor and respect for His holy name.

The Day of Inspection

(Exodus 39:1, 5, 7, 21, 31-32, 42-43)

I. Concentration: on "as the Lord had commanded Moses"

This phrase occurs seven times in Exodus, chapter 39.

II. Meditation: on the inspection process (vv. 32-43)

1. The inspection did not occur until all the work had been finished. *The final judgment of our works will not happen until after the world ends, for until then our influence will continue to have some impact.*
2. The materials were examined carefully. *The materials with which we build will be tried to see if they match God's specifications: gold, silver, and precious stones, rather than wood, hay, and stubble, I Cor. 3:12.*
3. The quality of our workmanship also will be evaluated. *God will judge our degree of faithfulness and our motivations, Mt. 25:19; I Cor. 13:1-3.*
4. "Moses looked over all the work, and indeed . . . just so they had done it. And Moses blessed them," v. 43. *We will be rewarded or punished "just so" (justly; exactly) according to our works, II Cor. 5:10.*

III. Meditation: on the spiritual implications of this chapter

1. God reveals His will about every detail of our lives, if we will have "ears to hear," Mt. 11:15.
2. Whenever God reveals His will to persons, He expects them to obey His word immediately and completely.
3. When God assigns His chosen people a task to perform, He also provides the necessary materials and the gifting ("know-how") to get the job done right.
4. There will come a day when the Lord will inspect the work which His servants have done; He will judge their work according to His revealed pattern and specifications.

IV. Applications: as a Christian, I need to realize that . . .

1. The Great Architect of the Universe someday will come to evaluate whether I have built according to His "blueprint."
2. My spiritual service will be tested to see whether it is permanent or temporary; Jesus wants me to bear fruit that "remains," Jn. 15:16.
3. My works will not be evaluated in comparison to someone else's accomplishments; rather, my works will be judged in comparison with my potential . . . what I did compared what I could have done through total faithfulness and obedience to the Lord.
4. The Lord's words of commendation: "Well done, you good and faithful servant," will be a blessing indeed! *My future assignment in heaven will be determined by the degree of my faithfulness to the Lord here on earth, Mt. 25:21.*

God's Glory Filled the Tabernacle

(Exodus 40:1-38)

I. Concentration: on the main events of this chapter

1. God told Moses to erect and arrange the tabernacle, vv. 1-15.
2. Moses immediately obeyed the Lord's directions, vv. 16-33.
3. God's cloud covered the tabernacle of meeting, and the glory of the Lord filled the tabernacle, vv. 34-35.
4. The cloud by day and the fiery pillar by night was given to guide and comfort the Israelites, vv. 36-38.

II. Meditation: on the timing of this memorable day

1. This event happened on the first day of the first month of the second year . . . Israel's first year as a nation began two weeks before the original Passover night, vv. 2, 17; Ex. 12:2-6.
2. Israel's journey from Egypt to Mount Sinai took three months, Ex. 19:1.
3. All preparations for worshipping God in the tabernacle, including Moses 40 days to receive the Ten Commandments (maybe 80 days since he made two trips), took a total of about nine months.
4. The Israelites departed from Mount Sinai toward the Promised Land of Canaan on the 20th day of the second month in the second year . . . after they had observed the second Passover, Num. 9:1-5; 10:11-13.

III. Revelation: on the spiritual implications seen in this chapter

1. Even with exact obedience in constructing the tent and all its furnishings and anointing them and the priests with holy oil, the work was not finished and the tabernacle was useless.
2. Everything they had done was vain and empty until God's glory and Presence filled the tabernacle.
3. When God's Spirit is manifested in glory and power, no man can enter in or function normally, v. 35; II Chron. 7:1-3.
4. The Presence of the Lord was visible to every man, woman, and child of the house of Israel, bringing them, no doubt, great comfort and assurance, as well as divine illumination and guidance, vv. 36-38.

IV. Applications: as a Christian, I need to . . .

1. Follow God's commands in complete obedience, even though I may not yet see His miraculous hand at work.
2. Realize that "All is vain unless the Spirit of the Holy One comes down," *(from the gospel song, "Brethren, We Have Met to Worship")*.
3. Humbly fall before the Lord Almighty to worship Him in fear, awe, and holy reverence.
4. Understand that the Holy Spirit is available to all believers to bring them comfort, assurance, enlightenment, guidance, and strength.

The Burnt Offering

(Leviticus 1:1-17)

I. Concentration: on the Book of Leviticus

1. "Leviticus" means "matters pertaining to the Levites."
2. Leviticus links holiness to everyday life; "holy" appears more than 80 times in the book.
3. The first five chapters are devoted to five different "offerings" (sacrifices), each addressing a different issue (problem or hindrance) which prevented fellowship with God and which could be removed by a sacrifice to restore holy communion with God.
4. Each of these five sacrifices pictures something which Christ has done for us on the cross: (1) Burnt Offering, Lev. 1, (2) Grain Offering, Lev. 2, (3) Peace Offering, Lev. 3, (4) Sin Offering, Lev. 4, and (5) Trespass Offering, Lev. 5.

II. Meditation: on the Burnt Offering

1. The Israelite worshipper was to bring a male animal of the herd or flock, without blemish, v. 3. *(Poor persons could bring a bird, vv. 14-17.)*
2. The animal was to be a freewill offering; the worshipper was to place his hand on the animal's head, symbolically transferring his life to the animal to be offered as a sacrifice to bring atonement between man and God, v. 4.
3. The priest was to kill the animal and sprinkle its blood on the altar and near the door of the tabernacle, v. 5.
4. The animal's body was to be completely consumed by the fire on the altar . . . "a burnt sacrifice, an offering made by fire, a sweet aroma to the Lord," vv. 9, 13, 17.

III. Revelation: on the spiritual significance of this burnt offering

1. Christ was the spotless Lamb of God offered for us, Jn. 1:29; I Pet. 1:19.
2. Christ took our sins upon Himself at the cross, II Cor. 5:21.
3. Christ's blood brings spiritual life, forgiveness, and atonement for our souls, Lev. 17:11; I Pet. 1:19.
4. Christ completely and totally poured out His soul unto death, Isa. 53:12.

IV. Applications: as a Christian, I need to . . .

1. Worship Jesus Christ, the holy and spotless Lamb of God, Rev. 5:12.
2. Repent and confess my sins daily, receiving Christ's forgiveness and cleansing, I Jn. 1:9.
3. Pattern my life after the holiness and purity of the Lord, I Jn. 3:2-3.
4. Follow Christ's example by pouring out my life in total surrender to His will, Phil. 2:17; II Tim. 4:6.

The Grain Offering

(Leviticus 2:1-16)

I. Concentration: on the elements of the grain offering

    1. Flour - finely ground grain, v. 1.
    2. Oil - olive oil was poured upon the flour, v. 1.
    3. Frankincense - the perfumed ingredient used on the incense altar in the tabernacle was added, v. 1; Ex. 30:34.
    4. Salt - every grain offering was to be seasoned with salt, v. 13.

II. Meditation: on the pictures of Christ in these items

    1. The grain baked into bread represents Christ, the bread of life, Jn. 6:35.
    2. The oil pressed from the olives may portray the extreme pressures and stresses of Christ's suffering for mankind; the oil also represents the presence of the Holy Spirit as a vital part of true worship.
    3. The frankincense usually pictures the worship and intercessory prayers ascending to God as a sweet smelling aroma. *The wise men presented this sacred substance as an offering to the Christ child, Matt. 2:11.*
    4. The salt symbolized a lasting, preserving quality and was used in "sealing" a covenant or agreement; salt represents a wholesome, beneficial, tasty quality of life or speech, Matt. 5:13; Mk. 9:49-50; Col. 4:6; Num. 18:19; II Chron. 13:5; Ezek. 43:24. *Christ gives "flavor" to life, and His presence in His people preserves society from death and decay.*

III. Revelation: on the spiritual lessons in this chapter

    1. The grain offering teaches that God is the Creator and Provider of every good thing to sustain life.
    2. The grain offering teaches that mankind should return a portion of God's blessings to Him as an expression of gratitude and thanksgiving.
    3. Only a handful of the grain offering was burned on the altar; the rest of the offering was given to the priests for food. *God's plan is for His ministers to support their families on part of the offerings given by His people, I Cor. 9:9-14.*
    4. The four ways of preparing the bread from the flour before presenting it as an offering (vv. 4, 5, 7, 14) teaches that different kinds of service are acceptable to God as expressions of true worship.

IV. Applications: as a Christian, I need to . . .

    1. Feed daily on Jesus Christ, my source of spiritual life and nourishment.
    2. Be a good steward of God's blessings by faithfully bringing to Him His tithes and my offerings.
    3. Present myself (all that I am, all that I have, and all that I can be) as a living sacrifice to God, which is my holy, acceptable, perfect, and reasonable service of spiritual worship unto Him, Rom. 12:1-2.
    4. Exhibit in my life the qualities of oil, frankincense, and salt . . . being like a sacrifice of poured-out, healing oil; like the sweet-smelling aroma of intercessory prayer; and like life-preserving salt in a decaying world.

The Peace Offering

(Leviticus 3:1-17)

I. Concentration: on the occasion of making a Peace Offering

The Peace Offering was an optional sacrifice, which could be brought in conjunction with a confession or vow or simply as a freewill offering of gratitude (Lev. 7:11-21). The spiritual meaning of the Peace Offering and its relationship with Christ is discussed in detail in Leviticus 7.

II. Meditation: on the ceremonial regulations

1. The animal must be without blemish before the Lord, vv. 1, 6.
2. The worshipper laid his hand upon the animal's head before the priest killed it, vv. 2, 8, 13.
3. Aaron's sons, the priests of the tribe of Levi, sprinkled the blood of the sacrifice on the altar, vv. 2, 8, 13.
4. The fat and certain internal organs of the animal were removed and burned on the altar, vv. 3-5, 9-11, 14-16.

III. Revelation: on the spiritual significance of these practices

1. The animal without blemish foreshadowed the coming Lamb of God.
2. The worshipper identified himself with the sacrifice.
3. The sprinkled blood symbolized the giving of a life to secure the forgiveness of sins.
4. "All the fat is the Lord's," v. 16, refers to a custom going back to Abel's acceptable offering in Genesis 4:4. Fatness in the Bible represents health and prosperity (Prov. 13:4; 15:30; 28:25; and Isa. 30:23). *Heathen nations ate the fat of their sacrifices as part of their religious ceremonies (Deut. 32:38), but God's chosen people were to be different, separated, and holy. The Hebrew prohibition against eating blood and fat (Lev. 3:17) kept those parts of the sacrifice holy unto the Lord . . . the blood represented "life" and the fat symbolized the "best and prosperous" part of the offering.*

IV. Applications: as a Christian, need to . . .

1. Present myself to the Lord as a blood-washed, holy sacrifice, Rom. 12:1-2.
2. Identify my life with Christ's life: *"I have been crucified with Christ; it is no longer I who live, but Christ lives in me; and the life which I now live in the flesh I live by faith in the Son of God, Who loved me and gave Himself for me,"* Gal. 2:20.
3. Receive daily forgiveness and cleansing through repentance and confession of my sins, I Jn. 1:9.
4. Give the best that I have in holy worship unto the Lord, Who is the source of all that I have, Jas. 1:17.

The Sin Offering

(Leviticus 4:1-35)

I. Concentration: on "unintentional" sins

The significance of this sacrifice is its cancellation of guilt, even for unintended sins or sins of ignorance. God makes provision to cover sins we may have forgotten to confess or sins we didn't even know or recognize we committed! "Father, forgive them," Jesus said, "for they do not know what they do," Lk. 23:34.

II. Meditation: on persons covered by the Sin Offering
1. The anointed priest, vv. 1-12.
2. The entire congregation (nation) of Israel, vv. 13-21.
3. The ruler (king) of the people, vv. 22-26.
4. An individual of the common people, vv. 27-35.

III. Revelation: on the unique features of this sacrifice
1. The Sin Offering for the priest and the congregation was a young bull; for the ruler, it was a male goat kid; for a common person, it was a female goat kid, vv. 3, 14, 23, 28.
2. As part of the ritual for the priest's and the congregation's Sin Offering, the priest dipped his finger in blood, sprinkled it seven times in front of the veil, applied blood to the incense alter, and poured the rest of the blood at the base of the altar of burnt offering. The sacrifice for the ruler or for an individual did not include putting the blood near the veil or on the incense altar inside the tabernacle.
3. The carcasses of the sacrificed bulls (for the priest and for the congregation) were carried outside the camp and burned on a wood fire where the ashes of the sacrifices usually were dumped. The bodies of the sacrificed goats were treated as were the Peace Offerings in Leviticus 3.
4. Apparently, the unintentional violations of the holiness code (and the covenant relationship) by the High Priest and by the entire nation of priests (Ex. 19:6) were considered to be more serious than were the unintentional violations committed by a secular ruler or by a common individual citizen.

IV. Applications: as a Christian, I need to . . .
1. Realize that God makes provision for the forgiveness of all my sins, even the unintentional and unrecognized ones.
2. Recognize that as a spiritual leader (a teacher), I am subject to a stricter judgment due to the larger scope of my influence, Jas. 3:1.

The Trespass Offering

(Leviticus 5:1-19)

I. Concentration: on the specific sins mentioned in this chapter

1. Refusal to report a crime or to testify as a witness is a sin, v. 1.
2. Touching an unclean animal makes a person unclean and guilty, v. 2.
3. Touching certain human waste products also defiles a person, v. 3.
4. Swearing thoughtless or meaningless oaths . . . or failure to fulfill vows made . . . makes a person guilty, v. 4.

II. Meditation: on some particulars about the Trespass Offering

1. The Trespass Offering in other Bible translations is called the Guilt Offering or the Reparation Offering.
2. The Trespass Offering ritual is very similar to the Sin Offering, and both offerings were made for similar types of violations of the Old Testament laws of holiness.
3. The Trespass Offering pictures the basic spiritual principles necessary for a person to receive Divine forgiveness and restoration:
1. Realize or recognize his guilt, vv. 3-4.
2. Confess that he has sinned, v. 5.
3. Come to the High Priest, who offers a blood sacrifice to atone for the sin, vv. 6-13.
4. Make restitution for the harm he has done to others by his sin, and pay whatever material and spiritual penalties which may be required, vv. 15-18.
4. The Trespass Offering is concerned primarily with restitution, with the guilty person expected to repay what he had taken illegally, plus 20 percent of the value (as a fine), plus a ram for a spiritual sacrifice.

III. Revelation and Applications: as a Christian, I need to . . .

1. Recognize the extent of my sins in God's eyes . . . including my unclean thoughts, words, deeds, and even my sins of omission: knowing to do good but not doing it, Jas. 4:17.
2. Repent of my sins and confess them to the Lord, I Jn. 1:9.
3. Receive cleansing by the blood of Jesus Christ, I Jn. 1:7.
4. Make restitution whenever possible; accept the just penalty imposed by the state for my crimes; serve the "probation" time required by the church before my restoration to full spiritual fellowship.

Carry the Ashes Outside the Camp

(Leviticus 6:1-30)

I. Concentration and Meditation: on the additional details about the sacrifices

    1. The regulations about the Trespass Offering (Lev. 5) are expanded to include penalties for persons guilty of robbery, stealing, and extortion: restitution plus a 20 percent fine plus a ram for the sacrifice, vv. 1-7.

    2. The priests were given instructions about maintaining the altar fire and disposing of the ashes of the Burnt Offerings, vv. 8-13; Lev. 1.

    3. Instructions were given regulating the eating of the Grain Offering by the priests, vv. 14-23; Lev. 2.

    4. Instructions were given about the vessels used in the Sin Offering and   about eating the meat of the sacrifices, vv. 24-30; Lev. 4.

II. Revelation: on the significance of the Burnt Offering regulations

    1. The priest was to put on clean white linen garments when he officiated at the altar, vv. 10-11. *Christ, our High Priest, is clothed in holiness and righteousness; we also are to be clothed in His righteousness as we minister in His name.*

    2. The priest was to carry the ashes of the Burnt Offerings outside the camp to a clean place, vv. 10-11. *Christ removes the "ashes" of our sins as far away as the east is from the west, never to be remembered against us any more, Psa. 103:12.*

    3. The ministry of the priest was to be performed daily: removing the ashes, laying the wood, burning the fat, vv. 9, 12. *Just as Christ always lives to make continual intercession for us, so also we are to take up our cross daily, Heb. 7:25; Lk. 9:23.*

    4. The fire on the altar was to be kept burning day and night: "it shall never go out," vv. 9, 12-13. *This symbolized that God's grace, mercy, and forgiveness are always available for repentant sinners.*

III. Applications: as a Christian, I need to . . .

    1. Put off the "old man" garments of sin, and put on the "new man" of true righteousness and holiness, Eph. 4:22-24.

    2. Know that God has forgiven and forgotten my sins (*He has taken them away and dumped them like yesterday's cold ashes!*); likewise, I must forgive and forget all the sins which others have committed against me, Mt. 5:12, 14-15; 18:21-35.

    3. Daily spend quality time with the Lord Jesus in Bible study and quiet meditation, in intercessory prayer and spiritual communion.

    4. Continually be in the state of humble repentance, allowing the purifying fire of the Holy Spirit to burn out the dross of my soul, Mal. 3:2-3; Mt. 3:11; I Cor. 3:12-15.

The Diet of the Priests

(Leviticus 7:1-38)

I. Concentration: on the main themes of this chapter

1. Additional regulations about Trespass, Sin, and Grain Offerings, vv. 1-10.
2. Additional regulations about Peace Offerings, vv. 11-21.
3. Regulations forbidding the eating of fat and blood, vv. 22-27.
4. Regulations about the portions of the sacrifices which belonged to the priests (Aaron and his sons), vv. 28-38.

II. Meditation: on what, when, and where the priests were allowed to eat

1. Priests were allowed to eat part of the Trespass, Sin, Grain, and Peace Offerings . . . but not any of the Burnt Offerings, which were wholly dedicated to God and completely consumed by the fire on the altar.
2. Priests were allowed to eat parts of some of the sacrifices only on the same day they were offered, v. 15; other sacrifices could be eaten on the first and second days, but the leftovers were to be burned on the third day, vv. 16-18. *(Some regulations had only religious significance; other regulations were given for health reasons.)*
3. The priests who officiated at the sacrifices and who ate of the offerings were required to be ceremonially clean and pure . . . emphasizing God's requirement of holiness; the priests also were required to eat these sacrifices only within the holy place (v. 6) which maintained the sacredness of the offerings set apart to the Lord.
4. Any person of the nation of Israel, who ate fat or meat from which the blood had not been drained, was to be "cut off from his people," (vv. 25, 27) . . . exiled, excommunicated, and shunned, because these portions of the animal had particular spiritual significance to the Lord God. *(See notes on Leviticus 3.)*

III. Revelation and Applications: as a Christian, I need to . . .

1. Perceive the spiritual truths that God allows me to partake of His abundance and blessings with thanksgiving, and that everything belongs to Him, so that my worship must include a complete "living sacrifice" of myself on the altar of "Burnt Offering," Rom. 12:1-2.
2. Understand that all of God's commands, laws, and regulations are designed for my good . . . spiritually and/or physically.
3. Live a life of holiness according to God's word: "You shall be holy, for I am holy," Lev. 11:44; and "Pursue . . . holiness, without which no one will see the Lord," Heb. 12:14.
4. Persons who do not come to Almighty God in His way are lost and doomed, Jn. 3:16-18; 14:6; Acts 4:12.

Stay in God's Tabernacle Seven Days!

(Leviticus 8:1-36)

I. Concentration: on the consecration of Aaron and his sons

1. The ceremony was done in obedience to the direct commands of the Lord God Almighty, vv. 1-5, 36.
2. The consecration of the priests was to be observed by the entire congregation (nation) of Israel, v. 4.
3. Detailed instructions were given about the priestly garments, the sacrifices to be offered, the anointing with oil, and the applying of the blood to the right ear, the right thumb, and the right big toe of Aaron and his sons, vv. 5-32.
4. The priests were required to spend seven days and nights within the tabernacle before beginning their ministry, vv. 33-35.

II. Meditation: on the significance of this ceremony

1. Although every person has a built-in spiritual urge to worship God, true worship can occur only as persons receive God's revelation of Himself and choose to obey and serve Him in His way.
2. The ways of God are filled with marvelous truths and mysterious revelations; yet they are to be observed and taught so that every child and adult can come to some degree of understanding of the holiness of the Lord, and so that the office of God's chosen and anointed servants may be magnified in the eyes of all the people.
3. The garments, the sacrifices, the oil, and the blood all had spiritual meaning for the immediate situation (ordination of the priesthood), but they also contained Messianic prophesies to be fulfilled in Jesus Christ. *(See notes on Exodus 29.)*
4. All God-called, ordained ministers should spend a complete, perfect period of time (symbolically, seven days) in the presence of the Lord before beginning their public service.

III. Revelation and Applications: as a Christian, I need to . . .

1. Study God's word and be open to His revelation so that I may better know and experience Him, and so that I may genuinely worship Him in spirit and in truth, Jn. 4:23-24.
2. Live a clean, pure, and holy life before the Lord and before the people, so that my life is a true reflection of Christ living in me, Ga. 2:20.
3. Look for the spiritual implications in every object and in every event or circumstance I encounter; cultivate an awareness of the presence of the living Christ in every moment, receiving from Him: eyes with spiritual discernment, ears tuned to hear His voice, and a heart warmed by His Spirit.
4. Spend daily quiet time with the Lord, learning from Him, before I go forth to teach and to minister in His name.

When Fire Falls from Heaven

(Leviticus 9:22-24)

I. Concentration: on God's fire falling on man's sacrifices

The Bible speaks a number of times about fire falling from heaven. Only four times, however, does God's fire fall on man's sacrifices. Paul says that Old Testament writings are for our learning . . . are examples for our admonition and instruction, Rom. 15:4; I Cor. 10:11. In this light, we examine these four falling-fire occasions to discover what they signify.

II. Meditation: on the occasions of these four falling-fire sacrifices

1. Fire fell on Aaron's sacrifice, Lev. 9:24. Here Aaron and his sons have just been set apart for service as priests, having carefully followed God's instructions for preparing themselves and the sacrifices for worship.
2. Fire fell on David's sacrifice, I Chron. 21:26. Here David, in repentance and confession, asked God to have mercy on the nation, for God had sent His death angel as punishment for David's sin of prideful disobedience in conducting a census in spite of God's prohibition.
3. Fire fell on Solomon's sacrifice, II Chron. 7:1. Here Solomon had just finished construction of the temple; the Ark of the Covenant had been brought into the holy of holies, and the people were praising the Lord and offering sacrifices.
4. Fire fell on Elijah's sacrifice, I Kgs. 18:38. Here Elijah confronted the prophets of Baal on Mount Carmel in a contest to demonstrate which god was the True and Living One.

III. Revelation: on the purposes of God's fire falling

1. God's fire fell on Aaron's sacrifice to exhibit God's glory upon the presentation of an acceptable sacrificial offering of true worship.
2. God's fire fell on David's sacrifice to signify God's mercy and grace . . . the end of punishment and the beginning of blessing.
3. God's fire fell on Solomon's sacrifice to confirm God's sovereign choice of a place where His manifest presence would dwell.
4. God's fire fell on Elijah's sacrifice to demonstrate God's power and superiority over false gods.

IV. Applications: as a Christian, I need to know that . . .

1. God's glory will be exhibited in me when I come to experience the full efficacy of Christ's atonement, and when I present myself as an acceptable sacrifice, Rom. 12:1-2.
2. God's mercy and grace (forgiveness, cleansing, and restoration) will become operative in me when I truly repent of my willful sin against the Lord God, I Jn. 1:9.
3. God's sovereign choice to confirm His presence will be manifested in me when I invite Him to fully occupy His temple (my body), I Cor. 6:19.
4. God's power will be victoriously demonstrated in me when I boldly take my stand against the enemy, Satan, Jas. 4:7.

Nadab and Abihu

(Leviticus 10:1-12)

I. Concentration: on Aaron's sons

1. Aaron had four sons: Nadab, Abihu, Eleazar, and Ithamar, Ex. 6:23.
2. The two older sons (Nadab and Abihu) were more actively involved in the priesthood, Ex. 24:1, 9.
3. Nadab and Abihu died without fathering children, Num. 3:4.
4. Nadab and Abihu died because they offered "profane" fire before the Lord, Num. 26:60-61. *"Profane fire" means fire which was not "holy" from the altar, as commanded by the Lord.*

II. Meditation: on the duties of the priesthood:

1. To magnify the holiness of God before the people,
2. To glorify God before the people, and to minister unto Him,
3. To offer sacrifices and lead people in worship of God, and
4. To teach spiritual principles to the people, including:
   1) Priests themselves must distinguish between holy and unholy, between clean and unclean, v. 10; Ezek. 22:26,
   2) Priests were to teach God's law to the people, v. 11,
   3) Priests were to teach the people how to discern for themselves between the holy and the unholy, Ezek. 44:23, and
   4) Priests were to be examples of abstinence from alcoholic beverages, v. 9; Ezek. 44:21.

III. Revelation: on the spiritual implications from this chapter

1. Apparently, it was drunkenness which caused Nadab and Abihu to sin.
2. Drunkenness is not an acceptable excuse or reason for sinful actions.
3. Their severe punishment was not for the sin of getting drunk, but for treating holy things in a profane, common, vulgar manner rather than according to God's instructions.
4. By their deaths, they taught valuable lessons about God's standards of holiness and His righteous judgment.

IV. Applications: as a Christian, I need to . . .

1. Realize that I am called to be a holy priest of the Lord God, and that I am always "on duty."
2. Set a clear example of abstinence (non-use of alcohol and other drugs).
3. Be able to distinguish personally between right and wrong, between good and evil, between holy and unholy.
4. Teach and equip other persons to have such spiritual perception also.

Unclean Foods and Untouchable Animals

(Leviticus 11:1-47)

I. Concentration: on the forbidden creatures listed in this chapter

1. The Israelites were forbidden to eat certain animals such as the camel, the hare, and the swine, vv. 1-8.
2. The were forbidden to eat certain sea creatures . . . those without fins and scales (like the eel and the octopus), vv. 9-12.
3. They were forbidden to eat certain birds, such as the eagle, the buzzard, the ostrich, the owl, etc., vv. 13-19.
4. However, they were allowed to eat insects, such as locusts, crickets, and grasshoppers, vv. 20-23.
5. They were forbidden from even touching certain other animals, such as those which walk on four paws (lions and tigers), vv. 26-27.
6. They were forbidden from touching creeping things, such as the mole, the mouse, and the lizard, vv. 29-31.
7. They also were forbidden from touching any creature that crawls on its belly, such as snakes, v. 42.

II. Meditation: on why such prohibitions were given to the Israelites

1. Some laws were given to bring identity to the Israelites . . . to make them different from the surrounding heathen nations, who worshipped some of the forbidden creatures listed.
2. Some laws were designed simply to insure the health of the community.
3. Some laws were given as a test of their obedience to God.
4. Some laws were given to emphasize a conscious, continual awareness of God's holy presence in their daily lives, vv. 44-45.

III. Revelation: on the spiritual implications of these regulations

1. God's people are commanded to "Come out from among them and be separate, says the Lord. Do not touch what is unclean, and I will receive you," II Cor. 6:17.
2. All God's laws, precepts, rules, and regulations are given for man's benefit.
3. Every command of God contains an element of testing, to determine man's degree of obedience and the motivation of his heart.
4. All aspects of our daily lives should remind us constantly that we are creatures of God, Who is holy and Who desires for us also to be holy.

IV. Applications: as a Christian, I need to . . .

1. Live a clean, pure, holy life before the Lord, daily asking Him for forgiveness and cleansing, I Jn. 1:9.
2. Know that God is not so concerned with my keeping dietary laws, etc. as He is concerned about the spiritual integrity of my heart, I Sam. 16:7.
3. Understand that in Mark 7:18-19, Jesus declared that all foods are clean.
4. Recognize that the Bible does not support nor mandate vegetarianism; in fact, God commanded Peter to "kill and eat" unclean animals in Acts 10:13. *(See I Tim. 4:1-5.)*

The Ritual After Childbirth

(Leviticus 12:1-8)

I. Concentration: on the regulations specified in this chapter

1. When a woman gave birth to a son, she was ceremonially unclean seven days, just as during her menstrual period, v. 2; 15:19.
2. On the eighth day, the boy child was to be circumcised, v. 3.
3. The mother of a son continued her purification period another 33 days (totaling 40 days) before she was allowed to worship, v. 4.
4. When a woman gave birth to a daughter, she was unclean for two weeks plus 66 days (totaling 80 days) of exile from the place of worship, v. 5.

II. Meditation: on the purification process

1. When the 40 days or 80 days were over, the new mother brought a lamb for a burnt offering and a young bird as a sin offering, v. 6.
2. The priest sacrificed and burned the lamb completely as a sign of the mother's thanksgiving and total dedication to the Lord, vv. 6-7.
3. The priest sacrificed the pigeon or turtledove to cancel guilt and to make atonement (a covering) for sin, bringing restoration after the violation of the holiness code, vv. 6-7.
4. Persons who were too poor to offer a lamb were allowed to offer two birds, rather than a lamb and a bird, v. 8.

III. Revelation: on the spiritual implications seen here

1. Although male and female are equal in the sight of God (Gal. 3:28), there are innate differences in their God-given roles and functions.
2. The ritual uncleanness or impurity connected with the birth process is part of the spiritual curse pronounced on Eve for her sin in the Garden of Eden, Gen. 3:16; I Tim. 2:15.
3. The 40-day testing/purification period was required for both the mother and the child (a total of 80 days), but the rite of circumcision for the male child brought him immediately under the blessing of the Covenant, removing his "uncleanness" and negating the usual required 40-day waiting period before purification.
4. Mary and Joseph followed these regulations with the infant child Jesus, Lk. 2:21-24. *(Apparently the wise men had not yet arrived with their valuable gifts within the 40 days after Jesus' birth (Mt. 2) because His parents offered the "poor" sacrifice of two birds.)*

IV. Applications: as a Christian, I need to . . .

1. Respect equally all persons, male and female, and honor their differing roles and functions within the plan of God.
2. Realize that, like everyone, I was born in sin, and that I need a Savior.
3. Thank the Lord for His atonement, bringing me into the New Covenant relationship with Him.
4. Realize that salvation is available to all persons, and is not linked to the economic status of the individual.

The Law Concerning Leprosy

(Leviticus 13:1-46)

I. Concentration: on the term "leprosy" in the bible

1. This chapter deals with the diagnosis of 21 afflictions of the skin which are referred to in the inclusive term "leprosy."
2. The generic term "leprosy" applied to skin disorders from psoriasis to true leprosy, with symptoms ranging from white patches on the skin to running sores to the loss of fingers and toes.
3. Leprosy rendered its victims ceremonially unclean and unfit to worship God; anyone who came into contact with a leper also was considered to be unclean.
4. Lepers were isolated (quarantined) by the priest to protect the health of the rest of their family and the community, v. 4.

II. Meditation: on the condition of a person with leprosy

1. A leper was considered to be unclean, unholy, untouchable . . . as was the body of a corpse, v. 44.
2. A leper was identified as unclean by his deliberately torn clothes and by his bare head, v. 45.
3. A leper was required to cry out "unclean" whenever anyone approached him, v. 45.
4. A leper was required to dwell alone, outside the camp, v. 46.

III. Revelation: on how Jesus treated lepers

1. Jesus physically touched and healed lepers, Mk. 1:40-42.
2. Jesus commanded his disciples to cleanse lepers, Mt. 10:8.
3. Jesus commended the faith of the one leper who returned to say "thank you" out of the ten lepers He had healed, Mt. 17:11-19.
4. Jesus made a leper the hero of one of His parables, Lk. 16:19-31.

IV. Applications: as a Christian, I need to . . .

1. Recognize that persons without Christ have the spiritual "leprous" disease called sin, which ultimately will bring them death.
2. Reach out in mercy and compassion to touch and minister to "lepers," in spite of their uncleanness, loneliness, and isolation from God.
3. Realize that our Great High Priest can pronounce "lepers" healed from their deadly disease of sin, give them a clean new garment of righteousness, return them to the fellowship of the family of God, and replace their "unclean" testimony with words of praise and glory and witness to Almighty God.
4. Repent daily of my own "leprous" sins, allowing the Lord to use me (a healed leper) to bring others to Him for cleansing also.

Ceremonial Cleansing of Healed Lepers

(Leviticus 14:1-20)

I. Concentration: on the ritual purification of an impure leper

    1. Two birds were presented: one was sacrificed and the other was covered with blood and released, vv. 4-6.

    2. The leper was to wash himself and his clothes, and to shave his hair, beard, and eyebrows, vv. 8-9.

    3. The priest applied the blood of a sacrificial lamb to the leper's ear, thumb, and big toe, vv. 12-14.

    4. The priest then applied holy oil to the leper's ear, thumb, big toe, and head, vv. 15-19.

II. Meditation and Revelation: on the spiritual symbolism observed here

    1. Symbolism of the two birds:

        1) The sacrificed bird showed that the penalty of sin is death, and that without the shedding of blood there is no salvation.

        2) The living bird was dipped in blood and released, showing that when a person is forgiven, his sins are taken away.

    2. Symbolism of the bathing and shaving:

        1) Bathing pictured the act of repentance . . . taking off old, soiled garments and washing spiritually.

        2) Shaving represented public confession and humiliation; it pictured Godly sorrow and the making of a new start.

    3. Symbolism of the blood:

    The applied blood portrayed spiritual cleansing, which affected a man's hearing, his works, and his walk.

    4. Symbolism of the oil:

    The anointing oil represented the Holy Spirit, Who empowers a man's spiritual hearing, deeds, walk, and thoughts.

Note: When Jesus healed the leper in Lk. 5:12-14, He commanded him to show himself to the priest and to make the offering which was commanded by Moses in the law. See also Mt. 8:2-4; Mk. 1:40-44; and Lk. 17:14.

III. Applications: as a Christian, I need to . . .

    1. "See" that all my sins are forgiven and taken away by Christ.

    2. Live in a continual state of repentance and humility before God.

    3. Hear, act, and walk as a person who is "under the blood" of Christ.

    4. Listen, behave, move, and think as a person filled and empowered by the Holy Spirit.

The Law Concerning Bodily Discharges

(Leviticus 15:1-33)

I. Concentration: on the bodily discharges mentioned in this chapter

    1. The matter produced from festering sores, vv. 1-15.

    2. An emission of semen, vv. 16-18.

    3. Blood from the monthly menstrual period, vv. 19-24.

    4. Bleeding beyond the customary period of the menstrual cycle, vv. 25-30.

II. Meditation: on the uncleanness associated with these conditions

    1. Ceremonial impurity could be caused by normal as well as abnormal bodily functions.

    2. Persons who associated with or touched unclean persons (or things touched by unclean persons) became unclean, vv. 5-12, 18-27.

    3. A burnt offering and a sin offering were required to make atonement, to bring cleansing, to restore the impure person to a proper standing within the community, and to allow the individual to worship God, vv. 14-15, 29-30.

    4. These regulations were given as public health measures, but mainly to emphasize God's holiness, vv. 31-33.

III. Revelation: on the spiritual implications of these regulations

    1. Ordinary and commonplace occurrences of life can contaminate the lives of people . . . their minds and souls, as well as their physical bodies.

    2. The uncleanness (and vulgarity) of others can cause God's people to become impure also.

    3. A blood sacrifice by our Great High Priest is necessary for our cleansing.

    4. God is holy, and He requires His people also to be holy . . . to live pure lives, separated from the contamination of the world.

IV. Applications: as a Christian, I need to . . .

    1. Be sensitive to the fact that I am a sinful person, and that I live in the midst of sinful people, Isa. 6:5.

    2. Guard my Christian influence, striving always to be a good example to other persons, I Tim. 4:12-16.

    3. Live in a continual state of humble repentance, confessing my sins and asking Jesus for forgiveness and cleansing, I Jn. 1:9.

    4. Be holy . . . in heart, mind, speech, and action . . . always choosing to walk in His steps as I consider the question, WWJD: "What would Jesus do?" I Pet. 2:21.

The Day of Atonement

(Leviticus 16:1-34)

I. Concentration: on the High Priest's work on the Day of Atonement (Yom Kippur)

1. The High Priest bathed himself in water, symbolizing cleansing, v. 4.
2. He dressed in white linen, symbolizing purity, v. 4.
3. He sacrificed a bull as a sin offering for himself and for his family, vv. 3, 6.
4. He burned incense, forming a cloud in the Holy of Holies, v. 16.
5. He sprinkled blood from the bull on the mercy seat, v. 16.
6. He cast lots over two goats, v. 8.
7. He chose one of the goats as a sin offering; sacrificed it and sprinkled its blood on the mercy seat for the sins of the nation, v. 15.
8. He mixed blood from the bull with blood from the goat; applied the mixed blood to the horns of the altar, v. 18.
9. He took the second goat (the scapegoat); confessed the sins of the nation over its head; ordered it to be led away into the wilderness and released, vv. 21-22.
10. He bathed again and dressed in his usual garments, vv. 23-24.
11. He offered a burnt offering for himself and for the nation, symbolizing total consecration unto the Lord, v. 24.
12. He ordered that the remains of the sacrificed bull and goat be burned outside of the camp, signifying that the work was complete, vv. 27-28.

II. Meditation and Revelation: on the spiritual significance of this solemn ceremony

1. For the ceremony to accomplish its spiritual purpose, the High Priest had to be pure. *Christ, our High Priest was sinless, II Cor. 5:21; Isa. 53:9; Heb. 9:14; I Pet. 1:19.*
2. The blood sprinkled on the mercy seat taught: that the wages of sin is death (Rom. 6:23); that without the shedding of blood there is no remission of sin (Lev. 17:11; Heb. 9:22); and that God's mercy is available to all through the death of His Son (I Pet. 1:2).
3. The scapegoat pictured the nation's sins of the past year being taken away "as far as the east is from the west," Psa. 103:12.
4. Traditionally, at the close of the ceremony of the Day of Atonement, the High Priest extended his arms and proclaimed to the assembled congregation of Israel: "It is finished!" This forecast Christ's cry of triumph from the cross, Jn. 19:30.

III. Applications: as a Christian, I need to . . .

1. Worship the Lord Jesus Christ, the Great High Priest and the Lamb of God, Who takes away the sin of the world, Jn. 1:29.
2. Recognize that the Lord suffered and died for me personally, and come to Him daily in repentance and faith.
3. Thank Him that my sins have been taken away, not for a year, but forever . . . never to be remembered against me anymore, Mic. 7:19.
4. Rest in the assurance of Christ's finished work for me.

"Kosher" or Ritually Correct Meat

(Leviticus 17:1-16)

I. Concentration: on the "kosher" regulations

1. Orthodox Jews may eat only the flesh of certain specified animals (Deut. 14) which have been slaughtered without pain to the beast and with speed and sharp instruments.
2. All traces of blood must be removed by draining, washing, soaking, and salting.
3. Neither milk nor milk products (such as cheese) may be eaten with meats, and meat must not be cooked in milk or butter.
4. Only such "koshering" according to Jewish ritual produces clean and wholesome food.

II. Meditation: on the main principles emphasized in this chapter

1. The gravest sin in Israel was idolatry, v. 7; Ex. 20:3-6; Deut. 6:4.
2. The sacrifices which pagans make to false gods are offerings made to demons, v. 7; Deut. 32:17.
3. Blood represents life; it is life; it sustains life, v. 14.
4. The blood of the Jewish sacrifices was unique; persons who consumed blood were excluded from the Covenant relationship, vv. 10, 14; the blood of hunted or trapped animals was to be covered with dust, v. 13.

III. Revelation: on the spiritual significance of the blood

1. Blood is the life-flow principle of God's creatures; God forbids making this element (blood) into something commonly consumed daily without regard to any spiritual implications . . . such eating/drinking of blood is vulgar and unholy.
2. Blood is connected to life; the shedding of blood is connected to death; here a physical thing (blood) portrays a spiritual reality (life).
3. Christ's shed blood (death) removes man's sin, bringing God and man together in new spiritual life . . . called the atonement.
4. There is a uniqueness to the precious shed blood of Jesus Christ which we should hold sacred, and upon which we need to meditate regularly.

IV. Applications: as a Christian, I need to . . .

1. Obey God's commands so that I may remain under the covenant of His promises and continue to receive His spiritual blessings.
2. Realize that the wages of my sin is death, but that the gift of God is eternal life through the atoning blood of Christ.
3. Thank God that "the blood of Jesus . . . cleanses us from all sin." I Jn. 1:7.
4. Keep the atonement central in my daily devotions and meditations.

Laws of Sexual Morality

(Leviticus 18:1-30)

I. Concentration: on the prohibitions in this chapter

1. Sexual intercourse with blood relations, step-relations, and in-laws was forbidden, as was adultery . . . sexual intercourse with another person's spouse, vv. 6-20. (*"To uncover his nakedness" means to have sexual intercourse.*)
2. Human child sacrifice ("pass through the fire to Molech") was forbidden, v. 21; 20:3-5; II Kgs. 23:10; Jer. 32:35. (*Compare with II Kgs. 17:31; 21:6; Jer. 7:31; 19:5; II Chron. 28:3; Psa. 106:38; Ezek. 16:21;23:37.*)
3. Homosexuality was forbidden as "abomination," v. 22; 20:13; Rom. 1:27.
4. Bestiality (sexual relations with animals) was forbidden as "perversion," v. 23; 20:15-16; Ex. 22:19; Deut. 27:21.

II. Meditation: on the reasons for these prohibitions

1. The "Exodus" involved not only bringing the Jews out of Egypt, but also bringing Egypt (Egyptian pagan practices) out of the Jews v. 3.
2. These evil practices also were practiced in the pagan religions of the Canaanites in the Promised Land, vv. 3, 24-28.
3. These prohibitions were given to magnify the sanctity of the Israelite's family relationships within the plan of God.
4. God's chosen people were to be pure and holy, as God Himself is holy.

III. Revelation: on the spiritual implications of these laws

1. People whom God has chosen and delivered are responsible to obey Him.
2. Sin defiles an individual and a nation, removing them from the Covenant blessings of God, vv. 29-30; Prov. 14:34.
3. The home and family is the basic, God-ordained foundation of society, and God's people are to live sexually pure lives of faithfulness to their marriage vows.
4. God-like, holy living reveals something of the character of the Lord Whom we worship to the unbelievers and pagans who observe our conduct.

IV. Applications: as a Christian, I need to . . .

1. Serve the Lord faithfully and in obedience to His commands.
2. Daily repent and confess my sins to receive forgiveness and cleansing, and to remain under the canopy of His spiritual blessings.
3. Live a pure, holy, faithful, Christ-like life.
4. Let my daily walk before God be a living testimony which backs-up my verbal witness to those who need a Savior.

Applying the Ten Commandments

(Leviticus 19:1-37)

I. Concentration: on the references here to the Ten Commandments (Ex. 20)

    1. Worship no other Gods before the Lord - v. 2.
    2. Make no idols nor engage in false worship - vv. 4-8.
    3. Reverence God's holy name - v. 12.
    4. Observe the Sabbath Day - vv. 3, 30.
    5. Honor your parents - vv. 3, 32 (elderly).
    6. Do not murder - vv. 17-18.
    7. Do not commit adultery - vv. 20-22, 29.
    8. Do not steal - vv. 11-12, 35-36.
    9. Do not lie - vv. 11, 16.
    10. Do not covet - v. 20.

II. Meditation: on other major emphases in this chapter

    1. Worship the Lord your God: "I am the Lord" is stated fifteen times in this chapter (vv. 2, 3, 4, 10, 12, 14, 16, 18, 25, 28. 30, 32, 34, 36, 37).
    2. "You shall love your neighbor as yourself," v. 18 . . .
        1) The Israelites were to leave part of their crops in the fields to feed the poor, vv. 9-10.
        2) The Israelites were to care for the deaf and the blind, and to deal justly with all persons, great or small, vv. 14-15.
        3) Jesus taught this principle of loving others as you love yourself in Matt. 7:12, Matt. 22:37-40, and Lk. 10:29-37.
        4) Paul also cites Leviticus 19:18 in Rom. 13:8-10 and Gal. 5:14.
    3. Do not involve yourself in pagan practices:
        1) Regulations concerning fruit trees (vv. 23-25) were given as a precaution against certain heathen worship rites.
        2) The prohibition against eating blood was repeated, v. 26.
        3) Occult practices were forbidden: divination, soothsaying, mediums, and familiar spirits, vv. 26, 31.
        4) Certain haircuts and beards associated with pagan customs, as well as body mutilations and tattoos, were forbidden, vv. 27-28.
    4. Be holy and separate! The prohibitions against mixing different species of animals, seeds, and cloth garments were constant reminders to the Israelites that they were set apart and different from the other nations of the world because they were God's chosen people.

III. Revelation and Applications: as a Christian, I need to . . .

    1. Recognize that the Creator of the universe is the deliverer of my soul, and worship Him in spirit and in truth.
    2. In the light of God's love for me, love Him and love others, I Jn. 4:19.
    3. Avoid even the appearance of evil, I Thes. 5:22.
    4. Live a life of purity before God, receiving His continual cleansing for my sins, I Cor. 6:16-18; I Jn. 1:9.

Observations on the Death Penalty

(Leviticus 20:1-27)

I. Concentration: on the divine authority behind the death penalty laws

1. The laws and the penalties for breaking the laws originate with the Lord God Almighty, the Creator of the universe, v. 1.
2. God, Who is the source of all life, also has the power and authority to end life whenever His creatures violate His strict standards of holiness, vv. 7-8, 24, 26.
3. Since God is holy and everything that He does is holy, then the death penalty He commands is a holy act done for a holy purpose.
4. The death penalty was a drastic, but necessary, practice to preserve the separation of God's chosen people from the pagan practices of the heathen people inhabiting the land of Canaan.

II. Meditation: on the spiritual crimes calling for the death penalty

1. Persons who sacrificed children and other human beings were to be executed, vv. 2-4.
2. Persons who engaged in occult, idolatrous, demonic practices were to be executed, vv. 6, 27.
3. Persons who cursed their parents were to be executed, v. 9.
4. Persons who committed certain sexual sins (adultery, incest, homosexuality, and bestiality) were to be executed, vv. 10-21.

III. Revelation: on reasons that God classifies these as capital offenses

1. Human sacrifice is both murder and idolatry, violating Commandments I, II, and VI, Ex. 20:2-8, 17-18.
2. Occult practices not only are idolatry, they are acts of worship of the devil, God's archenemy, Satan, Lev. 17:7; Deut. 32:17.
3. The proper family relationship (including respect for parents) is absolutely necessary because the home is the major, fundamental building block of society; if the homes fail, the nation collapses, Ex. 20:12.
4. Sexual sins violate not only Commandment VII, but they also break down God's original order establishing the family to populate the earth, Gen. 1:28.

IV. Applications: as a Christian, I need to . . .

1. Be holy . . . for the Lord my God is holy, and He commands me to be like Him, v. 7.
2. Recognize that I am a sinner, a violator of God's laws; allow the Lord to "sanctify" me . . . to cleanse and set me apart for His service, for He is "Jehovah-M'Kaddesh" - "The God Who Sanctifies," v. 8; Ex. 31:13.
3. Thank the Lord for my inheritance . . . a spiritual land flowing with milk and honey, v. 24.
4. Rest in the blessed assurance that the Lord is my God, and that He claims me as His own, v. 26.

Regulations for the Conduct of Priests

(Leviticus 21:1-24)

I. Concentration: on the specific rules found in this chapter

1. The ordinary priests were not allowed to defile themselves by contact with the dead, except if the deceased person was a near relative, vv. 1-4.
2. The priests were forbidden from shaving their heads, shaping their beards, or cutting (mutilating) their flesh, v. 5.
3. The priests were not to profane (by word or deed) the name of the Lord God, v. 6.
4. The priests were allowed to marry only virgins, vv. 7, 13-15.
5. The daughters of priests were to remain sexually pure until marriage, under penalty of death, v. 9.
6. The high priest was not to go near (mourn) any dead person, not even his closest relatives, vv. 10-12.
7. No man with any physical defect was allowed to serve as a priest, although those with defects were allowed to partake of the sacrifices, vv. 17-24.

II. Meditation: on the implications of these regulations

1. Since contact with the dead made a person unclean (ceremonially unfit to worship God), the priests (especially the high priest) were to keep themselves holy before the Lord, and thus always qualified to offer sacrifices for the people. (*As ministers of spiritual life, they were to avoid contact with death: see #'s 1 and 6 above.*)
2. Certain pagan customs were prohibited so that the priests could remain holy and separated from the heathen people around them. (*See #'s 2 and 3 above.*)
3. Since the priesthood was hereditary, the genealogical line was to be kept pure . . . including the wives and daughters of the priests. (*See #'s 4 and 5 above.*)
4. Just as the sacrificial offerings were to be without spot and blemish, so also those priests offering the sacrifices were to be without physical defect, vv. 6, 8. (*See #7 above.*)

III. Revelation and Application: on these spiritual truths

1. Christ, our great High Priest, conquered death forever, I Cor. 15:55-57; Heb. 7:25; therefore, I also need to walk in new life, Rom. 6:4.
2. Christ's life was without sin, II Cor. 5:21; therefore, I too need to walk in purity . . . receiving continual cleansing through His blood, I Jn. 1:7.
3. Christ's genealogical line was made up of sinful men and women, showing that God came to earth as a human being to identify with mankind, Mt. 1:1-17; so as David, I also was born in sin (Psa. 51:5), but Christ has made me a child of God, Jn. 1:12.
4. Christ was the perfect sacrifice, I Pet. 1:19; therefore, I am to present myself as a living sacrifice . . . "holy, acceptable to God," Rom. 12:1.

Acceptable and Unacceptable Offerings

(Leviticus 22:1-33)

I. Concentration: on the basic principles of making acceptable offerings

1. The priests themselves had to be clean and holy, ceremonially pure and properly consecrated for service, v. 2.
2. The priests had to receive and offer the sacrifices in strict obedience to God's revealed will and plan, v. 9.
3. The sacrificial offerings had to be presented by the people of their own free will, without coercion, vv. 18-19, 21, 29.
4. The animals presented to be sacrificed had to be without any blemish or defect . . . "perfect," vv. 19-24.

II. Meditation: on the reasoning behind these principles

1. True worship of the holy God requires that the priest ministering the worship must himself be holy. *The minister must be right!*
2. True worship requires that the ceremony be done exactly as commanded by the holy God being served. *The method must be right!*
3. True worship must be done voluntarily from the heart, not through force or fear of reprisal. *The motive must be right!*
4. True worship requires that the offering being given as a sacrifice must be "perfect" . . . God deserves and demands that man brings the very best possible. *The meaning must be right!*

III. Revelation on the Messianic implications seen here

1. Jesus Christ, our great High Priest after the order of Melchizedek, is far superior to the priesthood of Aaron and his sons, Heb. 7:20-8:2.
2. The Lord Jesus offered an eternal sacrifice according to the will of God the Father, Heb. 9:24-28; 10:5-7.
3. God the Father is "seeking" persons to worship Him in spirit and truth, Jn. 4:23-24; however, He gives mankind free-will, and the choice to worship, or not, is up to the individual, Jn. 3:16-18; Rev. 22:17.
4. Christ Jesus was the perfect sacrificial Lamb of God, dying to take away the sins of the world, Jn. 1:29; I Pet. 1:19; Heb. 10:8-10.

IV. Applications: as a Christian, I need to . . .

1. Praise the Lord Jesus Christ, the Son of God, my great High Priest, Who "always lives to make intercession" for me, Heb. 7:25.
2. Come daily to Him in repentance, confession, and faith to receive His forgiveness and cleansing, I Jn. 1:7, 9.
3. Worship Him in spirit and in truth, freely and from my heart!
4. Follow in His steps (I Pet. 2:21), offering my body as a living sacrifice, Rom. 12:1-2.

Why Christians Worship on Sunday

(Leviticus 23:1-44)

I. Concentration and Meditation: on the Feasts of the Lord (vv. 1-2)

1. Sabbath, v. 3 - Commandment IV; the one day out of each week set aside for worship, Scripture study, reflection and meditation, family fellowship, doing of good deeds, rest and refreshing, and, of course, cessation of work . . . memorializing both the Creation and the Exodus, Ex. 20:8-11; Deut. 5:12-15.
2. Passover, v. 5 - 1st month, 14th day (March or April); to commemorate deliverance from the death angel in Egypt.
3. Unleavened Bread, v. 6 - 1st month, 15th to 21st days (March or April); to commemorate the Exodus events.
4. First Fruits, v. 10 - on the Sunday occurring during the Feast of Unleavened Bread (March or April); to celebrate the beginning of the spring barley harvest.
5. Pentecost (Feast of Weeks), v. 16 - on the Sunday seven weeks (50 days) after First Fruits (May or June); harvest festival.
6. Trumpets, v. 24 - 7th month, 1st day (September or October) New Year's celebration called "Rosh Hashanah."
7. Day of Atonement, v. 27 - 7th month, 10th day (September or October); day of fasting and national mourning for sins, called "Yom Kippur."
8. Tabernacles ("Booths"), v. 34 - 7th month, 15 to 22nd days (September or October); to commemorate the 40 years of wilderness wandering.
9. Dedication, Jn. 10:22 - 9th month, 25th day (December); Feast of Lights called "Hanukkah" to celebrate Jewish Independence during the Maccabean period between the Old and New Testaments.
10. Purim ("Lots"), Esther 9:17-26 - 12th month, 14th and 15th days (March) celebrating deliverance during the time of Persian rule.

Note: Jewish males were required to attend the Feasts of Unleavened Bread, Weeks, and Tabernacles each year, according to Deut. 16:16.

II. Revelation and Applications: for Christians living under the New Covenant

1. Christians observe Sunday as their day of worship and rest in fulfillment of the Jewish First Fruits festival, which always was celebrated on the day following the Sabbath. Christ's resurrection on Easter Sunday was the "firstfruits" of those who have died, according to I Cor. 15:20.
2. Christians observe Sunday also in fulfillment of Pentecost, the other Jewish festival which was celebrated on the day after the Sabbath. The Holy Spirit empowered the church on Pentecost Sunday, Acts 2.
3. The disciples customarily met on Sunday, according to Acts 20:7.
4. Believers worshipped and gave their offerings on Sunday, according to I Cor. 16:2.

Note: Following Passover, Easter falls on the 1st Sunday after the first full moon on or after March 21 . . . always between March 22 and April 25.

"The Mind of the Lord"

(Leviticus 24:1-23)

I. Concentration: on the tabernacle lamps and the loaves of bread

1. Specific responsibility was assigned to Aaron and his sons to make sure that the lamp in the tabernacle always was filled with olive oil so that the light shone continually, vv. 1-4.
2. The ignited oil of the Holy Spirit produces a glowing radiance in us (God's lampstands) to help light up the darkness . . . but the oil needs to be continuously replenished: "Be continually being filled with the Spirit," Eph. 5:18.
3. Aaron and his sons also were responsible each week for baking the twelve loaves of bread displayed in the tabernacle, which they were allowed to consume as food in the holy place, vv. 5-9.
4. Jesus is the "Word" which nourishes us spiritually if we partake of it regularly and in a holy place . . . a spot dedicated to the worship of God and to the meditation on His Word while listening for His will to be revealed, Jn. 1:1; 6:35; Matt. 4:4; Psa. 119:11; 19:14.

II. Meditation: on "the mind of the Lord" shown to Moses (v. 12)

1. Verses 10-23 must be understood in the context of God's holy enlightenment and miraculous provision for His people, as seen in verses 1-9 (lamp and bread).
2. During a fight, a certain man blasphemed the name of the Lord (spoke irreverently; took God's name in vain, cursed and swore) vv. 10-11.
3. The penalty for breaking Commandment III (Ex. 20:7) had not been specified, so the man was held under guard until "the mind of the Lord" was shown to the Israelites through Moses, v. 12.
4. The last verses of this chapter are God's words which equate the sin of blasphemy (verbal violence against God) with murder (physical violence against man); both called for the death penalty.

Yet God also here sets strict bounds for penalties for other crimes so that the punishment would fit (but not exceed) the seriousness of the offense, ("an eye for an eye"). This limited punishment principle applied to property damage and personal injury, and it was to be administered justly to both the Israelites and to the foreigners living among them.

III. Revelation and Applications: as a Christian, I need to . . .

1. Depend upon the Holy Spirit to give enlightenment to my spirit; receive the "Bread of Life" for nourishment for my soul.
2. In times of confusion or uncertainty, wait for the Lord to reveal His will on how and when to proceed.
3. Realize that spiritual sins of attitude and speech are just as serious in God's sight as are physical sins, such as murder, Matt. 5:21-30.
4. Advocate justice based upon the principles taught in the Scriptures.

The Year of Jubilee

(Leviticus 25:1-55)

I. Concentration: on the year of liberty (v. 10)

1. The Year of Jubilee was the 50th year, after seven cycles of seven years; it was signaled by a ram's horn blown on the Day of Atonement, v. 9.
2. It was to be a time of rest for the soil as well as for the people, v. 11.
3. During Jubilee, all land was to revert to the original owner, vv. 10-34.
4. During Jubilee, every Israelite who had sold himself into slavery because of poverty was to be freed along with his family, vv. 39-46.

II. Meditation: on these God-given blessings of freedom

1. These blessings of freedom are spiritually connected to the forgiveness of sins accomplished by the sacrifices on the Day of Atonement.
2. The year of rest for the land not only was the method of soil conservation, it also taught the Israelites to live that year in faith that God would satisfy their needs.
3. God intended for the original distribution of the Promised Land to the Twelve Tribes to remain intact; their family inheritance was to be a permanent gift of God.
4. Permanent slavery (indentured servanthood or "share-cropping") was made impossible by this law of Jubilee.

III. Revelation: on the spiritual implications of these blessings

1. Man's sins always bring bondage, but God's forgiveness brings freedom.
2. God provides for the needs of all His creatures . . . the partial gleaning provisions (vv. 18-22; Ex. 23:11) were given to feed the poor and the beasts of the field.
3. The land ownership regulations discouraged excessive, permanent accumulations of real estate, and they eliminated pauperism. *Land was never actually sold; it was leased for a maximum of 49 years.*
4. Family and tribal identity was preserved because individuals in every generation were given the opportunity to make a fresh start.

IV. Applications: as a Christian, I need to . . .

1. Rejoice and celebrate every day of every year because Jesus came to proclaim perpetual Jubilee (the eternal "year" of God's favor), Isa. 61:2; Lk. 4:19.
2. Be generous and charitable in my giving to help the poor and needy around me, expressing my faith in God's faithful provision for me by sharing rather than hoarding His blessings.
3. Recognize that ownership of private property does not violate God's laws and purpose; realize, however, that material possessions must not be acquired by oppression or deceit, and that material possessions are far inferior to spiritual blessings.
4. Receive God's promised provision for a chance to make a new beginning daily through His grace, mercy, and forgiveness.

Divine Rewards and Punishments

(Leviticus 26:1-46)

I. Concentration: on the main themes in this chapter

1. Obedience to God brings divine blessings, vv. 1-13.
2. Disobedience to God brings divine punishment, vv. 14-26.
3. Continued and repeated disobedience brings increasing destruction, and ultimately national captivity and exile, vv. 27-39.
4. Humble confession and repentance brings divine forgiveness and restoration, vv. 40-46.

II. Meditation: on the promised blessings for obedience

1. Prosperity: abundance and fruitfulness, vv. 3-5, 10.
2. Victory and peace, vv. 6-8.
3. Family growth (children) and happiness, v. 9.
4. Spiritual communion and fellowship with God, vv. 11-13.

III. Revelation: on God's dealings with disobedience and rebellion

1. God uses terror, disease, sorrow, and enemy attacks to discipline His people in an effort to bring them back to Him, vv. 14-17.
2. Continued disobedience brings "seven times more" punishment: humiliation, drought, famine, and fatigue, vv. 18-20.
3. More disobedience and sin brings "seven times more" retribution: plagues and wild beasts to destroy children and livestock, and to disrupt travel and commerce, vv. 21-22.
4. If these punishments fail to bring reformation, God will increase the pressure "yet seven times" . . . with warfare casualties, siege, pestilence, and starvation, vv. 23-26.
5. Finally, God will chastise disobedience another "seven times" bringing cannibalism, total destruction of their cities, desecration of their holy places of worship, and complete and utter desolation of the Promised Land, vv. 27-35.
6. When this tragic captivity and exile occurs, the few remaining refugees will barely exist in poverty and perpetual fear, vv. 36-39.

IV. Applications: as a Christian, I need to . . .

1. Obey the commands of the Lord; whenever I sin against Him, come immediately in humble confession and repentance to ask for forgiveness and restoration.
2. Recognize that God is merciful and long-suffering, repeatedly giving me opportunities to respond positively to His discipline.
3. Realize that God's holiness and righteousness demand that justice be served: "The wages of sin is death," Rom. 6:23.
4. Thank the Lord for His New Covenant of grace: "The gift of God is eternal life in Christ Jesus our Lord," Rom. 6:23.

Consecrated, Redeemed, Devoted

(Leviticus 27:1-34)

I. Concentration: on the technical terms used in this chapter

1. "Consecrate" (v. 2) - voluntary dedication of a person or a thing for the service of the Lord.
2. "Vow" (v. 2) - act of swearing or promising a "consecrated" person or thing to God.
3. "Redeem" (v. 13) - to purchase or buy back; in this context, it refers to paying a specified amount of money in place of actually giving the person or thing to God as originally consecrated by a vow.
4. "Devoted" (v. 28) - an offering (man, animal, field, etc.) which was given exclusively and irrevocably to the Lord; it was "most holy" and could not be "redeemed."

II. Meditation: on the "redemption" values (in silver shekels)

1. Persons, vv. 1-8 . . .

Ages:			
1 month to 5 years:	male - 5 shekels;	female - 3 shekels	
5 years to 20 years:	male - 20 shekels;	female - 10 shekels	
20 years to 60 years:	male - 50 shekels;	female - 30 shekels	
60 years and above:	male - 15 shekels;	female - 10 shekels	

2. Animals, vv. 9-13 - appraised value plus one-fifth (20%).
3. Houses, vv. 14-15 - appraised value plus one-fifth (20%).
4. Fields, vv. 16-25 - appraised value plus one-fifth (20%); determined by the amount of barley seed needed to sow it, multiplied by the number of years until the Year of Jubilee.

III. Revelation: on the persons or things covered by exceptional regulations

1. The firstborn of the animals were "devoted" to the Lord as a sign of His deliverance from the death angel on the night of the Passover in Egypt, vv. 26-27; Ex. 13:2, 12.
2. Voluntary "devoted" offerings could not be redeemed.
3. Persons sentenced to be executed could not be redeemed, v. 29.
4. Tithes of seed, fruit, and animals could be paid in money by adding one-fifth (20%) to the value.

IV. Applications: as a Christian, I need to . . .

1. Be careful not to make any zealous, rash vows; keep all pledges and promises made unto the Lord.
2. Do not misuse the Lord's pledging regulations as a means to cheat (or fail to support) family members or to avoid fulfilling other honorable debts and obligations, Mk. 7:9-13.
3. Recognize that true justice in the eyes of God does not allow wealthy persons to "buy" (or redeem) their way out of a death penalty conviction and sentence.
4. Honor the Lord by giving Him the tithe, because everything I have comes from Him, even my ability to work and earn money, Deut. 8:18.

Course #3

The First Census of Israel

(Numbers 1:1-54)

I. Concentration: on the time frame of these events

1. The Israelites arrived at Mount Sinai exactly three months after they left Egypt, Ex. 19:1.
2. The tabernacle was completed nine months later, in the first month of the second year, Ex. 40:17.
3. The Book of Numbers begins a month later, 1:1.
4. Nineteen days later, after completing the census, Israel left Sinai en route to the Promised Land, Num. 10:11.

II. Meditation: on the results of the census

Tribe	Leader	Number of men age 20 and above
1. Reuben	Elizur	46,500
2. Simeon	Shelumiel	59,300
3. Judah	Nahshon	74,600
4. Issachar	Nethanel	54,400
5. Zebulun	Eliab	57,440
6. Ephraim	Elishama	40,500
7. Manasseh	Gamaliel	32,200
8. Benjamin	Abidan	35,400
9. Dan	Ahiezer	62,700
10. Asher	Pagiel	41,500
11. Gad	Eliasaph	45,650
12. Naphtali	Ahira	53,400
Total		603,550

III. Revelation and Applications:

1. **The Lord is a God of order.** *He has a plan and purpose to accomplish through His people who must be organized for battle, v. 45.*
2. **The Lord chooses leaders.** *God selected twelve tribal chiefs from among the more than 600,000 men.*
3. **The Lord magnified the importance of every individual within the community.** *Each person "counts" in the eyes of God.*
4. **The Lord issues a special calling to those whom He chooses to serve Him in full-time ministry.** *The priestly tribe of Levi was not included in this military census; the principle (which applies even today in the United States) is that persons who are dedicated to the holy service of God are exempt from service in the army, vv. 47-54.*

The Israelite Camp and Battle Formation

(Numbers 2:1-34)

I. Concentration: on the nation's use of identification banners

    1. "Standard," 1:52; 2:2; 10:14, 18 - a military flag identifying each tribe's cohort of troops armed for battle.

    2. "Emblem," 2:2 - a non-military sign identifying a tribe, clan, or family.

    3. Isa. 59:19 - "When the enemy comes in, like a flood the Spirit of the Lord will lift up a <u>standard</u> against him."

    4. Ex. 17:15 - "Moses built an altar and called its name "Jehovah-Nissi . . . The Lord is my <u>banner</u> (of victory)."

II. Meditation: on the places assigned to the tribes within the encampment

    1. The tabernacle and the Levites camped in the center of all the tribes, v. 17.

    2. Judah, Issachar, and Zebulun camped on the east, vv. 3-9.

    3. Reuben, Simeon, and Gad camped on the south, vv. 10-16.

    4. Ephraim, Manasseh, and Benjamin camped on the west, vv. 18-24.

    5. Dan, Asher, and Naphtali camped on the north, vv. 25-31.

III. Revelation: on the tribal order when marching into battle

    1. The eastern group (186,400 men) led the army of Israel. *Judah, the largest and the kingly tribe, led the troops, accompanied by two other sons of Judah by his first wife, Leah: Isaachar and Zebulun.*

    2. The southern group (151,450 men) marched second. *Reuben, Jacob's oldest son, led this group, accompanied by the second son, Simeon, both children of Leah; the third tribe of this group (Gad) was a descendant of Leah's maid, Zilpah.*

    3. Next marched the tribe of Levi with the tabernacle. *Levi was Jacob's third son, also a child of his wife, Leah.*

    4. The western group (108,100 men) followed the Levites and the tabernacle. *This group, Ephraim (the leader) and Manasseh (Joseph's sons) and Benjamin, all were descendants of Jacob's favorite wife, Rachel.*

    5. The northern group (157,600 men) made up the rear ranks of the army. *This group all were descendants of maids of Jacob's wives: Dan (the leader) and Naphtali from Bilhah, and Asher from Zilpah.*

IV. Applications: as a Christian, I need to . . .

    1. Identify myself clearly with the people of God, marching beneath the banner of the cross.

    2. Put the abiding presence of the living God at the very center of my life.

    3. Realize that God has planned a specific place for me to dwell and to do battle against His enemies.

    4. Submit to God's authority, and faithfully and obediently take the place which He has assigned to me. *Note: God's place of highest authority (Judah, the kingly tribe) also was the place of the most responsibility and danger . . . at the head of the army in the forefront of the battle. This arrangement reveals a divine spiritual principle.*

The Census of the Tribe of Levi

(Numbers 3:1-51)

I. Concentration: on the main divisions of this chapter

    1. "Records" (v. 1) is a technical term for genealogy; Aaron's four sons are listed here: Nadab and Abihu (who died for their sins, Lev. 10:1-2)) and Eleazar and Ithamar, vv. 1-4.

    2. God ordained that the tribe of Levi was to serve in the tabernacle and certain of them were ordained to be His priests . . . they all were consecrated unto the Lord, vv. 5-13.

    3. The three clans of Levi are listed, and each clan is given specific duties for ministering in the tabernacle, vv. 14-39.

    4. The tribe of the Levites was dedicated to the Lord in place of the firstborn males of all the Israelite families, vv. 40-51. *Since there were only 22,000 male Levites compared to 22,273 firstborns in the other tribes of Israel, 5 silver shekels each was paid to "redeem" the extra 273 persons . . . a total of 1,365 shekels.*

II. Meditation: on the census of the Levites

    1. Gershon (7,500 males) under their leader Elisaph camped west of the tabernacle; they were in charge of the external coverings of the tent.

    2. Kohath (8,300 males) under their leader Elizaphan camped south of the tabernacle; they were in charge of the Ark and other holy furnishings.

    3. Merari (6,200 males) under their leader Zuriel camped north of the tabernacle; they were in charge of the structural pieces of the tent.

    4. Moses and Aaron and their sons (of the Kohath clan) camped east of the tabernacle; they were the priests in charge of offering the sacrifices.

III. Revelation: on the "redemption" of the firstborn

    1. The firstborn in Jewish culture were seen as God's special property.

    2. Because the firstborn belonged to the Lord, they were to be "sacrificed" (offered) to Him as a sign of their father's dependence and thanksgiving. *The sacrifice of firstborn animals pictured this same spiritual truth.*

    3. Human sacrifice, of course, was forbidden to the Israelites, but symbolically, the entire Levite tribe was consecrated (totally dedicated; sacrificed) unto the Lord as a substitute for the nation's 22,273 firstborn sons.

    4. The 5-shekel "ransom fee" was to pay for the 273 extra firstborn Israelites. *This money was used to finance the tabernacle service.*

IV. Applications: as a Christian, I need to . . .

    1. Recognize that I belong exclusively to the Lord God.

    2. Find my specific assigned place of service and ministry for God.

    3. Thank the Lord Jesus Christ that He took my place as a substitute holy sacrifice for my sins; He "ransomed" me!

    4. Present my body as a living sacrifice unto God, Rom. 12:1-2.

Job Descriptions for the Levites

(Numbers 4:1-49)

I. Concentration: on the major sections of this chapter

1. God specified the duties of the Levitical clan of Kohath, vv. 1-20.
2. God specified the duties of the Levitical clan of Gershon, vv. 21-28.
3. God specified the duties of the Levitical clan of Merari, vv. 29-33.
4. A census was taken to determine the number of Levites eligible for service in the tabernacle, between the ages of 30 and 50, vv. 34-49.

II. Meditation: on the job descriptions of the Levitical clans

1. Kohath: charged with transporting the most holy things of the tabernacle. *All the items were to be covered and either have poles inserted into rings or placed on a carrying beam by Aaron and his sons, so that the Kohathites had no need to touch the holy things. Eleazar, Aaron's older surviving son was given the responsibility for the holy oil, v. 17.*
2. Gershon: responsible for the external coverings of the tabernacle, under the supervision of Ithamar, the second surviving son of Aaron, v. 28.
3. Merari: duties related to the structural pieces of the tabernacle and the surrounding court, under supervision of Ithamar, v. 33.
4. Census of the male Levites, ages 30 to 50 years: Kohath - 2,750; Gershon - 2,630; Merari - 3,200; Total - 8,580.

III. Revelation: on the spiritual implications of these instructions

1. God has a specific task for each and every one of His servants.
2. The assigned responsibilities are inter-dependent . . . all assignments are vitally necessary to get the job done.
3. God assigns lines of responsibility and authority; He chooses certain persons to oversee the work of His other servants.
4. Persons given responsibility for the holy things of the Lord must have a certain degree of maturity: Levitical ministers had to be at least 30 years of age. *Even Jesus Christ did not begin His ministry until He reached the age of 30, Lk. 3:23.*

IV. Applications: as a Christian, I need to . . .

1. Realize that there is no place in the Christian kingdom for spectators; each individual has a personal responsibility to serve God.
2. Recognize the importance of the "unsung" laborers; without them, the more prominent servants of the Lord would not be able to perform their duties and fulfill their responsibilities.
3. Respect spiritual authority in the church, and be a submissive Christian.
4. Continually grow toward maturity in Christ, Eph. 4:13, 15; II Pet. 3:18.

Jealous Husbands and Unfaithful Wives

(Numbers 5:11-31)

I. Concentration: on the ritual described in this chapter

1. A husband who suspected his wife of adultery could accuse her to the priest, bringing along a grain offering.
2. The priest would uncover the wife's head, put her under oath, and make her swear to her faithfulness to her husband.
3. The wife agreed to the curse pronounced by the priest if she were lying ("Amen," she vowed); then she drank holy water containing dust from the floor of the tabernacle.
4. During the ceremony, the wife held the sacrificial grain offering in her hands; the priest then took it from her and offered it on the altar, thus involving the Lord God in the trial by ordeal.

II. Meditation: on the results of this trial by ordeal

1. If the woman was guilty, she had sworn a false oath before the Lord.
2. In that case, she was punished directly by the Lord: the curse came upon her . . . violent illness, swelling of her body, and barrenness.
3. If the woman was innocent, she had sworn the truth before the Lord.
4. In that case, she was declared free of suspicion (silencing forever her husband's groundless accusations); the blessings of the Lord came upon her, allowing her to bear children.

III. Revelation: questions of doubt and affirmations of faith

1. Was this trial by ordeal unfair to women? *No, because of the loving and just character of the Lord, Who is involved in the process.*
2. Does God know a person's heart, and does He reveal it to others? *Yes, God is omniscient, and He does reveal His secrets to men, Dan. 2:47.*
3. Did this ancient trial by ordeal really work? *Yes, because God is omnipotent, and He used His miraculous power to bring the wife either a blessing of health or a cursing of illness.*
4. Are these verses in Numbers 5 really God's word or are they merely priestly "mumbo-jumbo?" *Numbers, chapter 5, along with all other chapters and verses in the Bible, is part of God's holy, inspired, and infallible Scripture.*

IV. Applications: as a Christian, I need to . . .

1. Worship the Lord, Who is holy, righteous, just, and merciful.
2. Be open to God's revelation of truth to my heart.
3. Accept as fact that God is a worker of miracles . . . in the Old Testament, in the New Testament, and in this present day.
4. Accept, believe, study, and practice the teachings of the Bible . . . which is the true and accurate Word of God.

The Law of the Nazirite Vow

(Numbers 6:1-21)

I. Concentration: on the Nazirite vow

1. "Nazirite" means "to separate" . . . both men and women could be separated for service unto the Lord for a specific time, or for an entire lifetime, vv. 1-2.
2. The first aspect of the Nazirite vow was abstinence from the fruit of the vine, vv. 3-4. *(Priests, also, were to be abstainers from alcoholic beverages, Lev. 10:9-11; Ezek. 44:21, 23.)*
3. The Nazirite vow also involved abstinence from cutting one's hair, v. 5.
4. The third requirement of the Nazirite vow was abstinence from defilement by contact with a dead body, vv. 6-12.

II. Meditation: on Biblical examples of Nazirites

1. Samson, Judg. 13-16.
2. John the Baptist, Lk. 1:13-17; Mk. 1:6.
3. The Apostle Paul, Acts 18:18.
4. Four men in Jerusalem, Acts 21:23-26.

III. Revelation: on renewal after a Nazirite became unclean

1. He had to shave his head, v. 9.
2. He had to present sacrifices to God . . . sin, burnt, and guilt (or peace) offerings; grain and drink offerings were part of the peace offering ceremony, vv. 10-17.
3. He had to take the hair from his shaved head and put it in the fire on the altar as a sign of his rededication, v. 18.
4. He had to start again counting his dedicated days as a Nazirite . . . making a new beginning, a fresh start, v. 12.

IV. Applications: as a Christian, I need to . . .

1. Live a life of separation before the Lord: abstaining from alcoholic beverages, from vanity and pride related to personal appearance, and from spiritual contamination by association with unclean, decaying, death-dealing things of human existence.
2. Repent whenever I break my vow of consecration unto the Lord . . . repent with humility as inwardly genuine and as outwardly evident as would be shaving my head and going out into public.
3. Receive forgiveness, cleansing, and restoration through the blood sacrifice of the Lord Jesus Christ.
4. Rededicate myself unto God and begin again . . . thanking the Lord that He gives us "second chances."

Offerings of the Tribal Leaders

(Numbers 7:1-89)

I. Concentration: on the offerings made by the tribal leaders

    1. The offerings for the work of the tabernacle (vv. 2-9):
        1) All were given at the same time, on one day.
        2) Six covered carts, one from every two leaders.
        3) Twelve oxen, one from each leader.
        4) Two carts and four oxen were given to the Gershon clan to transport the hangings of the tabernacle and court; four carts and eight oxen were given to the Merari clan for transporting the boards and frames of the tabernacle and court.

Note: the Kohath clan received no carts and oxen because they carried the most holy furnishings on their shoulders by means of poles.

    2. The offerings for the altar (vv. 10-88):
        1) Given one tribe at a time during a 12-day ceremony.
        2) The tribal leaders and their order of appearance matched the military listing in Numbers, chapter 2.
        3) Each leader gave an identical offering: a silver platter and a silver bowl full of a flour-oil grain offering, a gold pan full of incense, and 21 animals for the burnt, sin, and peace offering sacrifices.
        4) These offerings were to be used in the daily ceremonies of the Hebrew sacrificial system of worship.

II. Meditation: on the events of these dedication days

    1. Moses began the ceremony by anointing and consecrating the tabernacle, its furnishings, the altar, and its utensils, v. 1.
    2. The ceremony was practical as well as spiritual: the items offered were useful as well as symbolic of the Lord God whom they served.
    3. All tribal leaders participated equally: every person should serve the Lord and all are equal in His sight, regardless of their relative standing, size, or worth.
    4. When everything was completed in exact obedience to God's commands, the Lord met Moses at the Mercy Seat and spoke to him there, v. 89.

III. Revelation and Applications:

    1. Just as Moses consecrated the tabernacle unto the Lord God, *I also should present my body (my tabernacle, my temple) holy unto the Lord, Rom. 12:1-2; I Cor. 3:16-17.*
    2. My true worship of God not only involves spiritual praise unto Him, *it also involves practical service which benefits my fellow human beings.*
    3. The Lord demands my best in service to Him; *He judges me not on my accomplishments but on my degree of faithfulness.*
    4. God reveals Himself to man; *I can hear Him speak to my heart at the Mercy Seat . . . at the place of atonement where I receive grace through Christ's shed blood.*

Dedicating the Levites for Service

(Numbers 8:5-26)

I. Concentration: on the beginning of the service by the Levites

1. Prior to this, only Moses, Aaron, and his sons served the tabernacle.
2. Now the other men of the tribe of Levi were set aside to assist in the tasks of operating the worship system of ancient Israel.
3. The Levites first were ceremonially cleansed by sprinkling them with water of purification and by washing their clothes, vv. 5-7.
4. The Levites also were told to shave all the hair from their body as a symbol of being cut off from anything unclean, v. 7.

II. Meditation: on the ordination ceremony of the Levites

1. The representatives of Israel laid their hands on the Levites, vv. 10, 20.
2. The Levites were presented like a "wave offering" (6:20), which was the portion of the sacrifice that belonged to the officiating priest. *Symbolically, the Lord gave the Levites to Aaron and his sons to assist them in their work, v. 19.*
3. Two young bulls were sacrificed: one as a sin offering and the other as a burnt offering, vv. 8, 12.
4. "To make atonement" (vv. 12, 19) meant that the Levites represented the firstborn of all the Hebrew families which were to be dedicated ("sacrificed") unto the Lord, vv. 16-18.

III. Revelation: on the spiritual implications of this ceremony

1. The laying on of hands symbolized that the Levites were identified as official spiritual representatives of the nation.
2. The function of the Levites was more practical than that of the priests, whose function was more spiritual; this explains the differences in the ordination ceremonies of this chapter and in Leviticus, chapter 8.
3. The Levites formed a protective buffer between the tabernacle and the Israelites, so that no plague (heavenly curse) would come upon the nation by unholy persons entering God's holy place.
4. The minimum age for Levitical service was reduced from age 30 (Num. 4:3) to age 25 (Num. 8:24) and later to age 20 (I Chron. 23:3) . . . probably to meet the increased demands of the sacrificial system of worship. *Retirement from active duty occurred at age 50, vv. 25-26.*

IV. Applications: as a Christian, I need to . . .

1. Magnify my position as a priest of the living God.
2. Realize that no matter how menial my service may be, it is to be rendered as "unto the Lord," Rom. 14:6-8; Col. 3:23.
3. Recognize that my assigned place of service for the Lord is designed to bring a spiritual benefit (a blessing) unto His people.
4. The principles and truths of God are unchanging, but the methods of service need to be flexible to meet the needs of the current situation.

Divine Guidance

(Numbers 9:1-23)

I. Concentration: on the two types of divine guidance seen in this chapter

    1. The first instance involved observing the Passover, vv. 1-14.

    2. Certain Israelites found themselves ceremonially unclean and thus prohibited from observing the Passover at the proper time, vv. 6-7.

    3. Moses inquired of the Lord about the problem, and the Lord gave him practical, divine guidance, vv. 8-14.

    4. The second instance involved the pillar of cloud and fire over the tabernacle which showed the nation when to move, vv. 15-23.

II. Meditation: on the Passover incident

    1. God's will was revealed to Moses to allow persons who were prevented from observing the Passover on the proper day (1st month, 14th day) to keep the feast a month later.

    2. One extenuating circumstance involved ceremonial uncleanness caused by a person being defiled by touching a human corpse . . . such as caring for a relative who died just before Passover.

    3. The second extenuating circumstance involved a person who was away on a journey, making it impossible for him to observe Passover properly with his family.

    4. These exceptions to the rule were to be kept within strict guidelines . . . clean persons or those not away on a journey who failed to observe Passover were to be excluded from the camp and from the covenant relationship with God.

III. Revelation: on the pillar of cloud and fire

    1. The pillar first appeared to guide and protect the Israelites at the time of the Exodus from Egypt, Ex. 13:21-22; 14:19-20.

    2. In Ex. 40:34-38, the pillar descended on the completed tabernacle, and led the people to Mount Sinai.

    3. This Scripture passage (Num. 9:15-23) fore-shadowed the divine guidance of the Israelites during their years of wandering in the wilderness.

    4. When the Israelites finally crossed the Jordan River into the Promised Land under Joshua's leadership, the pillar of cloud and fire was removed and the ark showed them the way, Josh. 3:3-4.

IV. Applications: as a Christian, I need to understand . . .

    1. That God is much more interested in the condition of the heart of a worshipper than He is in the legalistic regulations.

    2. That God sees and knows whether I am truly "providentially hindered" from serving Him, or not.

    3. That in my early spiritual journeys with the Lord, He makes His will and way clear and obvious . . . giving simple instructions as to a child.

    4. That more experienced and mature followers of the Lord must learn to walk by faith, not by sight, II Cor. 5:7.

Departure from Sinai

(Numbers 10:1-36)

I. Concentration: on the main events in this chapter

1. The Lord gave Moses instructions about making two silver trumpets to be used in giving signals, vv. 1-10.
2. The cloud moved, and the people set out from Mount Sinai toward the Promised Land, vv. 11-28.
3. Moses enlisted his father-in-law, Hobab the Midianite (Jethro, Ex. 3:1), to serve as a scout for enemies and future campsites, vv. 29-32.
4. At the beginning and ending of each day's journey, Moses invoked God's blessings upon the people, vv. 33-36.

II. Meditation and Revelation: on the spiritual implications of these events

1. The two silver trumpets signaled for the entire nation or for the leaders to assemble, for moving in and out of camp formation, for orders related to fighting battles, and to announce religious functions and holidays. *Christ's return will be heralded by a trumpet (I Thes. 4:16); the culminating events of God's final plan for the ages will follow the sounding of seven trumpets (Rev. 8-12); and a Christian's witness (testimony to the lost) is to be as clear as a trumpet call (I Cor. 14:6-9).*
2. On the 20th day of the second month of the second year (from the Exodus), the Israelites left Sinai where they had been given God's law, taught how to worship, organized to function as a theocracy, and prepared for battle against their enemies. *Spiritually, God trains His people today in these same four ways: to know His word, to worship Him in spirit and truth, to live daily as His subjects, and to do battle against the evil forces of Satan.*
3. Moses needed the endorsement and encouragement of Jethro (Ex. 18:7-12, 17-23); he also needed his experience and his "eyes" (Num. 10:31-32) . . . which would benefit both the nation and Jethro, who would share in God's blessings. *Likewise, younger spiritual leaders (ministers) can benefit from the approval, advice, "know-how," and vision of older, more mature leaders who have walked in God's ways for many years.*
4. In the morning, Moses prayed: "Rise up, Lord! Let Your enemies be scattered;" in the evening, he prayed: "Return, O Lord." *We need God's presence and power when the sun rises, and we need His rest and peace when the night falls.*

III. As a Christian, I need to . . .

1. Respond to God's trumpet calls each day in immediate obedience.
2. Prepare to be a well-trained, obedient follower of the Lord.
3. Respect my elders; be a good influence on the younger generation.
4. Start each day by invoking God's blessings; close each day with thanksgiving for His grace and mercy.

Griping and Complaining

(Numbers 11:1-35)

I. Concentration: on the people griping to Moses

    1. The instigators were the "mixed multitude," v. 4 . . . non-Jewish slaves from Egypt who accompanied the Israelites in the Exodus, Ex. 12:38.

    2. The complaining people were bored with manna, and they had an intense craving for the spicy foods of Egypt, vv. 4-6.

    3. Their complaining displeased God, because it demonstrated their basic sins of ingratitude and lack of faith, v. 1

    4. God's punishment upon the complaining people on the "outskirts of the camp" revealed that spiritually, they were living along the outer edges of the "canopy of God's covenant blessings," v. 1.

II. Meditation: on Moses' complaints to God

    1. "Why are You picking on me; what have I done wrong?" v. 11.

    2. "I'm not the parents of these people; where can I come up with what they are crying for?" vv. 12-13.

    3. I can't possibly do this job by myself; this burden of responsibility is too heavy for one man," v. 14.

    4. "It's all Your fault, God; if You really love me, please let me die," v. 15.

III. Revelation: on what the Lord God replied to Moses

    1. "I'll come down and talk with you," v. 17.

    2. "I'll give you some Spirit-filled assistants," v. 17.

    3. "I'll bless the people with so much meat that it will become a curse to them," vv. 18-20.

    4. I'll demonstrate to you that my power is unlimited (that the Lord's arm is not shortened)," v. 23.

IV. Applications: as a Christian, I need to understand . . .

    1. God sent His Spirit upon 70 chosen elders, who gave evidence of the Spirit of the Lord by prophesying, v. 25. *True Spirit-filled persons exhibit the presence of God in their lives by their God-inspired words.*

    2. Joshua jealously requested Moses to forbid two "outsiders" from prophesying, vv. 26-28. *Note the similarity between Moses' reply in this incident and Jesus' words in Mk. 9:38-40 and Lk. 9:49-50.*

    3. Moses responded in verse 29: "Oh, that all the Lord's people were prophets and that the Lord would put His Spirit upon them!" *This general outpouring of the Spirit upon all people also was prophesied in Joel 2:28-32, and fulfilled in Acts 2:4, 16-21.*

    4. God sent such an overwhelming number of quail that it became like one of the plagues in Egypt, vv. 31-34. *Sometimes God gives us what we beg and plead for, even though it may not be good for us . . . to teach us the valuable lessons that He knows best, and that His provision always is more than adequate to meet all of our needs.*

Rebellion of Aaron and Miriam

(Numbers 12:1-16)

I. Concentration: on the events of this chapter

1. Aaron and Miriam questioned the exclusive prophetic authority of their younger brother, Moses, vv. 1-3.
2. God affirmed Moses' special status above all other prophets, vv. 4-8.
3. God punished Miriam with leprosy, and Aaron confessed both their sins to Moses, asking him for mercy, vv. 9-12.
4. Moses prayed for her healing, and the Lord did so after a week's banishment from the camp, vv. 13-16.

II. Meditation: on these events

1. Both Aaron and Miriam had functioned in a prophetic role (Ex. 4:30; 15:20), but clearly they were to be under the authority of their brother, Moses. *A family squabble over Moses' wife caused them to dare to rebel against Moses' spiritual leadership.*
2. Unlike any other prophet who has ever lived, God spoke plainly and face-to-face with Moses. *God spoke to other prophets in visions and dreams.*
3. Only Miriam was afflicted with leprosy (perhaps because, as the oldest child she had been the instigator of this rebellion); yet Aaron, confessed that both of them had sinned. *This may be the second time that Aaron's position shielded him from punishment; see Ex. 32.*
4. Moses responded to Aaron's plea for mercy immediately and without a trace of vengefulness. *This illustrates Moses' humility, v. 3.*

III. Revelation: on the spiritual principles taught here

1. God establishes His line of authority according to His good will and pleasure; God's choices often ignore age or family relationships.
2. The Mosaic Law is above critique from the prophets; the Scriptures have a primacy over any and all prophetic gifts of the Holy Spirit.
3. Even Miriam's healing and public period of humiliation were under the guidelines established in Scripture: seven days of inspection by the priest in cases of leprosy, Lev. 13:33-34.
4. When a leader sins, it interrupts the spiritual progress of the entire congregation; Israel did not journey until after Miriam's time of separation and probation.

IV. Applications: as a Christian, I need to . . .

1. Respect and submit to the authority of God's chosen leaders.
2. Recognize that "words of prophesy" must neither contradict nor supersede Scripture.
3. Realize that restoration to a position of spiritual leadership, after a public sin, must follow an inactive period of repentance and reflection.
4. Reaffirm the impact of my influence: Moses' humble spirit brought God's approval and miraculous power; Miriam's sin delayed the nation's journey toward the Promised Land.

Twelve Spies Sent into Canaan

(Numbers 13:1-33)

I. Concentration: on the events of this chapter

1. In obedience to God's command to Moses, each tribe selected a man to go spy out the land of Canaan, vv. 1-6.
2. Moses gave them their orders, vv. 7-16.
3. The 12 spies spent 40 days spying out the land, vv. 21-25.
4. The spies presented their report to Moses and the people, with all 12 of them agreeing on the facts of what they observed . . . but disagreeing on whether they were able to take possession of the land, vv. 26-33.

II. Meditation: on some interesting details found here

1. The 12 chosen men were "heads" (leaders) in Israel (v. 3), but they were not the tribal chiefs named in Numbers 2.
2. The tribe of Ephraim chose Hoshea ("Salvation") whom Moses had renamed Joshua ("Jehovah is Salvation"), and who had commanded the original volunteer army and served as Moses' personal assistant (Ex. 17:9-13; 24:13; 33:11).
3. All the men in this expedition agreed on the facts of what they had observed: (1) the land was productive, (2) the people were numerous and strong, (3) they lived in large, fortified cities, and (4) some giants lived there, vv. 27-28, 32-33.
4. The "committee" exceeded its assigned authority: they had been charged only with reporting what they observed and bringing back samples of produce, not with making a recommendation about entering the land. *That decision already had been made by the Lord, v. 2.*

III. Revelation: on the differences between Caleb and Joshua and other 10 others

1. Caleb (v. 30), who also spoke for Joshua (Num. 14:6, 24, 30), saw the God who had delivered them from Egypt; the ten saw only giants.
2. Caleb and Joshua had faith; the ten were fearful doubters, v. 33.
3. Caleb and Joshua were positive and optimistic; the ten were negative and pessimistic.
4. Caleb and Joshua stood courageously against the majority; the ten were faithless cowards, who incited the mob into a lynching frenzy.

IV. Applications: as a Christian, I need to . . .

1. Realize that faith is not blind; it does not deny the reality of difficulty, but it declares the power of God to overcome the problems.
2. Beware of "majority rule" in spiritual matters; frequently God's will is not discerned by the worldly majority.
3. Recognize that a group of people usually is not to be trusted to know <u>what</u> God wants to accomplish; the group's value may lie in giving helpful advice on <u>how</u> to do a project.
4. When I attempt to walk and lead by faith, expect violent opposition from the faithless unbelievers who are among the people of God.

Israel Refuses to Enter Canaan

(Numbers 14:1-45)

I. <u>Concentration: on the main events in this chapter</u>

1. The nation reacted negatively to the report of the 12 spies, vv. 1-10:
   1) They decided to select a new leader and return to Egypt, v. 4.
   2) They started to stone Caleb and Joshua, v. 10.
2. Moses interceded for the rebellious people, vv. 11-25.
3. The Lord pronounced a death sentence on the rebelling adults, vv. 26-38.
4. In disobedience, the people then attempted to invade the land of Canaan, but were defeated, vv. 39-45.

II. <u>Meditation: on these dramatic events</u>

1. The fear and doubt of the nation contrasted sharply with the faith and assurance of Caleb and Joshua; only God's intervention prevented their execution. *Instead, the other ten spies were executed by God and only Caleb and Joshua were spared the Lord's judgment, vv. 36-38.*
2. Moses' prayer (v. 18) quoted the words of the Lord from Ex. 34:6-7 . . ."The Lord God, merciful and gracious, long-suffering . . . forgiving iniquity and transgression and sin."
3. The punishment for rebellion against the Lord was that His promised blessings were delayed for 40 years. *During this time of wilderness wandering, more than 600,000 men died . . . an average of over 40 funerals per day!*
4. The attempt to conquer the Lord's enemies without His accompanying presence, v. 44, was doomed to failure.

III. <u>Revelation: on the spiritual implications seen here</u>

1. As Caleb and Joshua proclaimed: "If the Lord delights in us, then He will give us this land . . . and the Lord <u>is</u> with us. Do not fear," vv. 8-9.
2. In response to Moses' intercession, we observe two aspects of the Lord's character: God is merciful, so He did not disinherit the nation; God is just, so the people who rebelled paid the death penalty for their sins.
3. The sins of the rebellious adults negatively affected the lives of their children for an entire generation.
4. Unless we obey God's will <u>on His timetable</u>, we shall surely fail. *(The Israelites had missed their chance, and God told them to turn south, away from the Promised Land and back into the desert, v. 25.)*

IV. <u>Applications: as a Christian, I need to . . .</u>

1. Live in faith and walk in obedience.
2. Base my prayers of faith on the character of the Lord God and on the promises of His word.
3. Live a Godly life of integrity today, for the sake of my children and grandchildren tomorrow.
4. Move <u>immediately</u> upon God's command . . . and <u>only</u> at that time!

Put Tassels on Your Garments

(Numbers 15:1-41)

I. Concentration: on the topics found in this chapter

1. The laws of grain and drink offerings were reviewed and more specific regulations were given, vv. 1-21.
2. The laws concerning unintentional sins, vv. 22-29, were stated in sharp contrast to the laws concerning presumptuous sins, vv. 30-31.
3. A Sabbath violator was executed according to the Law, vv. 32-36.
4. The Lord gave instructions for all Israelites to put a blue thread (ribbon) in the tassels on the hems of their garments to remind them of their covenant obligations under God, vv. 37-41.

II. Meditation: on these topics

1. The words, "When you have come into the land," vv. 2 and 18, inject a note of hope, that in spite of God's 40-year death penalty on Israel's sin, He still was preparing for His chosen people to enter into Canaan.
2. The Jewish sacrificial system brought forgiveness only for unintentional sins committed; deliberate, intentional, rebellious sins removed an Israelite from the covenant relationship, and there was no method for restoration . . . until the cross in the New Testament!
3. The execution of the Sabbath breaker not only carried out the assigned penalty for the crime against God (Ex. 31:14-15); it also served as a deterrent, as also was true of the execution of Achan in Josh. 7:10-26.
4. Symbols (such as tassels) sometimes come to be reverenced as the reality, rather than being merely reminders of deep spiritual realities.

III. Revelation: on the tassels on the corners of the Jewish garments

1. All Hebrews, not merely the priests, were told to wear tassels on their garments as a reminder of their <u>call</u> as a nation to be holy . . . not as a sign that they actually <u>were</u> holy.
2. In New Testament times, Jesus pronounced woes (curses) upon the hypocritical Pharisees, who pretended to be holy by "enlarging the borders of their garments," Matt. 23:5.
3. This "holy reminder" portion of Jesus' robe was the part touched by the woman who was healed of her infirmity, Matt. 9:20-21.
4. Other sick persons also prostrated themselves to the ground to touch the hem of Jesus' garment, as a sign of their faith in His special relationship to the holy God of Israel . . . and they also were healed, Matt. 14:35-36.

IV. Applications: as a Christian, I need to . . .

1. Live a life of purity and holiness as one of God's chosen people.
2. With integrity, practice what I preach, avoiding all hypocrisy.
3. Bow in humility before the King of Kings to receive his almighty power to meet my needs.
4. Point other hurting people to the One who can bring them help and hope.

How to Be a "Plague Buster"

(Numbers 16:1-50)

I. Concentration: on the chain of events in this chapter

1. Korah ("Bald"), accompanied by Dathan, Abiram, and 250 other leaders rebelled against the leadership of Moses and Aaron, vv. 1-3.
2. Moses dealt with Korah by devising a test to prove Aaron's divine calling; he rebuked Korah for despising his own ministry as a Levite, vv. 4-11.
3. Moses tried to deal with the two other rebel leaders, but they refused to appear before him, vv. 12-14.
4. The earth opened up to swallow the three leaders and their families; the fire of God consumed the 250 other rebels, vv. 15-35.
5. The censers carried by the dead rebels were hammered out and added to the brazen altar as a memorial sign that only the descendants of Aaron were to function as priests, vv. 36-40.
6. The people complained about God's treatment of the rebels; the Lord sent a deadly plague which was stopped by Aaron's making atonement for them . . . but 14,700 people died, vv. 41-50.

II. Meditation: on the charges (complaints) against Moses and Aaron

1. You take too much authority upon yourselves, vv. 3, 13.
2. You are not holier than we are; all God's people are holy; the Lord is with us too, not exclusively with you, v. 3.
3. You took us away from "milk and honey" (Egypt); you haven't led us into the Promised Land; we're going to die in the wilderness, vv. 13-14.
4. You want us to follow blindly ("put out the eyes"), but we refuse, v. 14.

III. Revelation: on becoming a "plague buster" (vv. 46-48)

1. Aaron obediently and immediately ran into the midst of the congregation who were dying of the plague.
2. He carried a censer of atonement . . . because censers had been the source of sin in the earlier dispute, revealing that God can sanctify and use even unworthy vessels to accomplish His purposes, II Tim. 2:21.
3. His censer contained fire, one of the symbols of the Holy Spirit.
4. The burning incense represented intercessory prayer rising in behalf of the dying people, Psa. 14:12.

IV. Applications: as a Christian, I need to . . .

1. Ignore criticism: the charges against Moses were groundless and foolish, but he allowed God to handle the punishment of the rebels.
2. Realize that one man's sin can bring doom upon God's people, v. 22; Jude 1:11 . . . Korah was responsible for the deaths of 15,000 people.
3. Recognize, also, that one man's obedience can bring deliverance . . . Aaron "stood between the living and the dead," v. 48, a picture of the saving work of the Lord Jesus Christ, I Cor. 15:22.
4. Serve as God's censer, filled with fire and incense, helping to stop sin's deadly plague in the midst of a dying world.

The Budding of Aaron's Rod

(Numbers 17:1-11)

I. Concentration: on God's instructions about the rods

1. Each tribal leader (Num. 1:5-15) was summoned to bring his rod (walking staff), v. 2.
2. Moses instructed each man to carve his tribal name on his rod, v. 2.
3. These 12 rods, along with Aaron's rod (labeled "Levi"), were placed in the tabernacle before the Ark ("Testimony"), vv. 3-4.
4. These rods were to be left overnight and examined on the following day to confirm God's selection of His spiritual leader (High Priest), v. 5.

II. Meditation: on the history of Aaron's rod

1. It was used in performing divine miracles during the time of the Exodus from Egypt, Ex. 7:8-13.
2. It was used in the wilderness wanderings to produce water from the rock, Ex. 17:1-7; Num. 20:7-11.
3. It was used in this chapter (Num. 17) to prove God's choice of Aaron, in response to the rebellion of the preceding chapter.
4. It was preserved as a permanent memorial in the Ark of the Covenant, along with the two tablets of the law (Ten Commandments) and the pot of manna, Heb. 9:4.

III. Revelation: on God's miraculous power flowing into a "dead stick" (v. 8)

1. Aaron's rod sprouted.
2. It put forth buds.
3. It produced blossoms.
4. It yielded ripe almonds . . . all in one night!

IV. Applications: as a Christian, I need to understand that . . .

1. God is sovereign; He chooses whom He will call to serve Him.
   I thank Him for choosing me.
2. God manifests His power through the miracles He performs.
   I worship Him for exhibiting His power in me.
3. God is the source of all life; He is the resurrection.
   I praise Him for giving me everlasting life.
4. God produces nourishing food out of a dead piece of wood.
   I serve Him by allowing Him to produce His fruit in me . . . a dead and useless stick.

A Tithe of the Tithe

(Numbers 18:1-32)

I. Concentration: on the main sections in this chapter

1. The Lord spoke to Aaron (rather than to Moses!), answering the Israelites' fearful question of Num. 17:12-13, and explaining how the lay people could bring sacrifices to God without dying: through the priests and Levites, vv. 1-7.
2. The Lord explained to Aaron that part of the offerings of the congregation were for the support of the priests, vv. 8-20.
3. The Lord also told Aaron that all of the tithes were to be given to the Levites as wages for their work of the tabernacle, vv. 21-24.
4. The Lord then spoke to Moses, commanding that the Levites give a tithe of the tithes they received unto Aaron and the priests, vv. 25-32.

II. Meditation: on Biblical principles about paying ministers

1. Payment for religious services rendered by priests and Levites was mandated by Mosaic Law, as in this text, and as illustrated in Deut. 25:4 . . . "You shall not muzzle an ox while it treads out the grain."
2. When Jesus sent out the seventy, He told them to accept charitable gifts from those they served because, "the laborer is worthy of his wages," Lk. 10:7.
3. Paul defended his right to be paid for his ministerial service in Corinth, (I Cor. 9:4-14), citing the command of the Lord that "those who preach the gospel should live from the gospel," (v. 14).
4. Paul told Timothy (I Tim. 5:17-18) that ruling and teaching elders in the church were worthy of "double honor" (double pay) . . . citing the quotes from both Moses (Deut. 25:4) and Jesus (Lk. 10:7).

III. Revelation and Applications: on the principle of the tithe

1. This passage (Num. 18:25-32) teaches that just as the common Israelites were commanded to pay tithes to the Lord by giving that sacred ten-percent to the Levites, so also the Levites were commanded to tithe their income to the Aaronic priesthood.
2. The law of the tithe preceded the Mosiac Law: hundreds of years before Moses, Abraham paid tithes to Melchizedek (Gen. 14:18-20), and Jacob pledged to give God a tithe of his increase (Gen. 28:22).
3. Even following the Babylonian captivity, Nehemiah led to people into a renewal of the covenant which required, among many other things, that the Levites were to give to God a tenth of the tithes they received from the worshipping people, Neh. 10:38.
4. This tithe principle, I believe, applies not only to all individuals (including ministers), but also to churches and other ministries: one-tenth of the total income received should be given to Godly causes outside the local operations . . . to Christian missionary endeavors and to other charitable enterprises.

The Red Heifer

(Numbers 19:1-22)

I. Concentration: on the special ceremony of purification

1. This chapter gives instructions concerning persons who have become ceremonially unclean by touching a corpse.
2. It was a particular problem at this time because of the deaths of so many persons in Num. 16:49.
3. Eleazar, Aaron's son, performed the ceremony . . . protecting the High Priest from any chance of defilement, vv. 3-4.
4. The careful separation of the High Priest from any contact with death emphasizes the truth that the Lord is the source of life . . . that He is the God of the living, not of the dead, Matt. 22:32.

II. Meditation: on the steps of this ritual

1. Eleazar sacrificed an unblemished red heifer outside the camp (compare Heb. 13:11-13), sprinkled its blood in front of the tabernacle, and completely burned the animal's body into ashes, vv. 3-5.
2. He also burned the implements used in the ceremony (cedar wood, hyssop and scarlet cloth); then he and his assistants washed themselves and their clothes, vv. 6-8.
3. The ashes then were stored in a clean place outside the camp, v. 9.
4. The ashes could be used by a person to purify himself, vv. 11-13, or another clean person could purify the unclean individual, vv. 17-19.

III. Revelation: on the spiritual implications of purifying an unclean person

1. The individual helping to purify the unclean person needed to be clean himself, v. 18.
2. This clean person mixed some ashes from the red heifer with running (literally "living") water and sprinkled the contaminated person and the objects he had touched, vv. 17-18.
3. This ceremony involved a period of a week, with the sprinkling being done on the third and seventh days, v. 19.
4. Following this ceremony and another bath, the contaminated person was pronounced clean and allowed to rejoin his family and to participate in the services of worship, v. 19.

IV. Applications: as a Christian, I need to . . .

1. See this red heifer cleansing ceremony (blood sacrifice, total dedication, and washing of the word, Eph. 5:26) as the Old Testament picture of Jesus' teaching about foot washing in John 13:6-10.
2. Allow the Lord to wash my feet daily from the contamination of the world; assist my fellow believers also to receive spiritual cleansing by my "washing their feet," Jn. 13:14.
3. Minister gently and humbly to those who have fallen into sin, Gal. 6:1-2.
4. Realize that God's forgiveness is immediate, but that restoration to full fellowship and a place of spiritual leadership takes time, Hos. 3:3.

The Tragedy of Missed Destiny

(Numbers 20:1-29)

I. Concentration: on the four tragic heartbreaks of Moses in this chapter

1. His only sister, Miriam, died and was buried in Kadesh, v. 1.
2. The Israelites contended again with Moses over the lack of water; he disobeyed God and struck the rock . . . which resulted in forfeiture of his opportunity to enter the Promised Land, vv. 2-13.
3. His negotiations for passage through the territory of the descendants of Esau (Edom) failed, and the Jews were forced to detour, vv. 14-21.
4. His brother, Aaron, also died and was replaced as High Priest by Eleazar, vv. 22-29. *Aaron was denied access into the Promised Land because of Moses' sin, according to verse 24.*

II. Meditation: on Moses' costly temper tantrum

1. Apparently a number of years had passed since the people had rebelled against entering Canaan (Num. 14), but Moses was particularly sensitive to their complaints here because this was the same place (Kadesh) where their first rebellion had occurred, bringing the 40-year punishment, v. 1; 13:26; Deut. 1:19.
2. The Lord commanded Moses to "speak to the rock" (v. 8), not to strike it as before as in Ex. 17:6.
3. Moses, with impatience, anger, and disobedience, struck the rock twice, and water did come out abundantly, v. 11.
4. Moses' sin involved both lack of faith and lack of reverence, v. 12.

III. Revelation: on the spiritual implications seen here

1. Moses failed to be open to the new way through which God wanted to act; rather, he did it the way he'd successfully done it before.
2. The old method worked, but God was displeased because Moses had presumed upon God's power; the Lord is not <u>obligated</u> to do a thing our way on our timetable!
3. God punished Moses because (1) he did not "believe" . . . that the Lord could or would send water from the rock merely in response to his spoken word, and (2) he did not "hallow" or reverence the Lord by strict obedience. *(Disobedience is irreverence!)*
4. The Lord changed the method of bringing water from the rock because symbolically the Rock was Jesus (I Cor. 10:4), and He was to be smitten only once, Heb. 7:27; 9:7, 12, 26, 28; 10:10.

IV. Applications: as a Christian, I need to . . .

1. Be flexible, allowing God to accomplish His purposes in new ways.
2. Avoid presumption: God will not allow me to place Him in a position where He is forced to do what I say or embarrass His reputation.
3. Exhibit my faith and reverence by obedience to the Lord's commands.
4. Realize that my disobedience may cause life's greatest tragedy: missing the blessing of fulfilling God's planned destiny for my life.

The Bronze Serpent on a Pole

(Numbers 21:1-35)

I. Concentration: on the contents of this chapter

1. The Israelites defeated the king of Arad, the Canaanite, vv. 1-3.
2. God sent poisonous snakes to kill the complaining people, and a bronze serpent was erected to provide healing, vv. 4-9.
3. The Jews journeyed from Mount Hor to Moab, vv. 10-20.
4. They defeated Sihon of Ammon, vv. 21-32, and Og of Bashan, vv. 33-35.

II. Meditation: on the bronze serpent events

1. Once again the people spoke against God, complaining about the manna saying, "Our soul loathes (detests) this worthless bread," v. 5.
2. Their frequent murmuring brought God's judgment, many people died, and the people asked Moses to pray for the removal of the fiery serpents, vv. 6-7.
3. The Lord instructed Moses to construct a bronze serpent and set it on a pole, so that everyone who was bitten could look and be healed, v. 8.
4. Moses obeyed, and persons who looked at the bronze serpent lived, v. 9.

III. Revelation: on the spiritual implications of these events

1. Sin against God (including ingratitude and complaining) brings His judgment; *such a bitter spirit is deadly to a nation and to a church.*
2. The people wanted God to remove the snakes, but He saved them in a different way; *usually the Lord does not remove our problems, but He provides a way through them which makes use of, and greatly strengthens, our faith.*
3. Moses' lifting up the serpent in the wilderness pictured Christ's being lifted up on the cross, so that *"whoever believes in Him should not perish but have eternal life," Jn. 3:14-15.*
4. Neither the object (the bronze serpent) nor the method (lifting it up on a pole) provided the healing and deliverance. *The miraculous power originated in the Lord God, and only those persons who looked in faith were saved . . . probably some doubted, refused to look, and died.*

(Note: Later, the Israelites foolishly began to worship the bronze serpent, and King Hezekiah had to destroy this religious relic, II Kgs. 18:4.)

IV. Applications: as a Christian, I need to . . .

1. Thank the Lord for all His blessings . . . especially His "Bread" that gives me nourishment and life.
2. Pray to the Lord when problems come, knowing He may not remove the difficulties, but that He has promised His strength to see me through.
3. Look to the Lord Jesus in faith, not only for salvation, but also for His provision for all my needs, Phil. 4:19.
4. Realize that yesterday's successful methods are not sacred; God never changes, but He accomplishes His divine purposes in different ways from day to day and from generation to generation.

God Can Use a Stubborn Donkey!

(Numbers 22:1-41)

I. Concentration: on the interesting events in this chapter

1. The Israelites camped across the Jordan River from Jericho; Balak, king of the Moabites, sent for a prophet, Balaam, to curse them, vv. 1-7.
2. The Lord told Balaam not to go curse the Jews, but Balaam finally was persuaded (bribed) by Balak's messengers to make the trip, vv. 8-21.
3. The Angel of the Lord blocked Balaam's path; his donkey balked and spoke to his master; the angel allowed Balaam to proceed with the strict warning to speak only the words given him by God, vv. 22-35.
4. Balak met Balaam, who repeated God's warning to him about cursing the Israelites; together they went to observe the Jewish camp, vv. 36-41.

II. Meditation: on being dumber than a donkey

1. Too much of the time, Balaam represents me, and the donkey represents the providential hand (and voice) of the Lord.
2. Although I know right from wrong, sometimes the allure of the world (honor, prestige, wealth, power) is tempting enough that I head down the road called "My Way" toward the sin-town of "Compromise."
3. Whenever that happens, God always places roadblocks in my path to detour me (I Cor. 10:13); yet my typical reaction is anger ("madness," II Pet. 2:15-16). I get mad" whenever . . .
   1) Circumstances delay by detouring me into a field, v. 23.
   2) Injury (or illness) puts me on "pause," v. 25.
   3) Everything comes to a complete stand-still, v. 27.
   4) The clear voice of God speaks a warning, frequently from an unexpected and unworthy source, like a donkey!
4. When I am blinded to spiritual reality (and dumber than a donkey), God prods me toward taking His escape route, rather than pursuing my own way toward destruction, as Balaam did.

III. Revelation and Applications: on how God uses stubborn donkeys, like me

1. God used a donkey as a prophet, Num. 22:28-30. *A donkey saw spiritual reality (the angel) and rebuked Balaam for his wrong-doing.*
2. God used a donkey as a pastor/teacher, I Sam. 9-10. *Lost donkeys led Saul to Samuel who directed the future king into a life-changing experience with the Holy Spirit, and into an awareness of God's destiny.*
3. God used a donkey as an evangelist, Matt. 21:1-5; Zech. 9:9. *A donkey "lifted up" Jesus in the midst of a crowd, and proclaimed Him as Christ.*
4. God used a donkey's jawbone as an instrument to defeat His enemies, Judg. 15:15. *Samson killed a thousand Philistines with the jawbone of a donkey; no doubt God also can find a way to use even me.*

Prayer: "Lord, help me not to be like a stubborn mule; rather, make me submissive and teachable," Psa. 32:8-9.

Blessing Rather than Cursing

(Numbers 23:1-30)

I. Concentration: on the events of this chapter

1. At Balaam's request, Balak built seven altars and sacrificed seven bulls and seven rams; Balaam left Balak and went to a desolate height where the Lord met him and gave him a prophetic word, vv. 1-6.
2. Balaam spoke the Lord's prophetic words of blessing upon Israel; Balak rebuked him, then gave him another chance to curse Israel from a different location where he could see only part of the assembled nation, vv. 7-14.
3. God gave Balaam a second prophecy, and Balaam pronounced a second word of blessing upon Israel, vv. 15-24.
4. Balak told Balaam to say nothing at all rather than to bless them; Balak gave Balaam a third chance to curse Israel from still another location, vv. 25-30.

II. Meditation: on Balaam's first prophecy

1. I cannot curse whom God has not cursed, v. 8.
2. The nation of Israel is unique; they are the people of God, v. 9.
3. The number of people is beyond counting (as "dust"), v. 10.
4. The nation will be blessed by the Lord ("die the death of the righteous"), and I wish my end could be the same, v. 10.

III. Revelation: on Balaam's second prophecy

1. Listen Balak! God is not a man; you cannot trick Him nor change His mind nor prevent what He has willed, vv. 18-19.
2. I have received God's command to bless the nation of Israel and I cannot reverse it, v. 20.
3. God has judged Israel, and they now stand faultless before Him, v. 21.
4. God is with the nation, as a King among them, v. 21.
5. God is overwhelmingly powerful ("strong as an ox"), v. 22.
6. No sorcery nor black magic can work against Israel's God, v. 23.
7. The people are a living witness and testimony of the power of God . . .   "Oh, what God has done!" v. 23.
8. The nation of Israel surely will conquer its enemies, v. 24.

IV. Applications: as a Christian, I need to . . .

1. Speak only the words of blessing which the Lord has put into my mouth.
2. Recognize that God's spiritual Israel stands before Him clothed in the righteousness of Christ, who dwells as a King among His subjects.
3. Realize that through the strength of the Lord, we shall triumph over Satan and his evil forces, which are powerless before our Almighty God.
4. Praise the Lord, and witness to those who are lost about what God has provided for them through His mercy and grace.

"A Star . . . A Scepter"

(Numbers 24:1-25)

I Concentration: on the events of this chapter

1. Balaam abandoned the use of sorcery; the Spirit of God came upon him; in an ecstatic trance, he pronounced another blessing upon the nation of Israel, vv. 1-9.
2. Balak, in anger, threatened Balaam's life; Balaam then prophesied that Balak's attempt to curse Israel would bring a curse upon his own nation of Moab, vv. 10-14.
3. In a second ecstatic trance, Balaam blessed Israel and uttered a Messianic p r o p h e c y, vv. 15-19.
4. Finally, Balaam pronounced three other independent oracles, emphasizing that the Lord God is in control of the fate of all the nations of the earth, vv. 20-25.

II. Meditation: on Balaam's ecstatic trances, vv. 3-4, 15-16

1. Balaam's experience was the direct result of the Spirit of the Lord falling upon him, v. 2.
2. Evidently he fell or prostrated himself under the weight of the manifest presence of the Lord: "falls down, with eyes wide open."
3. He heard the words of God and spoke them: ("utterance").
4. Not only physically, but also spiritually, his eyes were opened, and he saw a vision of the Almighty.

III. Revelation: on Balaam's Messianic prophecy, vv. 17-19

1. Balaam saw Jesus Christ in the distant future: "I see Him, but not now; I behold Him, but not near."
2. He saw the Messiah as a Star and a Scepter . . . as a light in the darkness and as a King.
3. Probably the wise men from the East were familiar with this ancient prophecy from the Fourth Book of Moses, so the appearance of a new star in the Hebrew portion of the sky signaled to them the birth of a Jewish king, Matt. 2:1-2.
4. This "One" prophesied by Balaam was to have "dominion" on the earth, v. 19; I Pet. 4:11.

IV. Applications: as a Christian, I need to . . .

1. Be open to the Holy Spirit of the Lord coming upon me to bring power and enlightenment . . . to give me God's words and a vision of His destiny for my life, Acts 1:8; 2:16-21.
2. Rejoice that the promised Messiah indeed has come . . . He is <u>now</u> and He is <u>near</u>! Heb. 13:8.
3. Like the wise men, bow in worship before the King, presenting worthy gifts to the One who is worthy, Rev. 4:11.
4. In obedience, humbly serve the Lord of Lords, Who has dominion over all of His creation, Phil. 2:9-11.

Zealous with Godly Zeal

(Numbers 25:1-18)

I. Concentration: on the events of this chapter

1. The Israelites joined with the Moabites in pagan worship of Baal, which included ritual sexual immorality, vv. 1-3.
2. At the Lord's command, Moses ordered the leaders of the apostasy to be hung, vv. 4-5.
3. Phinehas, the son of Eleazar and the grandson of Aaron, executed an Israelite who blatantly committed fornication with a Midianite woman (possibly a religious prostitute), thus stopping the plague (divine punishment) which already had killed 24,000 disobedient persons, vv. 6-15.
4. This seduction of Israel at Baal Peor was caused by the Midianites (probably on the advice of Balaam, Num. 31:8), so they were singled out by the Lord God for vengeance, vv. 16-18.

II. Meditation : on Phinehas, the "zealous" priest

1. He stopped a plague by executing blasphemers, Num. 25, and "it was accounted to him for righteousness," Psa. 106:28-31.
2. He led the Israelite army in a successful war against the forces of the Midianites, Num. 31:6-11.
3. He assisted Joshua in settling the dispute between the ten tribes who occupied the Promised Land and the two tribes who settled east of the Jordan River, Josh. 22:13-34.
4. He became Israel's third High Priest after the death of his father, Eleazar, who had succeeded Aaron, Josh. 24:33.

III. Revelation: on being "zealous with Godly zeal"

Zeal = intense enthusiasm for a cause; passionate ardor for a person.

1. Phinehas was zealous in defending the honor of the Lord from heathen defilement near the tabernacle, Num. 25:6.
2. "The zeal of the Lord of hosts" was prophesied to bring the Messiah . . . "Wonderful Counselor, Mighty God, Everlasting Father, Prince of Peace," Isa. 9:6-7.
3. Zechariah revealed the zeal of the Lord of hosts for His Holy City, Zion (Jerusalem), Zech. 8:1-5.
4. Jesus cleansed the temple (Jn. 2:13-17) in fulfillment of Psa. 69:9, "Zeal for Your house has eaten me up."

IV. Applications: as a Christian, I need to . . .

1. Zealously stand for the holiness of God against the world's wickedness.
2. Zealously worship the Messiah, the Son of God, the Savior of the world.
3. Zealously pray for the peace of Jerusalem, Psa. 122:6, in anticipation of someday dwelling in New Jerusalem, Heb. 12:22; Rev. 3:12; 21:2.
4. Allow the Lord to zealously cleanse His temple . . . my body, Rom. 12:1-2; I Cor. 3:16-17; 6:19-20; II Cor. 6:16-18.

The Second Census of Israel

(Numbers 26:1-65)

I. Concentration: on the new census

1. The new census was taken to help make the division of the land in Canaan equitable, whereas the first census (Num. 1) was to determine military strength, order of march, and battle formation, vv. 52-56.
2. The new census was necessary because all of the first generation of people who made the Exodus had died, vv. 64-65.
3. From this point forward, no more murmurings, complaints, or rebellions by the Israelites are recorded.
4. The problem of inheritance rights for families without male descendants is noted in v. 33; the case is adjudicated in Num. 27:1-12.

II. Meditation: on the results of the census (of males, age 20 and up)

1. The over-all male population decreased from 603,550 to 601,730.
2. Seven tribes increased in population: Judah, Isaachar, Zebulun, Manasseh, Benjamin, Dan, and Asher.
3. Five tribes decreased in population: Reuben, Simeon, Ephraim, Gad, and Naphtali.
4. The greatest change occurred within the tribe of Simeon which decreased from 59,300 to 22,200 . . . a net loss of 37,100 men.

III. Revelation and Applications:

1. The Israelites had increased from 70 men to 600,000 men during the 430 years in Egypt; this means that the male population doubled every generation of approximately 30 years. During the 40 years of wilderness wandering, however, the population remained static (actually declined by 1,820). Why? Many died by God's punishment, rather than by natural causes and old age: Num. 11, 14, 16, 21, & 26. *Lack of growth may be a sign of lack of faith or disobedience . . . in a church and in an individual's life.*
2. The decline of Simeon's tribe from 59,300 to 22,200 signals a serious flaw. *Often a statistical study can reveal the location of a spiritual problem, suggesting where the cause is and where to start seeking a solution.*
3. The sinner executed by Phinehas was Zimri, a leader of the tribe of Simeon, and the 24,000 men who died in that plague probably were those closely associated with Zimri . . . the Simeonites, Num. 25:9, 14. *The influence of one sinful person can do irreparable damage to a family, to a church, and to a nation.*
4. When Joshua divided Canaan among the tribes, he gave no particular plot of land to Simeon, merely allowing the persons of this weakened tribe to settle within the boundaries of Judah's territory, Josh. 19:1-9. *Even the promised purpose and destiny of God may be thwarted by one person's deliberate, blasphemous rebellion.*

Passing on the Torch

(Numbers 27:12-23)

I. Concentration: on God's instructions to Moses about a new leader to succeed him

"Succeed" = (1) to come immediately after, to follow in order, or to take the place of, and (2) to achieve one's aim, or to accomplish one's goals.

1. Choose Joshua, a man in whom is the Spirit, v. 18, Deut. 34:9. *The primary qualification for leadership is a Spirit-filled life.*
2. Set him before Eleazar and the congregation; inaugurate him, v. 19. *Ideally, the old leader is involved in inaugurating the new leader.*
3. Give him some authority, v. 20. *The transition should involve some real delegation of responsibility and authority.*
4. Instruct him in obtaining divine guidance, v. 21. *The top priority of training a successor is in the spiritual realm.*

II. Meditation: on the lessons to be learned from this passage of Scripture

1. Success involves succession. *I am only a success if my work outlives me.*
2. God makes the choice, from among faithful men of faith in whom is the Spirit. *Look for men with (1) faith in God, and (2) faithfulness to duty.*
3. The choice should be made publicly. *It should involve the old leader conferring some responsibility and authority upon the heir apparent.*
4. The retiring leader's main responsibility in the later years is to mentor his successor in "hearing" God. *Spiritual discernment is the vital step necessary before making a decision or taking an action.*

III. Revelation: on "triumphant transitions" in the Bible

1. Moses to Joshua (Num. 27:15-23) . . . delegating authority for leading God's people on a journey toward the Promised Land.
2. David to Solomon (I Chron. 22:5; 29:2) . . . giving plans and making preparations for the building of the temple.
3. Elijah to Elisha (II Kgs. 2:2, 9; I Kgs. 19:15-16) . . . imparting spiritual vision and power to impact a nation and the world.
4. Paul to Timothy (II Tim. 2:2; 4:5-8) . . . encouraging another person to fulfill God's destiny by faithful service in His kingdom.

IV. Applications: in transitioning my ministry, I need to . . .

1. Delegate some responsibility and authority to my successor as the journey toward the "Promised Land" continues.
2. Share with my successor the magnificent vision given to me by God, and make abundant plans and preparations for the future.
3. Allow my successor to accompany me to the sacred place of acquiring a heavenly vision and "doubled" spiritual power.
4. Encourage my successor by affirmation of his divine calling and gifting, and by setting an example of faithfulness and endurance.

God's Cycles of Time

(Numbers 28:1-31)

I. Concentration: on the offering regulations in this chapter

1. The daily offerings, vv. 1-8.
2. The Sabbath (weekly) offerings, vv. 9-10.
3. The monthly offerings, vv. 11-15.
4. The Passover offerings, vv. 16-25.
5. The offerings at the Feast of Weeks (Pentecost), vv. 26-31.

II. Meditation: on these offerings

1. These offerings were to be presented by the people as a whole (nation), rather than as individuals.
2. The burnt offerings twice daily (v. 4) marked the cycle of the day and night, symbolizing that the whole 24-hour period of each day was dedicated to the worship of the Lord.
3. A doubling of the daily offering ("besides the regular burnt offering," v. 10) marked the weekly Sabbath day, during which the Lord was to be worshipped according to Commandment IV, Ex. 20:8-11.
4. The beginning of each month (v. 11) marked an independent cycle of time, distinct from the 7-day week; it too had an appropriate expression of worship of the Lord. *Thus each day, week, and month was committed to the Lord by an act of worship.*
5. This chapter closes by mentioning the offering regulations for two of the nation's annual worship celebrations: Passover and Pentecost.

III. Revelation: on the spiritual implications seen here

1. Each morning and each evening, God's people should pause to worship and praise Him.
2. One day each week, God's people should rest from their work and meet with other believers to worship the Lord.
3. God's people also should worship Him as the calendar page of each new month is turned . . . time is a precious blessing from God, for "time is the stuff life is made of."
4. Annual worship celebrations by God's people are entirely appropriate and absolutely necessary, as reminders of His loving grace and mercy, and of His faithful provision of material and spiritual blessings.

IV. Applications: as a Christian, I need to . . .

1. Spend some quiet devotional time daily in personal worship of the Lord.
2. Set aside the Lord's Day each week, not only to rest from the week's labors, but also to worship Almighty God.
3. Reflect, as each month rolls by, on the brevity of life, and on the privilege and duty of investing my allotted time on earth in service for the kingdom of heaven.
4. Truly celebrate with joy and gladness (not dread and despondency) the Christian holidays each year . . . Merry Christmas! . . . Happy Easter!

Festivals of the Seventh Month

(Numbers 29:1-40)

I. Concentration: on the offerings described in this chapter

1. The Jews used two kinds of calendars: a civil calendar for birth dates and official contracts, and a sacred calendar for religious festivals. *All the religious holidays mentioned in Num. 29 occurred during the 7th month of the sacred calendar (first month of the civil calendar: September).*
2. The Feast of Trumpets offerings were specified, vv. 1-6.
3. The Day of Atonement offerings were specified, vv. 7-11.
4. The Feast of Tabernacles offerings were specified, vv. 12-40.

II. Meditation: on the sacrificial offerings of the Feast of Tabernacles

Day	Mo./Day	Bulls	Rams	Lambs	Goats
1	7/15	13	2	14	1
2	7/16	12	2	14	1
3	7/17	11	2	14	1
4	7/18	10	2	14	1
5	7/19	9	2	14	1
6	7/20	8	2	14	1
7	7/21	7	2	14	1
8	7/22	1	1	7	1

III. Revelation: on the symbolism of this festival

1. Tabernacles commemorated Israel's 40 years of wandering in the wilderness; worshippers at this festival lived in temporary booths for 8 days, each day representing a 5-year period in the desert.
2. The decreasing number of bulls sacrificed from day to day is significant because of the prevalence of pagan rituals involving this animal:
   1) The Egyptian god Apis of Memphis was a bull.
   2) The golden calf constructed by Aaron was a young bull, Ex. 32.
   3) The Canaanite god, Baal, was represented as a bull.
   4) King Jeroboam erected bulls at Bethel and Dan for Israel to worship, I Kgs. 12:26-30.
   It took God only a day to take Israel out of Egypt; it took Him many years to take Egypt out of Israel!
3. On the 7th day, 7 bulls were sacrificed, making a total of 70 during the week . . . again revealing the perfect nature of God's plans.
4. Whereas the number of bulls sacrificed decreased daily, the number of lambs sacrificed remained constant; this suggests the superiority of the sacrifice of the Lamb of God over any pagan approach to God.

IV. Applications: as a Christian, I need to . . .

1. Recognize the temporary nature of my life's journey here on earth.
2. Avoid the contamination of the world's view of God and His works.
3. Understand that all the minute details of God's plans are perfect.
4. Worship the Lamb of God, Who takes away the sins of the world.

Keeping Promises

(Numbers 30:1-16)

I. Concentration: on the laws concerning making and keeping vows

1. These laws came directly from the Lord to Moses, who spoke them to the heads of the tribes, vv. 1, 16.
2. No vows or oaths made by a man of Israel could be broken, under any circumstance, v. 2.
3. A vow made by an under-age daughter could be overruled by her father, if he acted immediately to disavow her oath on the day he heard of it; if the father failed to act that same day, her oath stood, vv. 3-5.
4. A vow made by a married woman could be overruled by her husband on the day he heard of it, or else it stood, vv. 6-8. *This regulation applied to a woman even if she had made the vow before her marriage.*
5. Widows or divorced women who had made vows while married were bound by these same regulations, vv. 9-12.
6. Underage girls whose vows were overruled by their fathers were forgiven by the Lord, with no penalty applied to her or her father.
7. All women whose adult vows had been overruled by their husbands were forgiven by the Lord, but the husbands had to bear their guilt for breaking the vows, vv. 13-15.

II. Meditation: on the obligation of keeping one's promises

1. All males, regardless of their ages, were held totally responsible for fulfilling their vows.
2. Unmarried females living at home were not held responsible for fulfilling their vows, if those oaths contradicted the will of their father.
3. Married women (including widows and divorcees) were not held responsible by God for failure to fulfill their vows, but their husbands who had negated their vows were guilty of the sin of oath-breaking.
4. Fathers and husbands could disavow any oaths made by their female dependents, but they had to take immediate action; delay of more than one day made the oath totally valid, binding, and obligatory.

III. Revelation and Applications: as a Christian, I need to . . .

1. Be very careful in making promises, and faithfully keep those which I have made, unless doing so would harm someone. *(See Judg. 11:30-40.)*
2. Recognize the Godly principle that underage children cannot be held totally responsible for their conduct; parents must accept this responsibility and be pro-active in controlling their children.
3. Understand that widows and divorcees have equal rights in the sight of God, Who is no respecter of persons.
4. Realize that there is no legal, moral, or ethical way for oaths (promises; contracts) to be made null and void without consequences . . . either the person making the obligation (or that person's controlling authority) must bear the responsibility.

God's Vengeance on the Midianites

(Numbers 31:1-54)

I. Concentration: on the events of this chapter

1. At the Lord's command, Phinehas the priest led 12,000 troops to defeat the Midianites; among the fatal casualties was Balaam, vv. 1-11.
2. The troops and the booty were purified, vv. 12-24.
3. The spoils of war were distributed: 50% to the military and 50% to the civilians; all were required to give a portion unto the Lord as an offering to the priests and Levites, vv. 25-47.
4. A special offering of thanksgiving was given, celebrating the fact that not one Israelite soldier was lost in the battle, vv. 48-54.

II. Meditation: on the biblical history of the Midianites

1. Midian, meaning "Strife," was the son of Abraham by his concubine, Keturah, Gen. 25:2.
2. It was the Midianites who bought Joseph from his brothers and sold him into slavery in Egypt, Gen. 37:28, 36.
3. Moses fled from Egypt into the land of Midian, where he married Zipporah, the daughter of Jethro (called Reuel), the priest of Midian, Ex. 2:15-21.
4. Hobab, the Midianite (Moses' father-in-law) guided the Israelites during the wilderness wanderings, Num. 10:29-32.
5. The Midianites were associated with the Moabites in seducing the Israelites into immorality and pagan worship at Baal-peor (Numbers 25:1-18), which resulted in the holy war of vengeance in Numbers 31.
6. Gideon fought and defeated the Midianites in Judges 6-8.
7. Although the Midianites never again threatened Israel, Midian did harbor Solomon's enemy, Hadad, I Kgs. 11:18.

III. Revelation and Applications: on the spiritual implications seen here

1. The Midianites were direct descendants of Abraham. *Being part of the family of a righteous person of faith does not guarantee that the children themselves will live Godly lives.*
2. Through Joseph, and later through Moses, God brought the Midianites into close contact and association with His chosen people. *God always deals graciously with sinful people, giving them numerous opportunities to come to faith in Him.*
3. Not even a close family relationship (such as Moses had with his in-laws) can shield rebellious, sinful people from the judgment and wrath of God. *Here the Lord ordered Moses to wipe out the evil Midianite nation in a holy war.*
4. The influence of an evil father can be evidenced for many generations. *Although the judgment and punishment of God upon the Midianites at Baal-peor was obvious and decisive, they continued to harass and fight against the Lord and His chosen people for centuries.*

Stopping Short of God's Destiny

(Numbers 32:1-42)

I. Concentration: on the events of this chapter

1. The tribes of Reuben and Gad requested permission from Moses to settle east of the Jordan River, rather than inside the boundaries of the Promised Land, proper, vv. 1-5.
2. Moses angrily accused them of committing the same sins (fear and doubt) which had caused the 40 years of wilderness wandering, vv. 6-15.
3. These tribes vowed to go into Canaan and fight until all the other tribes had received their inheritance, before they would return to their homes east of the Jordan, vv. 16-19.
4. Moses gave Reuben and Gad the inheritance they requested, under the condition that they would fight along side their brothers, as promised; the half-tribe of Manasseh also joined Reuben and Gad in occupying land east of the Jordan, vv. 20-42.

II. Meditation: on why Reuben and Gad wanted the land east of the Jordan River

1. It was more convenient; it was "here and now," v. 1.
2. It was fertile and prosperous, with green pastures for their cattle, v. 4.
3. It was a place of safety for their wives and children, because the enemies there already had been defeated, v. 17.
4. It gave them their personal choice, rather than forcing them to participate in the "lottery" by which God's decisions about land allotment to the tribes was made known, Josh. 13-19.

III. Revelation: on what "stopping short of God's destiny" cost these tribes

1. The families (wives and children) of Reuben, Gad, and Manasseh did not get to experience the miraculous crossing of the Jordan River, Josh. 3.
2. These families missed out on the renewal of the covenant and on the resumption of the rituals of worship of God, Josh. 4-5.
3. These families missed experiencing the great victory at Jericho, Josh. 6.
4. These three tribes left themselves exposed and vulnerable (outside the protective canopy of God's covenant of blessing), and they became the first of the 12 tribes to be invaded, defeated, and carried off into captivity, I Chron. 5:26.

IV. Applications: as a Christian, I need to . . .

1. Avoid choosing the convenient, easy, safe place, rather than following the Lord to the place which He has planned for me.
2. Trust in the grace and mercy of God, rather than refusing to move in faith by allowing Him to control my future.
3. Follow God's plan of destiny for my life, which will allow me and my family to worship the Lord, to live under His covenant, to experience His miraculous power, and to rejoice in His marvelous victories.
4. Realize that stopping short of God's destiny places me and my family in jeopardy . . . exposed and vulnerable to attacks by the enemy.

Israel's Journey from Egypt Reviewed

(Numbers 33:1-56)

I. Concentration: on the contents of this chapter

1. Moses wrote of the journeys of the nation of Israel, beginning with the Exodus from Egypt to their camping at Elim, vv. 1-9.
2. He detailed the route from Elim until Aaron's death at Mt. Hor, almost 40 years later, vv. 10-39.
3. Moses listed the rest of the wilderness wanderings from Aaron's burial until their arrival at the Jordan in the plains of Moab, vv. 40-49.
4. Moses spoke the Lord's commands to the Israelites about conquering   and occupying the Promised Land of Canaan, vv. 50-56.

II. Meditation: on the events mentioned here, and those omitted

1. Moses here recorded only two significant events: the miraculous provision of water, vv. 9, 14, and the death of Aaron, vv. 38-39.
2. These emphasized God's provision to sustain their lives for 40 years, and God's sentence of death upon the entire generation who rebelled and refused to enter the Promised Land.
3. Moses omitted recording two supremely important events: the deliverance from Egyptian bondage and the giving of the Law on Mt. Sinai.
4. There was no need the recount these two events because they had been built into the very fabric of the nation's life, as they observed Passover annually and as they participated daily in keeping God's laws and in worshipping Him through the sacrificial system.

III. Revelation: on the rules of spiritual conquest and occupation

1. The Israelites were ordered to completely destroy all idolatry and forms of heathen worship, vv. 51-52.
2. They were ordered to dispossess (drive out) all the ungodly inhabitants of the land, v. 53.
3. They were to divide the land according to God's blueprint, and to occupy and possess their divine inheritance, v. 54.
4. They were to continue to obey the Lord's commands, or they would live in constant turmoil and harassment from their enemies, vv. 55-56.

IV. Applications: as a Christian, I need to . . .

1. Destroy all the "idols" in my life . . . all those things which I worship, that come between me and my full allegiance to the Lord.
2. Cleanse the environment (the community and nation where I work, make my home, and raise my family) from all ungodly influences.
3. Recognize that my divine inheritance not only includes heaven in the future, but that it also includes living and "blooming where God has planted me" in the here and now. *I must recognize and live up to my present divinely destined privileges.*
4. Realize that God's spiritual peace and rest in this life is conditioned upon my obedience to His commands day by day.

The Boundaries of the Promised Land

(Numbers 34:1-29)

I. Concentration: on the events of this chapter

1. The Lord spoke to Moses, specifying the boundaries of the land of Canaan to be possessed by Israel, vv. 1-12.
2. Moses commanded the Israelites regarding the inheritance of the nine and a half tribes which settled west of the Jordan River, vv. 13-15.
3. At God's command, Moses appointed tribal leaders to divide the land among the Israelites, vv. 16-29.
4. Note: this ideal description of the territory of the Promised Land was never fully occupied, even during the largest expansion of the nation under David and Solomon. In fact, the Philistines continued to occupy the coastal areas throughout the entire period of the monarchy and the divided kingdom.

II. Meditation: on the borders of the Promised Land

1. The southern border included the wilderness of Zin to the southern tip of the Salt Sea (Dead Sea), vv. 3-5.
2. The western border was the Great Sea (Mediterranean Sea), v. 6.
3. The northern border included Mt. Hor and ran eastward to Hazor Enan, vv. 7-9.
4. The eastern border ran south from Hazor Enan to the Sea of Chinnereth (Lake Galilee), then followed the Jordan River south to the Salt Sea, vv. 10-12.

III. Revelation: on the men appointed to divide the land

1. Eleazar - the High Priest; son of Aaron, v. 17.
2. Joshua - one of the two surviving "elders," who was Moses' associate and chosen successor, v. 17.
3. Caleb - the other surviving "elder," representing the tribe of Judah, v. 19.
4. All the other tribal representatives had been under the age of 20 when the Israelites rebelled against God almost 40 years earlier, vv. 20-28.

IV. Applications: as a Christian, I need to . . .

1. Thank the Lord that all His promises to me shall be fulfilled; just as He prepared the Promised Land for the Israelites, He is preparing a place in heaven for me, Jn. 14:1-3.
2. Recognize that total victory over my spiritual enemies on this earth will not be achieved within my lifetime.
3. Realize that the reward for faithful service is greater opportunity and responsibility; as it was with Joshua and Caleb, so it is with Christ's followers, Matt. 25:21.
4. Understand that the destiny of God sweeps onward like a mighty river; my degree of faithfulness and obedience determines whether I participate as part of His current of divine purpose or whether I get left behind in a shallow eddy of frustration and uselessness.

Murder and the Death Penalty

(Numbers 35:1-34)

I. Concentration: on the contents of this chapter

1. The Lord through Moses gave instructions about the 48 cities in Canaan which were to be given to the Levites, including the common land surrounding the walls of those cities; six of these 48 Levite cities were to be designated as "cities of refuge," vv. 1-8.

2. The other verses of Numbers 35 regulate the function of the cities of refuge, and include specific regulations about the distinction between murder and manslaughter, and the punishment to be meted out to those found guilty, vv. 9-34.

II. Meditation: on the regulations concerning homicide

1. An individual who killed another person was entitled to a trial to determine whether it was murder or accidental death, v. 11.

2. The accused person was allowed to take asylum from retaliation by a victim's family until a trial was held, v. 12.

3. The "congregation" (probably appointed representatives from among the Israelites who formed a "jury") were the official legal authority to decide the case.

4. "Murder" was defined by these specific examples:
   1) Striking and killing a person with an iron implement, v. 16.
   2) Striking and killing a person with a stone in the hand, v. 17.
   3) Striking and killing a person with a wooden club, v. 18.
   4) "Hate" crimes, including pushing, ambushing, throwing or shooting a weapon, or striking with bare hands, which caused a person's death, vv. 20-21.

5. "Manslaughter" was defined by these specific examples:
   1) Pushing someone to his death without enmity (malice, hatred, or hostility), v. 22.
   2) Throwing a weapon without premeditation, v. 22.
   3) Throwing a stone which accidentally killed someone, v. 23.

6. The accused killer remained in "protective custody" in a city of refuge; he was taken to the place where the crime had been committed for trial; and he was returned to the city of refuge if the verdict rendered was manslaughter, vv. 24-25.

7. The "avenger of blood" was the official, legal executioner chosen by and from the family of the victim to kill the person convicted of murder (or to execute the person convicted of manslaughter if that person left the sanctuary of the city of refuge), vv. 19, 25-28.

8. The death sentence for murder only could be pronounced upon the testimony of at least two eye-witnesses; one witness was not considered sufficient for the death penalty, v. 30.

9. Ransom money was inadequate payment for the death of a person; neither a murderer nor a manslayer could "buy off" his sentence, vv. 31-32.

10. The length of "jail time" the person convicted of manslaughter spent in a city of refuge was in God's hands . . . determined by the length of life of the High Priest, vv. 28, 33-34. *Death had to be atoned for by death; the High Priest's death apparently was a substitutionary atonement for the life of the manslayer.*

III. Revelation and Applications:

1. A land (or a nation) can be polluted (spiritually defiled) by all the killings of human beings which are not appropriately prosecuted and justly punished, vv. 33-34.

2. . The death penalty for murder (both premeditated killings and those committed in angry passion) is the one and only penalty which fits the seriousness of the crime, and which emphasizes properly the value society places upon a human life . . . the life of the victim.

3. Justice in a murder case is more than merely a legal matter of concern to the state; it is a spiritual matter, and the laws of God should and must take precedence.

4. No "loop-holes" exist in God's righteous system of justice: guilty persons must receive their proper sentence and endure their just penalty . . . no paying of a "fine' to be released, and no being "paroled" earlier than serving the full term of their sentence.

Marriage of Female Heirs

(Numbers 36:1-13)

I. Concentration and Meditation: on the events of this chapter

1. The chief fathers of the tribe of Manasseh came before Moses and the other leaders of Israel with a problem, v. 1.

2. The problem related to one of the families of Manasseh, Zelophehad, who had five children, all daughters. The original judgment by Moses (Num. 27:1-11) was that the father's inheritance should pass to the daughters of the family in the absence of any male heirs. The problem mentioned here was the possibility of Manasseh tribal property being inherited by other tribes if the daughters of Zelophehad married outside the tribe of Manasseh, vv. 2-4.

3. Moses commanded the Israelites, according to the word of the Lord, that these women (Mahlah, Tirzah, Hoglah, Milchah, and Noah) were to marry only men from within the tribe of Manasseh; they obeyed this command and their inheritance remained within the tribe of their father's family, vv. 5-12. *Probably if any of these girls had disobeyed and married outside their own tribe, their father's inheritance would have been forfeited.*

4. The final verse of the Book of Numbers concludes the commandments and judgments of the Lord, just before the Israelites crossed the Jordan River toward Jericho, v. 13.

II. Revelation and Applications: on the spiritual implications seen here

1. Whenever a problem arises, people of faith first of all should seek spiritual guidance from the Lord. *"Seek first the kingdom of God and His righteousness, and all these things shall be added to you,"* Matt. 6:33.

2. The basic laws and principles given by the Lord are to be interpreted and applied to practical, day-by-day situations. *"In all your ways acknowledge Him, and He shall direct your paths,"* Prov. 3:6.

3. The directions from the Lord, when followed in humble obedience, bring the desired results to our problems and the needed solutions to our dilemmas. *"Come to Me, all you who labor and are heavy laden, and I will give you rest. Take My yoke upon you, and learn from Me, for I am gentle and lowly in heart, and you will find rest for your souls,"* Matt. 11:28-29.

4. The Lord takes care of all the necessary details of our lives, so that when we move forward at His command, His provisions and preparations are abundant and sufficient. *"I can do all things through Christ who strengthens me . . . My God shall supply all your need according to His riches in glory by Christ Jesus,"* Phil. 4:13, 19.

Moses' Farewell Addresses

(Deuteronomy 1:1-46)

I. Concentration: on the author and background of this book

1. "Deuteronomy" is a word taken from the Greek translation of this book, meaning "Second Law" or the repeating of the law.

2. Moses is the author of this book (1:1) and of the first five books of the Old Testament (31:9); Moses' authorship is acknowledged by Jesus, Peter, and Stephen, Matt. 19:7-8; Mk. 10:3-4; Acts 3:22; 7:37.

3. The Exodus occurred about 1440 B.C. so Deuteronomy likely was written about 1400 B.C. a month before Moses' death at age 120, and just before Joshua led the Israelites into the Promised Land, 1:3.

4. The book contains a series of four farewell addresses by Moses, exhorting Israel many times to "go in and possess" the Promised Land; the final chapter, probably written by Joshua, includes the 30 days of mourning after Moses' death.

II. Meditation: on the main events reviewed in this chapter

1. The time and place of Moses' farewell addresses were given, along with the purpose *("Moses began to explain this law," v. 5)*, vv. 1-8.

2. Moses reviewed the appointment of tribal leaders to assist him in administering justice to the people, vv. 9-18.

3. Skipping for a moment the giving of the Ten Commandments on Mt. Sinai (Horeb), Moses next recounted Israel's refusal to enter the Promised Land some 38 years earlier, vv. 19-33.

4. Moses then spoke of God's penalty for Israel's rebellion: wilderness wandering until the whole adult generation (except Joshua and Caleb) had died, vv. 34-46.

III. Revelation and Applications: on Moses' leadership and mine

1. Moses began his farewell address by once again sharing God's vision of promised blessings for His chosen people, v. 8. *As a Christian leader, I need to share regularly the vision which God has given to me about His purposes and plans for the ministry I lead.*

2. Moses reminded the people of their personal involvement in the leadership process . . . that they shared with him some ownership in the program of fulfilling God's destiny for them. *As a Christian leader, I need to involve others in the mission and plans which God has laid on my heart to accomplish . . . this is not a "one-man show!"*

3. Moses frankly spoke of mistakes and sins which had been committed in the past, which delayed the fulfillment of God's purpose, and which must be avoided in the future. *As a Christian leader, I need to recognize where we have gone astray, and guard against a repeat performance.*

4. Moses pointed out the penalties experienced for disobeying the Lord. *As a Christian leader, I need to encourage faith, obedience, and the pursuit of God's vision, while discouraging fear, doubt, and disobedience.*

You've Wandered Around Long Enough!

(Deuteronomy 2:1-37)

I. Concentration: on the contents of this chapter

1. Moses continued to recount the years of desert wanderings, reminding the Israelites of their passage through the territory of Esau, vv. 1-8.
2. Moses then spoke of Israel's journey through the land of Moab, vv. 9-15.
3. Moses continued telling of Israel's wilderness experiences, speaking to them of their encounter with the people of Ammon, vv. 16-25.
4. After Moses spoke of Israel's encounter with their distant relatives (Esau, Moab, and Ammon) without any harassing or meddling with them, he told of the defeat of King Sihon of Heshbon, one of the Canaanite nations which God had told Israel to destroy because of their heathen religious practices and gross sinfulness, vv. 26-37.

II. Meditation: on some spiritual principles seen in this chapter

1. The Lord God has a time-table for accomplishing His purposes: "You have skirted this mountain long enough; turn northward," v. 3.
2. God takes care of His chosen people and supplies all their needs: "These forty years the Lord your God has been with you; you have lacked nothing," v. 7.
3. God always remembers His promises and faithfully fulfills them to the letter . . . not allowing Israel to take any of the land which He had promised to Esau, v. 5, and to Lot's descendants: Moab, v. 9, and Ammon, v. 19.
4. God's judgment and punishment upon sinful persons is swift and severe . . . after a period of grace, during which sinners often obstinately harden their hearts, vv. 30, 34.

III. Revelation: on the implications of these principles

1. Since God has a time-frame for accomplishing His purposes, His people should be sensitive to His specific directions.
2. God's people should live by faith in His providential care.
3. All of God's promises shall be fulfilled.
4. God is patient and long-suffering, but someday He will come to judge the earth in righteousness.

IV. Applications: as a Christian, I need to . . .

1. Ask for and receive God's revelations of His will, Jas. 1:5.
2. Live and walk daily by faith, Rom. 1:17.
3. Know that what God says, He will surely do, II Pet. 3:8-9.
4. Realize that someday I shall stand before the judgment seat of Christ, Rom. 14:10, 12 . . . therefore, get right with God and stay right through continual repentance, confession, and faith in the Lord.

Moses Blamed Others for His Sins

(Deuteronomy 3:1-29)

I. Concentration: on the contents of this chapter

    1. Moses continued to review the history of Israel by telling of the defeat of Og, the king of Bashan, vv. 1-11.

    2. He then told of dividing the land east of the Jordan River to be the inheritance of the tribes of Reuben, Gad, and Manasseh, vv. 12-17.

    3. Moses commanded these three tribes to lead the battle for the Promised Land, and he encouraged Joshua to lead them to victory, vv. 18-22.

    4. Moses pleaded for God to allow him to enter the Promised Land, but God allowed him only to view it from Mt. Pisgah, vv. 23-29.

II. Meditation: on the sins of Moses

    1. God told Moses to speak to the rock, but Moses struck it, Num. 20:7-13.

    2. Moses' sin was rebellion against hallowing God, Num. 27:12-21.

    3. Moses blamed the people for losing his temper, disobeying God, and forfeiting his privilege of leading them into Canaan, Dt. 1:37.

    4. Even in this chapter, Moses failed to assume the responsibility for his sin: "The Lord was angry for me on your account," Dt. 3:26.

III. Revelation: on the spiritual implications seen in this chapter

    1. Man's disobedience to God's direct commands often brings unforeseen and far-reaching consequences, including frustration, disappointment, and missed destiny.

    2. The rock which brought forth water when smitten symbolized the Messiah, I Cor. 10:4, so Moses' smiting it a second time spoiled God's divine picture and resulted in Moses' punishment, Ex. 17:5-7.

    3. The request of Reuben, Gad, and Manasseh to settle outside of the Promised Land proper meant that they stopped short of God's destiny; this choice cost them dearly . . . see notes on Numbers 32.

    4. Although we cannot know for sure, Moses' failure ever to confess his sin against God and to assume full responsibility for his actions sealed his fate . . . God is full of mercy, grace, and forgiveness, so perhaps God would have allowed Moses the privilege of entering the Promised Land if he had truly repented.

IV. Applications: as a Christian, I need to . . .

    1. Obey the commands of the Lord.

    2. Look for God's providential hand at work revealing Jesus Christ.

    3. Never stop short of pursuing God's destiny for my life.

    4. Continually repent and confess my sins against the Lord; receive God's grace, mercy, and forgiveness.

Take Careful Heed to Yourself

(Deuteronomy 4:1-49)

I. Concentration: on the contents of this chapter

1. Moses commanded the people to obey God's words, vv. 1-14.
2. Moses warned them against idolatry ("For the Lord your God is a consuming fire, a jealous God," v. 24), vv. 15-40.
3. Moses set apart three cities of refuge east of the Jordan River, vv. 41-43.
4. Moses gave an introduction to the Ten Commandments and to the ceremonial, civil, criminal, and social laws to be covered in the following 22 chapters, vv. 44-49.

II. Meditation: on some key verses in this chapter

1. "Surely this great nation is a wise and understanding people. For what great nation is there that has God so near to it, as the Lord our God is to us, for whatever reason we may call upon him?" vv. 6-7.
2. "Only take heed to yourself, and diligently keep yourself, lest you forget the things your eyes have seen, and lest they depart from your heart all the days of your life. And teach them to your children and your grandchildren," v. 9. *(Compare with vv. 15 and 23.)*
3. "But from there you will seek the Lord your God, and you will find Him if you seek Him with all your heart and with all your soul," v. 29.
4. "Therefore know this day, and consider it in your heart, that the Lord Himself is God in heaven above and on the earth beneath; there is no other," v. 39.

III. Revelation: on the spiritual implications of these key verses

1. There is a direct connection between a nation being great (composed of wise and understanding people), and that nation being near to God by calling upon Him in prayer.
2. Mature people of God should engage in careful, spiritual self-examination in the light of God's word and under the guidance of the Holy Spirit; not only should they "take heed," but they also are obligated to teach the next generations about the Lord.
3. The Lord God is available and approachable to those who seek Him sincerely and wholeheartedly, Jer. 29:11-14.
4. God's people must recognize His omnipresence and His uniqueness (There is no other God!); they should meditate upon Him daily.

IV. Applications: as a Christian, I need to . . .

1. Pray for the spiritual health of my nation and its leaders.
2. "Take heed" concerning the condition of my heart before God, and guard my influence upon the coming generations.
3. Worship the Lord God sincerely and whole-heartedly.
4. Meditate daily upon God and His word.

God: the Creator and the Deliverer

(Deuteronomy 5:1-33)

I. Concentration: on the contents of this chapter

1. Moses reviewed the events of the day when he stood on Mt. Horeb (Sinai) to receive the covenant from the Lord God, vv. 1-5.
2. Moses restated the Ten Commandments, originally given in Exodus 20.
3. In great fear, the people begged Moses to act as an intermediary between them and God, vv. 23-27 . . . in this role, Moses was a type of Christ, the "one Mediator between God and men," I Tim. 2:5.
4. The Lord heard their petition and affirmed Moses' role as the man to whom God would speak and the one who would relay God's word to His people . . . "that they may live and that it might be well with them," vv. 28-33.

II. Meditation: on the different reasons given for observing the Sabbath

1. "Remember the Sabbath day, to keep it holy. Six days you shall labor and do all your work, but the seventh day is the Sabbath of the Lord your God. In it you shall do no work . . . <u>For in six days the Lord made the heavens and the earth, the sea, and all that is in them, and rested the seventh day.</u> Therefore the Lord blessed the Sabbath day and hallowed it," Ex. 20:8-11.
2. "Observe the Sabbath day, to keep it holy, as the Lord your God commanded you. Six days you shall labor and do all your work, but the seventh day is the Sabbath of the Lord your God. In it you shall do no work . . . <u>And remember that you were a slave in the land of Egypt, and the Lord your God brought you out from there with a mighty hand and an outstretched arm;</u> therefore the Lord your God commanded you to keep the Sabbath day," Deut. 5:12-15.

III. Revelation: on the Sabbath day commandment

1. In Deuteronomy, Moses interpreted the Ten Commandments for the new situation in Canaan; this is an exposition or selective paraphrase, rather than a word-for-word recitation of the commandments.
2. The Exodus passage emphasizes observing the Sabbath day as a memorial to God, the Creator of the universe.
3. The Deuteronomy passage emphasizes observing the Sabbath day as a memorial to God, the Deliverer from Egyptian bondage.
4. In a further revelation, Jesus taught: "The Sabbath was made for man and not man for the Sabbath. Therefore the Son of Man is also Lord of the Sabbath," Mk. 2:27-28.

IV. Applications: as a Christian, I need to . . .

1. Apply God's word to every situation and circumstance of my life.
2. Praise the Lord God, the Creator of the universe.
3. Thank the Lord God, my Deliverer (Savior) from the bondage of sin.
4. Worship Jesus Christ, the Lord of all . . . including the Sabbath laws.

The Shema ("Hear, O Israel")

(Deuteronomy 6:1-9)

I. Concentration: on the "Shema"

1. "Shema" is a transliteration of the Hebrew imperative meaning, "Hear!"
2. The "Shema" refers to Deut. 6:4-9, which is the basic statement of the Jewish law . . . a confession of faith for the chosen people of God by which they acknowledged the one true God and His commandments.
3. Later worship practices combined Deut. 6:4-9 with Deut. 11:13-21 and Num. 15:37-41 to form the larger Shema, as the summary of the Jewish confession.
4. When Jesus was asked about the "greatest commandment," He answered by quoting the Shema, Mk. 12:29-30.

II. Meditation: on the benefits of keeping God's commandments

1. Long life, Deut. 5:33; 6:2, 24.
2. Prosperity, Deut. 5:33; 6:3, 24.
3. Godly children and grandchildren, Deut. 5:29; 6:2.
4. Fulfillment of God's promises (homeland; property), Deut. 6:18.
5. Victory over enemies, Deut. 6:19.
6. Eternal security, Deut. 5:29.
7. Divine blessings: "So that it might go well," Deut. 5:29, 33; 6:3, 18.

III. Revelation: on "phylacteries" (objects containing Scripture passages)

1. "Bind them as a sign on your hand," v. 8 . . . the Jews did this literally, but missed the spiritual meaning, that all the deeds of a person's hands should be guided by God's word.
2. "They shall be as frontlets between your eyes," v. 8 . . . again the Jews missed the true application, that the thoughts of a person's mind should be guided by the Scripture which has been memorized.
3. "You shall write them on the doorposts of your house and on your gates," v. 9 . . . more important than doing this literally, God's word should guide all the activities within the home, the business, and all the affairs of life's journey.
4. Jesus condemned the hypocritical Pharisees who pridefully enlarged their phylacteries to attract the praise of the common people, Matt. 23:2-7.

IV. Applications: as a Christian, I need to . . .

1. Love the Lord my God with all my heart, Deut. 6:5.
2. Love the Lord my God with all my soul, Deut. 6:5.
3. Love the Lord my God with all my strength, Deut. 6:5.
4. Love the Lord my God with all my mind, Mk. 12:30.

(When Jesus quoted the Shema in Mark's Gospel, He added the word "mind," meaning the understanding.)

"Little By Little"

(Deuteronomy 7:1-26)

I. Concentration: on the contents of this chapter

    1. Moses gave the Israelites God's instructions for dealing with the Canaanites when they entered the Promised Land, vv. 1-5.

    2. Moses spoke of God's special relationship with the Jews, vv. 6-11.

    3. Moses told the Israelites about God's blessings of obedience, vv. 12-15.

    4. Moses encouraged the people by reminding them of God's past victories and of His promises of future ones, vv. 16-26.

II. Meditation: on God's commands concerning the Canaanites

    1. Utterly destroy them . . . showing no mercy, v. 2.

    2. Make no covenant with them, v. 2.

    3. Do not inter-marry with them, v. 3.

    4. Wipe out all aspects of their heathen worship, v. 5.

(These harsh commands executed God's divine judgment upon sinful nations; they also removed future temptation for Israel to forsake their covenant relationship with God, to adopt these foreign gods, and to enter into idolatry.)

III. Revelation: on God's special relationship with the Jews

    1. The Jews were God's holy (separated) people, v. 6.

    2. The Jews were a chosen people, v. 6.

    3. The Jews were a treasured (valued; precious) people, v. 6.

    4. The Jews were a loved people, vv. 7-8.

    5. The Jews were a redeemed (delivered) people, v. 8.

    6. The Jews were a covenant people, v. 9.

    7. The Jews were a people blessed with God's mercy, v. 9.

IV. Revelation: on the blessings promised to God's people

    1. God promised to love them, v. 13.

    2. God promised to bless and multiply them, vv. 13-14.

    3. God promised to prosper them, vv. 13-14.

    4. God promised to give them health and healing, v. 15.

    5. God promised to give them courage, vv. 17-18.

    6. God promised to perform miracles in their behalf, v. 19.

    7. God promised them victory, vv. 19-22.

V. Applications: as a Christian, I need to . . .

    1. Recognize that I am a part of God's holy, chosen, treasured, loved people.

    2. Realize that God has redeemed me in mercy, and included me under His covenant of spiritual blessing.

3. Rejoice that God's blessings include prosperity (all my needs being met), healing, encouragement, and ultimate victory.

4. Receive God's providential care according to His own omniscient time-table: "The Lord your God will drive out those nations before you little by little; you will be unable to destroy them at once, lest the beasts of the field become too numerous for you," v. 22.

Purposes for "Wilderness Wanderings"

(Deuteronomy 8:1-20)

I. Concentration: on selected key verses in this chapter

1. "You shall remember that the Lord your God led you all the way those forty years in the wilderness, <u>to humble you and test you, to know what was in your heart</u>, whether you would keep His commandments or not . . . <u>to do you good in the end</u>," vv. 2, 16.
2. "So He humbled you, allowed you to hunger, and fed you with manna   which you did not know nor did your fathers know, that He might   make you know that <u>man shall not live by bread alone; but man lives by every word that proceeds from the mouth of the Lord</u>," v. 3.
3. "You should know in your heart that <u>as a man chastens his son, so the Lord your God chastens you</u>," v. 5.
4. "Then you say in your heart, 'My power and the might of my hand have gained me this wealth.' And you shall <u>remember the Lord your God, for it is He who gives you power to get wealth</u>," vv. 17-18.

II. Meditation: on God's purposes for our "wilderness wanderings" (vv. 2, 16)

1. To humble us . . . to break our prideful spirits.
2. To test us . . . to examine of commitment and faithfulness.
3. To know what is in our hearts . . . to weigh our motives.
4. To do us good . . . to develop strength and endurance in us.

III. Revelation: on the spiritual truths taught in this chapter

1. God's people should feed on His word, memorizing it as a defense against sin, v. 3; Psa. 119:9, 11; Matt. 4:4, 7, 10.
2. God's discipline always is given in love; His chastening always is for our own good, v. 5; Heb. 12:5-11.
3. God's people should bless His name for His goodness toward us, being very careful not to forget to say "thank you," vv. 10-11.
4. God's people should understand that the Lord owns everything and that we are merely stewards; that, in fact, we are not "self-made financial successes" but God has given us the strength and ability to work and earn money, vv. 17-18.

IV. Applications: as a Christian, I need to . . .

1. Read, study, memorize, and meditate on God's word daily.
2. Receive God's corrective discipline with the proper spiritual under-standing: that it always is given in love, and for my own good.
3. Always be thankful for the Lord's blessings, gratefully expressing to Him my sincere appreciation for His providential care.
4. Work faithfully at my assigned tasks, with the humble recognition that both my job and my ability to work are gifts from the Lord.

The Power of Intercessory Prayer

(Deuteronomy 9:1-29)

I. Concentration: on the contents of this chapter

1. Moses bluntly stated three times that the Israelites were receiving the Promised Land from God <u>not</u> because of their righteousness, vv. 1-6.
2. To emphasize this truth, Moses reminded them of the golden calf incident of rebellion against the Lord, vv. 7-17.
3. Moses related his intercessory prayer for the people and for Aaron (which is not recorded in Exodus), vv. 18-21.
4. Moses then reminded the Israelites of several other times when they had disobeyed the Lord, yet were spared destruction because of his intercessory prayers, vv. 22-29.

II. Meditation: on why God allowed the Jews to conquer and occupy Canaan

1. It was <u>not</u> because of Israel's righteousness and purity of heart, vv. 4-6.
2. It was <u>not</u> because of Israel's yielded and submissive spirit, v. 6.
3. It <u>was</u> because of the wickedness of the Canaanites, vv. 4-5.
4. It <u>was</u> because the Lord had promised the land to Abraham, Isaac, and Jacob, v. 5.

III. Revelation: on the power of intercessory prayer

1. Moses spent 40 days in prayer and fasting before the Lord, after the people had made and worshipped the golden calf; God heard Moses' prayers and refrained from destroying them, nor did He "blot out their name under heaven," vv. 14, 18-19.
2. Moses' intercession for his brother, Aaron, who largely had been responsible for the idolatry, was answered by the Lord, v. 20.
3. Moses also had prayed for the Lord to forgive Israel's sins at Taberah (Num. 11:1-3), at Massah (Ex. 17:7), at Kibroth Hattaavah (Num. 11:4, 34), and at Kadesh Barnea (Num. 13:3), vv. 22-29.
4. Moses was an example of the truth of James 5:16 . . . "The effective, fervent prayer of a righteous man avails much."

IV. Applications: as a Christian, I need to . . .

1. Recognize that truly effective intercessory prayer takes much time and usually should include fasting, Matt. 17:21.
2. Pray for even the most notorious guilty sinners, particularly for those in places of government leadership and religious influence.
3. Intercede for individuals and nations, not on the basis of their worthiness, but plead for them on the basis of God's mercy and grace, and upon His promises to forgive and cleanse.
4. Trust in Jesus Christ, who is my Intercessor and my Mediator, I Tim. 2:5; Heb. 7:25; 9:15.

He Is Your Praise and He Is Your God!

(Deuteronomy 10:1-22)

I. Concentration: on the contents of this chapter

1. Moses told of his second trip up Mt. Sinai, where the Lord God again wrote the Ten Commandments on tablets of stone (to replace the ones Moses had broken), vv. 1-5, 10-11.
2. Moses related the death of his brother, Aaron, and reviewed the Lord's separating of the tribe of Levi to be the worship leaders of the nation, vv. 6-9.
3. Moses emphasized the essence of God's laws, vv. 12-13, 16, 19-20.
4. Moses magnified the Lord, and spoke of His divine power and His purpose for the nation of Israel, vv. 14-15, 17-18, 21-22.

II. Meditation: on the divine assignments given to the tribe of Levi (v. 8)

1. They were "to bear the ark of the covenant of the Lord" . . . to be in charge of God's revealed word, which later included the ministry of teaching these laws to the people.
2. They were "to stand before the Lord" . . . to serve as the mediator between God and the people.
3. They were "to minister to Him" . . . to offer the sacrifices and offerings unto the Lord, which had been presented by the people; to officiate as the people worshipped God.
4. They were "to bless in His name" . . . to speak God's words of assurance, encouragement, comfort, and grace unto the people.

III. Revelation: on God's requirements of His people

1. Fear the Lord, vv. 12, 20.
2. Walk in His ways, v. 12.
3. Love Him, v. 12.
4. Serve Him with all your heart and soul, vv. 12, 20.
5. Obey Him, v. 13.
6. Yield your will to Him, v. 16.
7. Love other people, and care for their needs, v. 19.
8. Hold fast unto the Lord (in a close, intimate relationship), v. 20.
9. Reverence His name whenever you take an oath, v. 20.
10. Praise Him, v. 20 . . . "He is your praise!"

IV. Applications: as a Christian, I need to . . .

1. Fear, walk, love, serve, obey, yield to, hold fast to, reverence, and praise the Lord my God.
2. Worship the Lord "of the highest heavens," Who loves me and Who chose me as one of His own, vv. 14-15.
3. Magnify the Lord . . . "The God of gods and Lord of lords, the great God, mighty and awesome," v. 17.
4. Follow the example of the God of justice and mercy by loving and caring for those needy and hurting persons around me, vv. 18-19.

God's Charge to the Spiritually Mature

(Deuteronomy 11:1-32)

I. Concentration: on the contents of this chapter

1. Moses reminded the adult generation of the Israelites that they had witnessed with their own eyes the mighty acts of God, vv. 1-7.
2. Moses restated God's promises to give the nation a good and prosperous land to be their home, vv. 8-17.
3. Moses charged the parents and grandparents to teach their children about God's miraculous deeds and His marvelous promises, vv. 18-25.
4. Moses called them to choose: either a blessing for obedience or a curse for disobedience, vv. 26-32.

II. Meditation: on some key verses in this chapter

1. "Know today that I do not speak with your children, who have not known and who have not seen the chastening of the Lord your God, His greatness and His mighty hand and His outstretched arm . . . but your eyes have seen every great act of the Lord which He did," vv. 2, 7.
2. "The land which you cross over to possess is . . . a land for which the Lord your God cares; the eyes of the Lord your God are always on it . . . I will give you the rain for your land in its season . . . I will send grass in your fields," vv. 11-12, 14-15.
3. "Therefore you shall lay up these words of mine in your heart and in your soul . . . You shall teach them to your children," vv. 18-19.
4. "Behold, I set before you today a blessing and a curse: the blessing, if you obey the commands of the Lord your God . . . and the curse, if you do not obey," vv. 26-28.

III. Revelation: on the spiritual truths and implications of these verses

1. God's mighty acts of deliverance and chastening are done in full view of discerning people.
2. God watches over His people; He cares for them and blesses them abundantly, supplying all their needs.
3. God commands His people to study, memorize, and teach His word to the next generation.
4. God's blessings or curses are conditional upon the choices people make: whether to obey or to disobey Him.

IV. Applications: as a Christian, I need to . . .

1. Cultivate spiritual perception with regard to God's hand at work in my life and in the world around me.
2. Trust in the Lord, Who compassionately provides for me every day.
3. Meditate daily upon the Scriptures, journaling God's revelations to me to be passed along to my children and grandchildren.
4. Choose to obey the commands of the Lord, thus positioning myself under the canopy of His blessings.

The Place Where the Lord Chooses

(Deuteronomy 12:1-32)

I. Concentration: on the place where the Lord chooses

    1. The Israelites were told to seek "the place where the Lord your God chooses . . . to put His name for His dwelling place; and there you shall go," v. 5.

    2. They were told to bring tithes and offerings to worship the Lord in that place, v. 11.

    3. They were to obey all the Lord's commands in that place, v. 14.

    4. They were to rejoice and celebrate with feasting in that place, v. 18.

II. Meditation: on some spiritual truths about that place

    1. It was to be a place of <u>purity</u> from all forms of sin and idolatry, vv. 2-4.

    2. It was to be a place of <u>submission</u> to God's divine authority, not anarchy: "every man doing whatever is right in his own eyes," v. 8.

    3. It was to be a place of <u>rest</u> . . . of peace, of security, of comfort . . . "home," vv. 9-10.

    4. It was to be a place where God and His people could <u>abide</u> and have spiritual communion and fellowship, v. 11.

III. Revelation: on the spiritual implications seen here

    1. God chooses the place where His people are to worship Him . . . "neither on this mountain, nor in Jerusalem . . . true worshipers will worship the Father in spirit and truth," Jn. 4:21, 23.

    2. God chooses the exact place where His people are to reside on the earth, Acts 17:26.

    3. God chooses the place where His people are to work, Matt. 20:1-16; 21:28.

    4. God chooses the place where His people are to dwell with Him throughout eternity, Matt. 25:31-46; Jn. 14:1-3.

IV. Applications: as a Christian, I need to . . .

    1. Worship the Lord my God with true sincerity and integrity of heart . . . in spirit and in truth.

    2. Thank the Lord for my house and for my home (family).

    3. Recognize that my position . . . my work of ministry . . . is a blessing from the Lord, and that He is the One Who gives me the power and strength to do my job, Dt. 8:18.

    4. Anticipate with joy and gladness the place which Jesus is preparing for me in heaven.

False Prophets and Dreamers of Dreams

(Deuteronomy 13:1-18)

I. Concentration: on the contents of this chapter

1. Moses closed the preceding chapter by warning against false worship, condemning child sacrifice as being a capital offense, 12:29-32.
2. Moses warned against false prophets and dreamers of dreams, who attempted to lead people away from God: such persons were to be executed, vv. 1-5.
3. Moses also warned against family members who attempted to lead people away from God: they were to be executed, vv. 6-11.
4. Finally, Moses commanded that cities, which allowed corrupt men to dwell there and to entice people to forsake God, be completely destroyed along with all the inhabitants, vv. 12-18.

II. Meditation: on prophets who have the power to perform signs and wonders

1. The wise men (sorcerers and magicians) of Egypt were able to perform certain miracles by their enchantments, Ex. 7:10-12.
2. It is possible for false prophets, who are not even known by the Lord, to do wonders in His name, Matt. 7:21-23.
3. "False christs and false prophets will rise and show great signs and wonders to deceive, if possible, even the elect," Matt. 24:24.
4. Such miraculous powers, false signs, and lying wonders are the works of Satan, II Thes. 2:9-12.

III. Revelation: on the spiritual implications seen here

1. Prophecy, dreams, and miracles are genuine, normal means which God uses to speak to His people.
2. However, not only true prophets, but also false prophets, can exercise such supernatural powers.
3. Gifts and powers are not the only (or even the main) test of being a true prophet; words and messages must be examined to discern whether they match what God says in the Scriptures, vv. 2-5.
4. We should examine (test; prove) the fruits of those who claim to speak for God . . . their life-style, character, and influence, as well as their teachings, Matt. 7:15-20; Gal. 5:22-23.

IV. Applications: as a Christian, I need to . . .

1. Be open and receptive to the Holy Spirit's prophetic revelations to me regarding my life and ministry.
2. Recognize that some so-called revelations may originate in my own mind, in someone else's well-meaning but misguided perceptions, or even from Satan, the deceiver.
3. Measure every prophetic word against the infallible standard of truth found in God's Holy Scripture.
4. Carefully examine the fruits of my own life, and the fruits of all other persons who claims to speak for God.

God's People Are to Be "Peculiar"

(Deuteronomy 14:1-29)

(The King James Version translates the word "special treasure" (Dt. 14:2) a "peculiar" in Tit. 2:14 and I Pet. 2:9. "Peculiar" means much more than "odd or strange;" it means "belonging solely to" or, as it is translated in various versions: "royal treasure" or "personal property" or "prized possession.")

I. Concentration: on the contents of this chapter

    1. Moses commanded the Israelites to be different from the heathen nations in the way they viewed life and mourned death, vv. 1-2.

    2. They were to be different in what they ate and how they ate it, vv. 3-21.

    3. They were to be different in the way they worshipped God, vv. 22-26.

    4. They were to be different in the way they cared for the poor and needy, the widows and orphans, the ministers and foreigners, vv. 27-29.

II. Meditation and Revelations: on how God's people are to be "peculiar"

    1. God's people believe in the resurrection and life after death; therefore, they should not mourn as those who have no hope, I Thes. 4:13-18.

    2. God gave His people certain dietary laws to identify them as holy people in the midst of heathen nations, to insure the health of the community, and to test their obedience . . . but God is more concerned with spiritual matters than with physical matters, such as food or drink, Mk. 7:18-19; Acts 10:13; I Tim. 4:1-5.

    3. God's law of tithes and offerings establishes Him as the source of all blessings; in the bringing of these tithes and offerings, His people acknowledge their dependence upon Him. *However, this passage (vv. 22-26) also keeps the law from being unduly burdensome by allowing worshipers to purchase their sacrifices in Jerusalem, rather than having to bring them from the far reaches of the nation; further, the giving of tithes was to be in an atmosphere of joyful celebration.*

    4. God's people are to be like Him in their generous spirit of giving to meet the needs of people . . . plus the caring for the underprivileged releases God's blessings to those who give, v. 29.

III. Applications: as a Christian, I need to . . .

    1. Live my brief life on earth in the light of spending eternity with the Lord, Eccl. 3:11; II Cor. 5:8.

    2. Know that "the kingdom of God is not eating and drinking, but righteousness and peace and joy in the Holy Spirit," Rom. 14:17.

    3. Worship Father God in spirit and truth, Jn. 4:23-24.

    4. Give generously and cheerfully to other persons in the name of Christ, Matt. 10:40-42; II Cor. 9:7-15.

Lessons about Giving and Forgiving

(Deuteronomy 15:1-23)

I. Concentration: on the contents of this chapter

1. Moses commanded the Israelites to cancel all debts at the end of every seven years; this regulation did not apply to money lent to non-Jews, vv. 1-6.
2. The Lord ordered the Jews to be generous in giving alms to the poor and needy, vv. 7-11.
3. Moses reviewed God's laws concerning bondservants: that they were to be released every seventh year with a liberal "severance payment"; if a bondservant so desired, he could voluntarily become a permanent "love slave" to his master's family, vv. 12-18.
4. The Lord commanded that all firstborn males of the herds and flocks (without defects) be sanctified (set apart; consecrated) . . . sacrificed unto the Lord, vv. 19-23.

II. Meditation: on the truths seen in this chapter

1. God provides a plan for His people to become debt-free: His people are to forgive the debts of their brothers and neighbors, releasing them from such economic bondage . . . in effect, this is charitable giving rather than lending money for interest.
2. God requires His people to exhibit compassionate hearts and open, generous hands . . . willingly helping the poor and needy without regard to whether they would be repaid, because the Lord promises to bless and prosper such charity.
3. Persons who voluntarily serve (work; minister) out of a motivation of love for the master are worth twice as much as a person who serves only for money. *(Paul was such a bondservant or "love slave," Rom. 1:1.)*
4. Since God owns the cattle on a thousand hills (Psa. 50:10), man is to acknowledge his stewardship under the Lord's ownership by giving the firstborn (the first and best part) unto the Lord as a sacrifice.

III. Revelation: on the spiritual implications of these truths

1. God has provided a way for my spiritual debts to be forgiven through the Redeemer, the Lord Jesus Christ.
2. God will abundantly bless His people who help the poor and needy.
3. A "love slave" is better than a hireling, Jn. 10:11-13.
4. God's people are to prioritize giving Him the best that they have.

IV. Applications: as a Christian, I need to . . .

1. Forgive others as God has forgiven me, Matt. 6:12, 14-15.
2. "Give and it shall be given unto you . . ." Lk. 6:38.
3. Serve the Lord with the one and only acceptable motive: love, I Cor. 13.
4. Dedicate my best, my all unto the Lord, Rev. 4:11.

The Three Annual Jewish Festivals

(Deuteronomy 16:1-21)

I. Concentration: on the contents of this chapter

1. Moses reviewed the Passover celebration and the Feast of Unleavened Bread, vv. 1-8.
2. He reviewed the Feast of Weeks celebration, vv. 9-12.
3. He reviewed the Feast of Tabernacles celebration, vv. 13-17.
4. He reviewed the establishment of the court system, along with stating the general guidelines for administering justice, vv. 18-21.

II. Meditation: on the three annual Jewish festivals

1. The Passover and the Feast of Unleavened Bread was a celebration of Israel's deliverance from Egypt and the commemoration of the establishment of the covenant community of God, Ex. 12; Lev. 23:5-8; Num. 28:16-25.
2. The Feast of Weeks, also called the Feast of Harvest (Ex. 23:16), the Day of Firstfruits (Num. 28:26), and Pentecost (Lev. 23:16) was a celebration of God's gracious providence in the harvest.
3. The Feast of Tabernacles, also called the Feast of Ingathering (Ex. 23:16; 34:22) was a harvest festival celebrated in the autumn when all the produce had been gathered; every sabbatical (seventh) year, the law was read to all Israel during this festival, 31:9-13.
4. All the males of the nation of Israel were commanded to gather three times each year for these festivals in the place which God chose (Jerusalem), vv. 16-17.

III. Revelation: on the spiritual implications seen here

1. God's people are to celebrate His deliverance from bondage and His establishment of a covenant relationship.
2. God's people are to celebrate His providential care, as He continually supplies all their needs.
3. God's people are to celebrate His divine guidance and protection during their days of wandering on the earth.
4. God's people are to prioritize worshipping the Lord regularly . . . in spite of any inconvenience involved.

IV. Applications: as a Christian, I need to . . .

1. Thank the Lord for His deliverance from bondage (salvation from sin) through Jesus Christ, and for the spiritual relationship I have as His born-again child by grace through faith.
2. Thank the Lord for supplying all my needs.
3. Thank the Lord for His guidance and protection.
4. Worship the Lord regularly and sincerely.

Advice to God's Chosen Leaders

(Deuteronomy 17:1-20)

I. Concentration: on the contents of this chapter

1. Capital punishment by stoning was required for idolaters on the testimony of at least two witnesses, vv. 1-7.
2. Local disputes could be appealed to the priests, Levites, and judges "in the place which the Lord chooses" (later revealed as Jerusalem, the capitol of the nation), and persons refusing to accept the judgment of the high court were to be executed, vv. 8-13.
3. The establishment of the monarchy was foreseen, and kings were forbidden to multiply horses, wives, and silver and gold . . . prohibitions which were violated by many of the kings of Judah and Israel, vv. 14-17.
4. Kings were ordered by the Lord to write personal copies of God's law for their own study, meditation, and guidance, vv. 18-20.

II. Meditation: on the advice to God's chosen leaders (vv. 18-19)

1. Write for yourself in a book a copy of God's word.
2. Keep this hand-written copy with you.
3. Read it every day.
4. Record the points of your spiritual journey in a journal, Num. 33:2.

III. Revelation: on the beneficial results of this discipline (vv. 19-20)

1. God is worshipped reverently.
2. God's word is obeyed carefully.
3. The heart is humbled genuinely.
4. The life is guided righteously.
5. The family is blessed abundantly.
6. Man's service is prolonged significantly.
7. His reputation is remembered eternally.

IV. Applications: as a Christian leader, I need to . . .

1. Daily read, study, meditate, and write God's word, keeping a spiritual journal of His personal revelations to me.
2. Faithfully obey God's word as an act of worship.
3. Live in a humble, spiritual relationship with God, seeking and following His divine guidance for my life.
4. Know that such discipline brings spiritual blessings . . . upon me personally, upon my family, and upon my ministry.

Recognizing True and False Prophets

(Deuteronomy 18:1-22)

I. Concentration: on the contents of this chapter

1. The tribe of Levi was to receive no land in Canaan; rather they were to dwell among the other tribes and be supported by their tithes and offerings, vv. 1-8.
2. The people were warned against pagan religious practices such as child sacrifice, witchcraft, sorcery, and spiritism, vv. 9-14.
3. Moses prophesied that God would raise up for Israel a Prophet from their midst, Who would speak God's words, vv. 15-20.
4. The people were told to examine the words of a prophet: if his words do not come to pass, he is a false prophet and his ministry is to be rejected, vv. 21-22.

II. Meditation: on the Prophet like Moses: Jesus Christ

1. Witnesses to the raising from the dead the son of the widow of Nain identified Jesus as the Prophet, Lk. 7:16.
2. Cleopas on the road to Emmaus identified Jesus of Nazareth as the Prophet mighty in deed and word, Lk. 24:19.
3. Peter, preaching in Solomon's temple after healing the lame man, quoted Deut. 18, identifying Jesus as the Prophet like Moses, Acts 3:22, 26.
4. Stephen, speaking to the mob before they stoned him to death, identified Jesus as the Prophet spoken of by Moses, Acts 7:37.

III. Revelation: on distinguishing between true and false prophets

1. True prophets receive a revealed word (message) from God, and they speak to the people all that the Lord commands, v. 18.
2. All the revealed words spoken by a true prophet do come to pass . . . none of his words "fall to the ground," I Sam. 3:19.
3. False prophets speak presumptuously the words which God has not revealed or commanded them to speak, vv. 20, 22.
4. If the words spoken do not happen (come to pass), that prophet is false; such a person is to be rejected, vv. 20, 22.

IV. Applications: as a Christian, I need to . . .

1. Worship Jesus Christ as the Prophet greater than Moses, Whose message fulfills and supersedes the law of Moses, Matt. 5:17; Heb. 3:1-6.
2. Be careful to speak only the words of truth which the Lord reveals to me.
3. Judge with spiritual discernment the words of those who claim to speak for God, measuring those words by the Scripture, I Cor. 14:29.
4. Refuse to listen to the so-called revelations of false prophets whose words do not come to pass and/or whose words contradict the Bible.

Landmark Regulations

(Deuteronomy 19:1-21)

I. Concentration: on the contents of this chapter

1. Moses ordered the establishment of three cities of refuge west of the Jordan, vv. 1-7. *(Earlier he had established three cities of refuge east of the Jordan, Dt. 4:41-43.)*
2. Moses allowed for three additional cities of refuge if expansion of the nation made it necessary, vv. 8-13. *(See notes on Numbers 35.)*
3. Moses prohibited the removing of landmarks: pillars or heaps of stones forming boundary markers for property lines, v. 14; Gen. 31:51-52.
4. Moses reviewed the laws concerning witnesses, perjury, and the limitation of penalties to fit the crimes committed, vv. 15-21.

II. Meditation: on "eye for eye, tooth for tooth" (v. 21)

1. The principle of *"lex talionis"* was used to prevent extreme brutality in exacting retribution, thus preventing execution for minor damages.
2. Mosaic law (Ex. 21:23; Lev. 24:20) limited vengeance to "<u>only</u> an eye for an eye" or "<u>not more than</u> a tooth for a tooth."
3. In Jesus' day, the Pharisees interpreted this law to mean that the guilty person was <u>required</u> to receive punishment equivalent to the damages which he had caused.
4. Jesus forbade any and all revenge by insisting on His disciples returning good for evil, Matt. 5:38-48.

III. Revelation: on removing "landmarks" (v. 14)

1. Landmarks refer to the original boundaries established by the Lord when He gave the twelve tribes their territory in the Promised Land (Josh. 13-21); landmarks also could apply to all boundaries established by God for His people, such as the Ten Commandments, for example.
2. Moving landmarks was as serious a sin as violence and robbery, Job 24:2 . . . shifting or "watering down" God's standards of righteousness and holiness also is a very serious sin.
3. The ancient landmarks of our fathers (Prov. 22:28) can be applied to the principles of the founders of our nation and to the fundamental beliefs of the Christian faith . . . none of which should be altered or removed.
4. The thwarting or the frustrating of God's plans and purposes also is a grave sin, comparable to removing a landmark, Hos. 5:10.

IV. Applications: as a Christian, I need to . . .

1. Flee to the Lord Jesus, Who is my "city of refuge."
2. As a guilty sinner, ask for the Lord's mercy and grace.
3. Love my enemies; do good to those who hate me.
4. Honor all the "landmarks" established by Almighty God.

The Rules of War

(Deuteronomy 20:1-20)

I. Concentration: on the contents of this chapter

1. The high priest was commanded to encourage the people to be courageous because the Lord God was with them, and He would conquer their enemies, vv. 1-4.
2. Several exemptions to compulsory military service were listed, vv. 5-8.
3. Instructions were given about the cities which the Israelites would besiege; some were allowed to surrender, while others were to be completely destroyed, vv. 9-18.
4. The Israelite soldiers were instructed not to use "scorched earth" tactics in warfare; they were ordered to preserve the trees capable of producing fruit for food, vv. 19-20.

II. Meditation: on the reasons behind the military service exemptions allowed

1. A man who had just built a new house (but not yet dedicated it) was exempted, lest he die in battle and his property would be inherited by another person.
2. A man who had planted a vineyard (but not yet eaten of it) was exempted, lest he be killed and someone else reap the fruit of his labors.
3. A man who was betrothed to a woman (but not yet married) was exempted, lest he become a casualty and someone else marry his fiancee and his family line cease.
4. A man who was a coward (fearful and fainthearted) was exempted, lest he demoralize the other soldiers.

III. Revelation: on the spiritual principles seen here

1. In the eyes of God, the establishment of a home takes priority over civic duties and societal responsibilities.
2. God's system of justice affirms the rule that a person is entitled to reap what he sows . . . "the laborer is worthy of his wages," Lk. 10:7;
3. I Tim. 5:18.
4. The Lord God's first command to human beings was to bear children and to raise them up to honor and glorify Him, Gen. 1:28; Psa. 78:5-7.
5. In the Lord's army . . . in spiritual warfare . . . soldiers who are overcome by fear and doubt do more harm than good, Eph. 6:10-18.

IV. Applications: as a Christian, I need to . . .

1. Get my priorities straight . . . God established the home as the basic building block of society, even before He established national entities or the church.
2. Be careful what I sow, because that is what I'll reap.
3. Train up my children, grandchildren, and succeeding generations in the nurture and admonition of the Lord, Eph. 6:4.
4. Stand faithfully and courageously as a good soldier of the Lord Jesus Christ, II Tim. 2:3-4; 4:7.

Spiritual Principles for Practical Matters

(Deuteronomy 21:1-23)

I. Concentration: on the contents of this chapter

1. Moses gave details about the legal and religious procedures to be carried out by the entire community to put away the guilt of innocent blood in the case of an unsolved murder, vv. 1-9.
2. Regulations were spelled out about Israelite men marrying and divorcing female captives, vv. 10-14.
3. The absolute right of a man's firstborn son to receive a double portion of the inheritance is clearly stated, vv. 15-17.
4. A stubborn, rebellious, disobedient, gluttonous, drunkard son who refused to heed the chastening of his parents was to be stoned, vv. 18-21.
5. Hanging was not a method of execution among the Jews, but sometimes the body of an executed person was hung on a tree until nightfall as a warning to the people that breaking God's laws was costly, vv. 22-23.

II. Meditation: on the spiritual implications of these practical regulations

1. Anonymous murder (along with other violent acts of bloodshed) involve the entire community in corporate guilt, and the community as a whole had to seek atonement; in this case, the heifer's neck was broken as a sign of the punishment the crime deserved.
2. God allowed the Israelite men to take foreign women captive, but they were to forsake paganism before marrying; note, however, that even foreign women captives had certain rights guaranteed by God's laws.
3. God demanded that families maintain the rights and privileges given to the firstborn son, which included not only a double portion of the father's property, but also the duty of family rule and spiritual leadership.
4. The Fifth Commandment about honoring parents is vitally important for maintaining an orderly society.
5. The Apostle Paul quoted Deut. 21:23, "He who is hanged is accursed of God," to draw an analogy to Christ, Gal. 3:13.

(Just as the corpse of the executed criminal was under the curse of God, so Christ hanging on the cross bore the judgment of God . . . the same shame as every condemned criminal. By taking upon Himself the curse of the law, Jesus redeemed us from that curse.)

III. Revelation and Applications: as a Christian, I need to . . .

1. Feel the weight of the blood-guilt of my nation over such violent acts as abortion; seek atonement through the blood of Christ.
2. Treat every person with justice and equality, with compassion and mercy.
3. Recognize that God has an orderly plan for the operation and government of my part of His world; find my proper place in His scheme of authority and submission.
4. Treat my parents and other elders with appropriate honor and respect.
5. Thank the Lord that He loved me and died for my sins.

Love, Holiness, Obedience, Faithfulness

(Deuteronomy 22:1-30)

I. Concentration and Meditation: on the contents of this chapter

1. Persons were ordered to avoid the human tendency not to get involved: they were not to ignore the situation when they saw their neighbor's animals straying; rather they were to take action to retrieve the animals, vv. 1-4.

2. Transvestism, a deviant form of sexual behavior, was forbidden; males and females were ordered to honor the dignity of their own gender by not adopting the appearance and role of the other, v. 5.

3. Preservation of natural resources was taught here, as persons were instructed not to consume both the mother bird and the eggs found in the nest, vv. 6-7.

4. Persons were instructed to take responsibility for protecting others from danger and accidents: a parapet (safety barrier or guard rail) was to be built around the edges of the flat roof of their houses, v. 8.

5. Different kinds of seeds were not to be sown in a vineyard, v. 9.

6. Persons were not to plow with an ox and a donkey together, v. 10.

7. Persons were not to wear a garment made of both wool and linen, v. 11.

8. Persons were to fasten tassels on the corners of their garments as reminders of God's commandments, v. 12; Num. 15:38-40.

9. Persons were taught to value virginity, rather than being ashamed of it; God places a high premium on sexual purity in sharp contrast to today's casual attitude toward sexual relationships, vv. 13-21.

10. Persons were instructed to detest and flee from adultery; they were to   honor marital fidelity, vv. 22-30.

II. Revelation and Applications: as a Christian, I need . . .

1. <u>Love</u>: I am my brother's keeper! Gen. 4:9; God expects His people to help others in need (#'s 1 and 4 above). *I must love and assist my neighbor as did the Good Samaritan, Lk. 10:30-37.*

2. <u>Holiness</u>: the people of God are to behave differently from the pagan society around them . . . "be holy," Lev. 11:45 (#'s 2, 3, 5, 6, and 7 above). *I must "be perfect, just as my Father in heaven is perfect," Matt. 5:48 . . . not sinless perfection in this life, but striving to follow the spiritually-mature, loving example of the heavenly Father.*

3. <u>Obedience</u>: God's people are to be continually mindful of His laws and seek to honor Him in all they do, I Cor. 10:31 (#8 above). *I must acknowledge Him in all my ways, Prov. 3:6.*

4. <u>Faithfulness</u>: the people of God are to live lives of sexual purity, obeying His commandment prohibiting adultery, Ex. 20:14 (#'s 9 and 10 above). *I must remain faithful to the vows (marriage and others) which I have taken before the Lord, Psa. 22:25; Eccl. 5:4-5.*

"No Unclean Thing Among You"

(Deuteronomy 23:1-25)

I. Concentration: on the contents of this chapter

1. Certain persons were to be excluded from admission to the "assembly," the worshipping community: those who were mutilated (eunuchs, Lev. 21:20), illegitimate persons, Ammonites and Moabites (unto the 10th generation), and Edomites and Egyptians (unto the 3rd generation), vv. 1-8.
2. During war, specific rules of hygiene were to be maintained as a symbol of purity, a requirement for God's presence to be among them, vv. 9-14.
3. Escaped slaves were to be given asylum, vv. 15-16.
4. Women and men of Israel were not to become prostitutes with the heathen cult fertility gods of Canaan; a female prostitute was called a "harlot" and a male prostitute was called a "dog," vv. 17-18.
5. Israelites were prohibited from charging interest on loans made to fellow Jews, but usury was allowed in dealing with foreigners, vv. 19-20.
6. All vows made before the Lord must be performed, vv. 21-23.
7. Gleaning by hand in a neighbor's vineyard or grain field was permitted, but not by filling a container or by using a sickle, vv. 24-25.

II. Meditation: on the basic principles seen here

1. There must be a separation between God's covenant people and the unbelievers (pagans, heathen).
2. God's people are to be pure and holy . . . even during war time.
3. God's mercy is to be extended even unto slaves.
4. God demands total faithfulness unto Him; idolatry or worship of false gods is spiritual adultery.
5. God's people are not to take unfair advantage of less fortunate brothers and sisters.
6. Not taking the Lord's name in vain (Commandment III, Ex. 20:7) includes the keeping of all promises made in God's name.
7. God's laws allowing gleaning was His method of providing food for the poor and needy. *(See Matt. 12:1, Mk. 2:23, and Lk. 6:1.)*

III. Revelation and Applications: as a Christian, I need to . . .

1. Live an exemplary life of separation, purity, and holiness (#'s 1 and 2).
2. Extend God's mercy, grace, and charity to others (#'s 3, 5, and 7).
3. Be totally committed unto the Lord, faithfully worshipping only Him (#4).
4. Set a spiritual watch over the words of my mouth, speaking only the truth in love, and keeping all my promises without fail (#6).

Every Detail of My Life Concerns God

(Deuteronomy 24:1-22)

I. Concentration: on the contents of this chapter

1. Moses dealt with divorce, remarriage, and the "honeymoon" period of one year following the wedding, vv. 1-5.
2. Moses interpreted the regulations concerning extending loans and holding various objects as collateral, vv. 6, 10-13, 17-18.
3. Moses discussed other practical matters in the light of God's laws: kidnapping as a capital offense, leprosy as a communicable disease, payment of wages promptly when they are due, and the principle of personal accountability rather than punishing the entire household for the crimes of one family member, vv. 7-9, 14-16.
4. Moses reviewed God's provision for feeding the poor and needy with grain, olives, and grapes, vv. 19-22.

II. Meditation: on the foundational principles seen here

1. The Lord is concerned with the husband-wife relationship within the family; He has established specific guidelines for maintaining godly homes and families.
2. The Lord expects and demands fairness and honesty by His people in all interpersonal and business dealings.
3. The Lord's commands have been given for the benefit of the individual and to maintain order within the community; these regulations are applicable in all matters from personal human rights to community health concerns, from paying wages to capital punishment.
4. The Lord has established the general principle that those who are blessed materially should care for the underprivileged of society.

III. Revelation: on the spiritual implications of these foundational principles

1. The godly home is the basic building block of society; it also is the picture of Christ's relationship with His bride, the church, Eph. 5:22-33.
2. The people of God are to exhibit His characteristics in their daily lives; this includes extending justice and mercy, Matt. 5:48.
3. The Lord is a God of order, and His dominion is to be acknowledged over each and every detail of our lives, Prov. 3:6.
4. The privilege of receiving God's blessings carries with it the duty and the obligation to love others and to be a blessing to them, I Pet. 3:9.

IV. Applications: as a Christian, I need to . . .

1. Maintain a godly home.
2. Exemplify God's mercy toward others.
3. Seek and follow God's will in every detail of my life.
4. Serve as a channel for God's blessings to flow to others.

Crime and Punishment

(Deuteronomy 25:1-19)

I. Concentration: on the contents of this chapter

1. Corporal punishment was allowed for persons found guilty of certain crimes by judges in open court, vv. 1-3.
2. A surviving brother was expected to marry his brother's widow to perpetuate the line of the deceased brother; refusal to do so could result in a court hearing and public, shameful disgrace, vv. 5-10.
3. Other issues were addressed and regulations were established concerning work animals, assault, and weights used in business, vv. 4, 11-16.
4. The Amelikites, who had attacked Israel during the wilderness journey, were to be totally annihilated, vv. 17-19.

II. Meditation: on Jewish laws on crime and punishment

Israelite law with respect to crime and punishment was different from the laws of other cultures in surrounding nations in several ways:

1. Israel did not consider crimes against property to be capital crimes.
2. Israel restricted the law of retaliation to the person of the offender only.
3. In theory, Israel did not observe class differences in enforcement of the law: nobility and commoner, priest and lay person were to be treated equally; even slaves and women had certain limited rights in Israel.
4. Israel could not substitute sacrifices for intentional breaches of the law; sin and guilt offerings were allowed only for unwitting sins, Lev. 4-5.

III. Revelation: on the punishments specified in this chapter

1. Flogging (scourging) of a condemned criminal was to be administered publicly as a deterrent to others; however, wicked men were not to be beaten to death, but rather the number of blows given was to be proportionate to the seriousness of the offense . . . no more than forty lashes, II Cor. 11:24.
2. Spitting in the face of a man who refused to raise up an heir to his dead brother was an act designed to humiliate the guilty man publicly.
3. Removing that irresponsible brother's shoe also was a public act symbolizing the community's reproach and God's judgment.
4. Cutting off the hand of a woman who deliberately tried to injure a man's genitals (vv. 11-12) revealed the depth of the Lord's intention for the Jews to bear children and to establish godly homes.

IV. Applications: as a Christian, I need to . . .

1. Recognize that I am a guilty sinner, deserving of God's punishment.
2. Thank the Lord for His overwhelming love for me, a sinner, Rom. 5:8.
3. Accept Christ's death as the atoning penalty paid for all my sins.
4. Rejoice in God's free gift of mercy and grace which removed my sins.

God Proclaimed Israel His Special People

(Deuteronomy 26:1-19)

I. Concentration: on the contents of this chapter

1. The first proclamation (accompanying the presentation of the firstfruits of the land of Canaan) acknowledged that the Jews now "have come to the country which the Lord swore to our fathers to give us," vv. 1-4.

2. The second proclamation was a review of the Jews' bondage in Egypt and God's miraculous deliverance, vv. 5-11.

3. The third proclamation (accompanying the presentation of the third year's tithe to support the Levites, the foreigners, the orphans, and the widows) asserted that the Israelites had obeyed all the Lord's commands, and asked God to bless them and the land, vv. 12-15.

4. Following these three proclamations, the Lord God proclaimed Israel to be His special people, blessed above all other nations, vv. 16-19.

II. Meditation: on God's proclamation (vv. 18-19)

"Today the Lord has proclaimed you to be His special people" . . . prized possession; personal property; royal treasure.

1. The Jews were people of *promise*, v. 18.

2. The Jews were to be people of obedience, v. 18.

3. The Jews were to be people set on high by God above all nations which He has made . . . exalted in praise, in name, and in honor, v. 19.

4. The Jews were a holy people (consecrated; set apart for a purpose), v. 19.

III. Revelation: on the spiritual implications seen here

1. Through the Israelites, God has revealed His promises of salvation and spiritual blessing to all mankind, Rom. 9:4.

2. Through the Israelites, God has revealed His commandments which are to be obeyed; God's law was "our tutor to bring us to Christ, that we might be justified by faith," Gal. 3:24.

3. Through the Israelites, specifically through the Messiah, the Son of David, God has exalted believers to the position of His children, Jn. 1:12; Gal. 3:26.

4. Through the Israelites, that is through Jesus Christ, believers are clothed with the righteousness and holiness of God, II Cor. 5:21; Gal. 3:13-14; Heb. 12:10, 14.

IV. Applications: as a Christian, I need to . . .

1. Stand in faith upon the eternal promises of God's word.

2. Obey the Lord's commands; but when I do sin . . . repent and confess; receive grace, mercy, forgiveness, and cleansing.

3. Strive to live a life which magnifies the Lord, Who has given me an exalted position of privilege: His "special" child.

4. Be holy in thought, attitude, word, and deed because the Lord God is holy, II Cor. 7;1; I Jn. 3:1-3.

Breaking God's Law Brings Curses

(Deuteronomy 27:1-26)

I. Concentration: on the contents of this chapter

1. When the Israelites crossed over the Jordan River into the Promised Land, they were to set up large stones and write God's laws upon them, vv. 1-10.
2. Six of the tribes (Simeon, Levi, Judah, Issachar, Joseph, and Benjamin) were to stand on Mount Gerizim to bless the people; the other six tribes (Reuben, Gad, Asher, Zebulun, Dan, and Naphtali) were instructed to stand across the valley on Mount Ebal to pronounce curses upon those who disobey God's law, vv. 11-26.

II. Meditation: on the "publishing" of God's laws

1. Since Moses would not be crossing over the Jordan into Canaan, he was joined here by elders and priests (vv. 1, 9) in addressing the people . . . impressing upon these men their future responsibilities as leaders, and impressing upon the people that they should obey these representatives as they spoke for God.
2. The large whitewashed stones were to serve as "billboards" so that all the people could read for themselves the commandments of God . . . this was new and significant!
3. At the place where the law was exhibited, the people were to erect an altar, thus joining the obedience of God's law with true and acceptable worship: obedience is worship, and worship requires obedience.
4. Worship of God not only involves obedience, it also involves sacrifice in the spirit of joyful celebration, v. 7.

III. Revelation: on the sins receiving the curses pronounced from Mount Ebal

1. Making graven images (idolatry), v. 15: Commandment II, Ex. 20:4.
2. Treating parents with contempt, v. 16: Commandment V, Ex. 20:12.
3. Moving a neighbor's landmark (stealing), V. 17: Commandment VIII,
4. Ex. 20:15.
5. Making the blind to wander off the road, v. 18; Lev. 19:14, 18.
6. Perverting justice (false witness), v. 19: Commandment IX, Ex. 20:16.
7. Committing sexual immorality (adultery), vv. 20-23: Commandment VII, Ex. 20:14.
8. Attacking a neighbor secretly or conspiring to slay an innocent person (murder), vv. 24-25: Commandment VI, Ex. 20:13.
9. Failing to confirm (ratify and obey) all the words of God's law, v. 26;
10. Gal. 3:10; Jas. 2:8-11.

IV. Applications: as a Christian leader, I need to . . .

1. Enlist and involve others to assume future leadership responsibilities.
2. Exemplify the spiritual connection between obedience and worship.
3. Magnify loving God and loving my neighbor, Matt. 22:35-40.
4. Say "Amen" to God's justice in punishing sin and disobedience.

God Commands "Overtaking" Blessings

(Deuteronomy 28:1-68)

I. Concentration: on the contents of this chapter

1. Moses lists God's blessings upon obedience, vv. 1-14.
2. Moses lists God's curses upon disobedience, vv. 15-68.

II. Meditation: on the lengthy series of curses recorded here

1. In the preceding chapter, the people were organized to pronounce curses on twelve specific sins, Dt. 27:15-26.
2. In this chapter of 68 verses, the last 54 verses list the horrible, devastating consequences of disobeying God's commands.
3. Paul comments about God's curses upon man's disobedience: *"For the wrath of God is revealed from heaven against all ungodliness and unrighteousness of men,"* Rom. 1:18.
4. The full weight of these curses would be upon believers today if it were not removed by Jesus Christ, Who *"has redeemed us from the curse of the law, having become a curse for us,"* Gal. 3:13.

III. Revelation: on the things that the Lord has promised His people

1. PROMINENCE AND POWER: *"The Lord your God will set you high above all the nations of the earth . . . You will lend to many nations, but you shall not borrow . . . The Lord will make you the head and not the tail; you shall be above only and not beneath,"* vv. 1, 12-13.
2. VICTORY: *"The Lord will cause your enemies who rise against you to be defeated before your face; they shall come out against you one way and flee before you seven ways,"* v. 7.
3. SPIRITUAL RELATIONSHIP: *"The Lord will establish you as a holy people to Himself,"* v. 9.
4. PROSPERITY: *"The Lord will grant you plenty of goods, in the fruit of your body (children) . . . livestock . . . produce . . . The Lord will open to you His good treasure, the heavens, to give the rain to the land in its season,"* vv. 11-12.

IV. Applications: as a Christian, I need to . . .

1. Choose to obey and receive God's blessings, rather than to disobey and bring God's curses upon myself.
2. Know that even if I run away from God's blessings (which I have no intention of doing), His blessings will pursue, overtake, and overwhelm me: *"All these blessings shall come upon you and overtake you,"* v. 2.
3. Realize that when I meet God's conditions of obedience, He commands the blessings to come my way, and what God says always comes to pass! *"The Lord will command the blessing . . . in all to which you set your hand,"* v. 8.
4. With a grateful heart, thank the Lord God for all His abundant and manifold blessings.

The Secret Things Belong to the Lord

(Deuteronomy 29:1-29)

I. Concentration: on some key verses in this chapter

1. "You have seen all that the Lord did before your eyes in the land of Egypt . . . the signs and those great wonders. Yet the Lord has not given you a heart to perceive and eyes to see and ears to hear, to this very day," vv. 2-4.
2. "All of you stand today before the Lord your God (leaders, elders, officers, men, children, wives, foreigners, servants) . . . I make this covenant and this oath, not with you alone, but with him who stands here with us today before the Lord our God, as well as with him who is not here with us today," vv. 10-11, 14-15.
3. "I make this covenant . . . that there may not be among you a root bearing bitterness or wormwood; and so it may not happen, when he hears the words of this curse, that he blesses himself in his heart, saying, 'I shall have peace, even though I follow the dictates of my heart (walk in stubbornness),'" vv. 18-19.
4. "The secret things belong to the Lord our God, but those things which are revealed belong to us and to our children forever, that we may do all the words of this law," v. 29.

II. Meditation and Revelation: on the spiritual implications of these verses

1. There is a huge difference between mere physical sight and spiritual discernment, I Cor. 2:9-16.
2. The Lord intends that all persons be given the opportunity to come under the canopy of blessing provided by His covenant . . . all persons, all ages, all classes, all nations . . . including those yet to be born ("him who is not with us today"), Jn. 17:20.
3. A right relationship with God is a matter of the attitude and the spiritual condition of the heart, Heb. 12:15; Acts 8:23.
4. God is omniscient (He knows all "secret" things); yet He has chosen to reveal some of those mysteries unto His people so that they may come to know, love, serve, and worship Him, Heb. 1:1-2; Amos 3:7.

III. Applications: as a Christian, I need to . . .

1. Ask the Lord for spiritual insight and divine wisdom, Jas. 1:5.
2. Thank God for my "New Covenant" relationship with Him through Christ; share the good news (gospel) message with everyone, as did the shepherds in Lk. 2:10-11, 20.
3. "Keep your (my) heart with all diligence, for out of it spring the issues of life," Prov. 4:23. *(See also Matt. 12:34; 15:18; Mk. 7:21; Lk. 6:45.)*
4. Allow the Holy Spirit to be my Teacher and to guide me into all truth, Jn. 15:26; 16:13; I Jn. 2:20, 27.

In Your Mouth and in Your Heart

(Deuteronomy 30:1-20)

I. Concentration: on the contents of this chapter

1. Moses spoke prophetically, seeing beyond a future Jewish captivity (in Babylon) brought on by disobedience to a period of repentance and restoration, vv. 1-6.
2. Moses described the Jews' future return from exile as a time of blessing and rejoicing, vv. 7-10.
3. Referencing the renewing of the covenant at Moab, Moses reminded the people that the commandment (law) of the Lord did not impose upon them conditions which they could not understand or fulfill; God's word was clear, practical, and realistic . . . so there was no excuse for disobedience, vv. 11-14.
4. Once again Moses repeated his basic call for the people to choose life, good, blessings, and prosperity, rather than death, evil, curses, and poverty, vv. 15-20.

II. Meditation: on the steps to future restoration

1. The Jews must remember that they are in captivity as a consequence of their disobeying the covenant with God, v. 1.
2. They must repent of their sins, v. 2.
3. They must wholeheartedly commit to obeying God's voice, v. 2.
4. God then would deliver them from captivity, v. 3.
5. God would have compassion upon them, v. 3.
6. God would bring them back to the Promised Land, v. 5.
7. God would circumcise their heart, v. 6 . . . a reference to the Messianic covenant when God would deal with man's spiritual problem through an internal transformation, Jer. 4:4; Ezek. 1:19.

III. Revelation: on the word "in your mouth and in your heart" (v. 14)

Paul quoted from Deut. 30:14, "The word is very near to you, in your mouth and in your heart," and he applied it to the word of faith which he preached, Rom. 10:8-10:

1. "If you confess with your <u>mouth</u> the Lord Jesus, v. 9.
2. "And believe in your <u>heart</u> that God has raised Him from the dead, you will be saved," v. 9.
3. "For with the <u>heart</u> one believes unto righteousness," v. 10.
4. "And with the <u>mouth</u> confession is made unto salvation," v. 10.

IV. Applications: as a Christian, I need to . . .

1. Recognize that my sins are against God and that "the wages of sin is death," Rom. 6:23.
2. Repent of my sins, turning from them and turning to the Lord.
3. Believe in my heart that Christ died for my sins, and that He arose in victory over sin, death, and hell.
4. Confess with my mouth that Jesus Christ is my Lord.

Moses Inaugurates Joshua

(Deuteronomy 31:1-30)

I. Concentration: on the contents of this chapter

1. Moses, at age 120, introduced Joshua to the nation of Israel as their new leader who would lead them into the Promised Land, vv. 1-8.

2. Moses wrote the Torah (the first five books of the Old Testament: Genesis through Deuteronomy), and gave it to the Levites for safekeeping with the instructions that every seven years it was to be read to all the people during the Feast of Tabernacles, vv. 9-13.

3. At the Lord's command, Moses and Joshua went into the tabernacle of meeting where, in a private ceremony, Joshua was commissioned as the new leader of Israel by the immediate presence of the Lord appearing in a pillar of cloud; the future apostasy of the Israelites was announced by the Lord so that Joshua would be aware of the danger and strive in his day to prevent it, vv. 14-21.

4. Moses wrote a praise song and officially inaugurated Joshua as the leader of Israel, vv. 22-30. *(Note: Joshua earlier had been designated as Moses' successor in Num. 27:23 and Deut. 1:38.)*

II. Meditation: on the central commands of this chapter

1. That the covenant between God and His chosen people be read regularly.
2. That the "Song of Moses" be written and taught to the people.
3. That the covenant document be placed beside the ark of the covenant and carefully preserved.
4. That Joshua be charged with the responsibility of leading the people in faithfulness to God's commands.

(All of these embody one significant spiritual concern: that Israel would forget her covenant with the Lord God and break it through disobedience.)

III. Revelation: on the spiritual implications seen here

1. God is faithful; He will never leave or forsake His people . . . if there is spiritual separation, it is because the people have moved away from God in disobedience, vv. 6, 8.

2. Everyone is to be taught the word of God, from the youngest child to the oldest senior adult, vv. 12-13.

3. One of the best teaching methods is to learn and sing songs about God and His marvelous works, v. 22.

4. God chooses leaders for His work, and He has a divine plan for a smooth transition into an new era under a new leader.

IV. Applications: as a Christian leader, I need to . . .

1. Trust in God's "great faithfulness," Lam. 3:23.
2. Study God's word and teach it to others.
3. Compose and sing songs of praise unto the Lord.
4. Seek God's leadership and timing about selecting, training, and inaugurating my successor in ministry.

The Song of Moses

(Deuteronomy 32:1-52)

I. Concentration: on some key verses in Moses' song

1. "Let my teaching drop as the rain, my speech distill as the dew, as raindrops on the tender herb, and as showers on the grass," v. 2.
2. "He is the Rock, His work is perfect; for all His ways are justice, a God of truth . . . righteous and upright is He," v. 4.
3. As an eagle stirs up its nest, hovers over its young, spreading out its wings, taking them up, carrying them on its wings, so the Lord alone   led him," vv. 11-12.
4. "Now see that I, even I, am He, and there is no God besides me; I kill and I make alive; I wound and I heal; nor is there any who can deliver from my hand," v. 39.

II. Meditation: on the truths of these selected verses

1. God's word (which is taught by faithful believers such as Moses) is like rain from heaven, producing a renewed spiritual life and an abundant harvest of blessing.
2. The Lord is characterized five times in this song as the Rock, a symbol of stability and reliability (vv. 4, 15, 18, 30, 31); this title emphasizes the unchanging nature of God, Heb. 13:8.
3. God "stirs up" His people to push them out of their comfort zone ("nest"), forcing them to stretch their wings and fly . . . to develop spiritual growth and maturity through exercising their God-given abilities.
4. There is only one God, and He alone is able to give us eternal life, healing from sickness or injury, and the security of eternal salvation.

III. Revelation: on the spiritual implications of these truths

1. Persons who desire to live productive lives here on earth must receive the spiritual, refreshing "rain" (living water) from God's word as administered by the Holy Spirit, Acts 3:19.
2. Jesus Christ is the "Solid Rock" upon which believers should build their lives, Matt. 7:24-27.
3. God wants His people to "soar" into the heavenly places, for that is their birthright, and to "fly" above earth's gravity (sin's downward pull), for that is their true spiritual nature, Psa. 90:10; Eph. 2:6.
4. Almighty "I AM" is the one and only, true and living God . . . the Alpha and Omega, the First and the Last, Who gives to believers the water of eternal life freely, Rev. 21:6; 22:13; Isa. 41:4.

IV. Applications: as a Christian, I need to . . .

1. Receive and channel to others God's life-producing word, II Tim. 2:15.
2. Hear and live-out the teachings of Jesus Christ, my Rock, I Cor. 10:4.
3. Fulfill God's spiritual destiny for me by mounting up with spiritual wings like an eagle, Isa. 40:31.
4. Worship the Lord my God in reverence and awe, I Tim. 1:17; Rev. 4:11.

Moses' Final Blessing on Israel

(Deuteronomy 33:1-29)

I. Concentration: on the contents of this chapter

1. Moses stated the grounds of his blessings upon the nation of Israel: "The Lord came . . . Yes, He loves the people," vv. 1-5.
2. Moses pronounced blessings upon the tribes: Reuben, Judah, Levi, Benjamin, Joseph (Ephraim and Manasseh), Zebulun, Issachar, Gad, Dan, Naphtali, and Asher, vv. 6-25.
3. Moses did not invoke a blessing upon the tribe of Simeon, perhaps because this tribe was soon to be absorbed by Judah, Josh. 19:2-9.
4. Moses concluded his blessings with praises to the eternal God and with joyous words of encouragement to the people, vv. 26-29.

II. Meditation: on some key verses in this chapter

1. "The Lord came . . . with ten thousands of saints," v. 2.
2. "The beloved of the Lord shall dwell in safety by Him, Who shelters him all the day long; and he shall dwell between His shoulders," v. 12.
3. "As your days, so shall your strength be," v. 25.
4. "The eternal God is your refuge, and underneath are the everlasting   arms," v. 27.

III. Revelation: on the wonderful promises given to us here

1. Jude (verses 14-15) wrote of Enoch's prophesy (quoted also in Deut. 33:2): "Behold, the Lord comes with ten thousands of His saints to execute judgment on all," which refers to Christ's coming to judge the world; the saints who accompany Christ to bring judgment are the angels, Matt. 16:27; 25:31.
2. God loves His chosen people, and He causes them to dwell close to Him in safety and security . . . in the place of absolute peace and confidence "between His shoulders," referring to the Lord's strong, burden-bearing capacity.
3. The Lord promises to supply strength to His people for all the days of their lives . . . Moses' "eyes were not dim nor his natural vigor diminished" even at the advanced age of 120 years, Deut. 34:7.
4. The Lord holds His beloved people securely in His "everlasting arms," Mk. 9:36; 10:16; Lk. 2:28.

IV. Applications: as a Christian, I need to . . .

1. Live in expectancy of the Lord's imminent return, I Jn. 3:2-3.
2. Draw near unto the Lord, as He draws near unto me, Jas. 4:8.
3. Depend upon the Lord's strength as I serve Him faithfully, Phil. 4:13.
4. Rest securely in the hands of God the Father, Jn. 10:27-30.

Moses' Death and Burial on Mount Nebo

(Deuteronomy 34:1-12)

I. Concentration: on the contents of this chapter

1. This last chapter of Deuteronomy, which contains the account of Moses' death and burial, probably was written by his successor, Joshua; Deuteronomy covers less than a two-month period, including the thirty days of mourning for Moses' death, Deut. 1:3; Josh. 4:19.
2. Moses viewed all of the Promised Land from the top of Mount Nebo, one in a range of mountains called Pisgah, vv. 1-4.
3. God buried Moses in an unmarked, unknown grave, and the people mourned his passing, vv. 5-8.
4. Joshua, who was "full of the Spirit of wisdom, for Moses had laid his hands on him," assumed the leadership of Israel, vv. 9-12.

II. Meditation: on Moses' final day on earth

1. Moses was allowed by God to see all the Promised Land of Canaan which the children of Israel would occupy . . . from the northern border (Dan) to the southern border (Zoar), and from the Jordan River westward to the Mediterranean Sea.
2. Moses heard the Lord reaffirming His promise to give all the territory he had seen to the descendants of Abraham, Isaac, and Jacob.
3. Moses died with the assurance that his divine mission would continue and be fulfilled through a trusted associate whom he had trained and to whom he had passed along the fullness of the Spirit of God.
4. The Lord buried Moses in an unmarked, unknown grave so that his body and grave-site would not become a place of worship or veneration; Moses' "epitaph" reveals God's unparalleled intimate fellowship with him: "There has not arisen in Israel a prophet like Moses, whom the Lord knew face to face," v. 10. *(See also Jude 1:9.)*

III. Revelation and Applications: as a Christian leader, I need to . . .

1. Allow God to reveal to me His vision of destiny for my life and for the continuation of the ministry He has assigned to me; *I need to realize that God wants to give me spiritual perception, allowing me to see more than I ever will experience here on earth.*
2. Have "ears to hear" God's promises and personal revelations of His will and purpose for my life; *I need to trust in the Lord, knowing that what He says, that He surely will do.*
3. Seek God's leadership concerning the future direction and leader of this ministry; *I need to receive such divine guidance not only so that I may bear fruit, but also so that my spiritual fruit may last (continue and endure), Jn. 15:16; I Cor. 3:9-15.*
4. Serve the Lord faithfully, motivated by love and with a sincere heart of integrity; *I need to give God the glory for all the worthy things He has been able to accomplish through my life, I Cor. 10:31; Gal. 6:14*

COME-REAP Biblical Studies

Genesis Examination   Student's Name: _____

1. According to I Thes. 5:23, a person is made up of body, soul, and spirit. Name the three aspects of the "soul." (Gen. 1)

   (1) _____   (2) _____   (3) _____

2. According to Jesus, Adam and Eve were two actual, historical, created persons. (Gen. 2) (Circle one)   True   False

3. Since God knows everything, why did He ask Adam and Eve a series of questions after they had sinned in the Garden of Eden? (Gen. 3)

   _____

   _____

4. Cain murdered Abel, and then asked God, "Am I my brother's keeper?" How would you answer this question? (Gen. 4)

   _____

5. What was so unusual about the man named Enoch? (Gen. 5)

   _____

6. Name two of the four major sinful conditions in Noah's world. (Gen. 6)

   (1) _____

   (2) _____

7. Noah took two animals of most of the species onto the ark, but he took seven animals of some species. Why did God instruct him to take seven of some of the animal species? (Gen. 7)

   _____

   _____

8. How much time passed between the day when Noah and his family entered the ark and when they exited from it? (Gen. 8) (Circle one)

   (1) 40 days   (2) 150 days   (3) 9 months   (4) More than a year

9. Why did God set His rainbow in the clouds following the flood? (Gen. 9)

   _____

   _____

10. Name Noah's three sons. (Gen. 10)

(1) _____ (2) _____ (3) _____

11. What does the word "Babel" (as in the Tower of Babel) mean? (Gen. 11)

_____

12. List two of the four promises God gave Abram when He called him. (Gen. 12)

(1) _____

(2) _____

13. When Abram separated from his nephew, Lot, what location did Lot choose? (Gen. 13)

_____

14. Abraham gave tithes to the King of Salem. By what other name is this King of Salem known? (Gen. 14)

_____

15. Complete this quotation from Gen. 15:6, "Abram believed in the Lord, and

_____

16. Name the two women involved in a domestic dispute within Abram's household. (Gen. 16)

(1) _____ (2) _____

17. What was the sign of the covenant which God mad with Abraham? (Gen. 17)

_____

18. Who were the three travelers who visited Abraham and Sarah, and who prophesied that the couple would bear a son in their old age? (Gen. 18)

_____

19. Lot and his wife, their two daughters, and the daughter's husbands (6 persons) were warned to flee from Sodom. How many actually escaped to safety? (Gen. 19)

(Circle one)   (1) Two   (2) Three   (3) Four   (4) Six

20. What identical sin did Abraham commit in Gerar (Gen. 20) which he also had committed in Egypt (Gen. 13)?

_____

21. Name the two sons of Abraham, born to Hagar and Sarah. (Gen. 21)

(1) _____ (2) _____

22. Why did Abraham call the place, where he was willing to sacrifice his son, by the Hebrew compound word, "Jehovah-Jireh"? (Gen. 22)

_____

_____

23. What was the occasion when Abraham officially and legally received a permanent "title deed" to a portion of the Promised Land? (Gen. 23)

_____

_____

24. Name "The Four Women at the Well" discussed in the notes on Genesis 24.

(1) _____   (2) _____   (3) _____   (4) _____

25. Identify the twin sons born to Isaac and Rebecca. (Gen. 25)

(1) Isaac favored: _____   (2) Rebecca favored: _____

26. Why did Isaac call the new well which he dug by the name "Rehoboth"? (Gen. 26)

_____

_____

27. Upon which son did Isaac pronounce the "Abrahamic Covenant" blessing? (Gen. 27)

_____

28. What New Testament person may be identified with Jacob's ladder? (Gen. 28)

_____

29. "They (seven years) seemed only a few days to him because of the love he had for her," Gen. 29:20. Identify the persons referred to in this quotation.

(1) "Him" refers to _____   (2) "Her" refers to _____

30. Name the twelve sons of Jacob (Tribes of Israel). (Gen. 30)

(1) _____   (2) _____   (3) _____   (4) _____

(5) _____   (6) _____   (7) _____   (8) _____

(9) _____   (10) _____   (11) _____   (12) _____

31. Laban and Jacob made a covenant and erected a pillar in Gen. 31. Name the pillar and give the meaning of its name.

(1) Name of pillar: _____

(2) Meaning: _____

_____

32. At Peniel, Jacob wrestled with God, Who changed his name to Israel. Define these two names. (Gen. 32)

   (1) Jacob: _____   (2) Israel: _____

33. In Gen. 33, Jacob crossed the Jordan River and settled near Shechem. What famous New Testament landmark, visited by Jesus, id identified with this place?

   _____

34. Why did Simeon and Levi massacre all the males of Shechem? (Gen. 34)

   _____

35. List two of the four possible spiritual meanings of the phrase "going back to Bethel." (Gen. 35)

   (1) _____

   (2) _____

36. List two of the possible four lessons to be learned from the man, Anah. (Gen. 36)

   (1) _____

   (2) _____

37. Describe one of Joseph's two dreams, and explain the interpretation. (Gen. 37)

   _____

   _____

38. Discuss briefly one of the four important spiritual lessons to be learned from Tamar. (Gen. 38)

   _____

   _____

39. What important principle about sin did Joseph proclaim at the time Potiphar's wife was attempting to seduce him to commit adultery? (Gen. 39)

   _____

   _____

40. In prison, Joseph interpreted the dreams of two servants of Pharaoh. (Gen. 40) Circle the one who was executed within three days.

   Butler   Baker

41. Why did Pharaoh have two similar dreams, both predicting seven years of plentiful harvest, followed by seven years of famine? (Gen. 41)

   _____

   _____

42. When Jacob's sons journeyed into Egypt to buy food, which brother remained at home with his father, and which brother remained in Egypt as a hostage until the brothers returned a second time? (Gen. 42)

(1) Brother, at home: _____   (2) Brother, a hostage: _____

43. When Joseph's brothers returned to Egypt a second time, why did he show extreme favoritism to his youngest brother? (Gen. 43)

_____

_____

44. What final test (or trap) did Joseph set to test his brothers' heart? (Gen. 44)

_____

_____

45. Discuss briefly how Joseph's original two dreams (when he was a boy) literally were fulfilled in Egypt. (Gen. 45)

_____

_____

46. Counting Jacob (Israel), and all his sons and grandsons, including Joseph and his two sons, how many Hebrew men settled in Egypt during this period of history? (Gen. 46) (Circle one)

(1) 40   (2) 70   (3) 144,000   (4) Too many to number

47. During the famine in Egypt, all land became the property of the state, and the citizens became "share-croppers." (Gen. 47) What percentage of their crops was paid as taxes to Pharaoh?

_____

48. Name Joseph's two sons, which became equal partners with their uncles to form the "twelve tribes of Israel." (Gen. 48)

(1) _____   (2) _____

49. On his death bed, Israel (Jacob) cursed his three oldest sons (Reuben, Simeon, and Levi) because of their sins. Name the next oldest brother, who was the first to receive his father's blessing, including a "royal" promise. (Gen. 49)

_____

50. What important request/order did Joseph issue before his death at the age of 110 years? (Gen. 50)

_____

_____

COME-REAP Biblical Studies

Exodus-Leviticus Examination   Student's Name _____

1. How long did the Israelites remain in Egypt? (Ex. 1)

   _____ years

2. The notes on Ex. 3 describe four places where a person can find "holy ground." Name two of these places.

   (1) _____

   (2) _____

3. Name the three signs which God gave to Moses in Ex. 4.

   (1) _____   (2) _____   (3) _____

4. Discuss one of the four reasons that Moses became discouraged in Ex. 6.

   _____

   _____

5. Discuss what is meant by Pharaoh's "hardening his heart," and then later by God "hardening Pharaoh's heart"? (Ex. 7)

   _____

   _____

6. From Ex. 8, name two of the four ways Satan attempts to get God's people to compromise.

   (1) _____

   (2) _____

7. To whom did God make this statement: "Indeed for this purpose I have raised you up, that I may show My power in you, and that My name may be declared in all the earth," Ex. 9:16?

   _____

8. What was God's main purpose in sending the ten plagues upon Egypt? (Ex. 10)

   _____

9. Name two of the four ways that the Passover lamb foreshadowed the ministry of Christ. (Ex. 12 and I Cor. 5:7)

   (1) _____

   (2) _____

10. What is the significance of "unleavened bread" in Ex. 13?

_____

_____

11. Name the four main elements of the Song of Moses in Ex. 15.

    (1) _____   (2) _____

    (3) _____   (4) _____

12. What does the word "manna" mean? (Ex. 16)

_____

13. List two of the four implications of spiritual warfare discussed in Ex. 17.

    (1) _____

    (2) _____

14. Jethro, Moses' father-in-law, is known by what two other names in the Bible? (Ex. 18)

    (1) _____   (2) _____

15. According to Jesus, what two great principles are the foundation of God's Law (Ten commandments)? (Ex. 20)

    (1) _____

    (2) _____

16. Why did God's law make cursing or striking one's parents an offense punishable by death? (Ex. 21)

_____

17. Who was the "Angel of the Covenant" in Ex. 23?

_____

18. According to Ex. 24, Moses took one man with him up into the mountain of God, while leaving two other men in charge of the people of Israel down in the valley. Name these three men.

    (1) _____   (2) _____   (3) _____

19. What did the "showbread" and the gold lampstand in the Tabernacle signify? (Ex. 25)

    (1) Showbread: _____

    (2) Gold lampstand: _____

20. What were the names of the two rooms within the Tabernacle? (Ex. 26)

    (1) _____   (2) _____

21. What did the two items on the high priest's breastplate (Urim and Thummim) provide, as indicated by the meanings of their names? (Ex. 28)

    (1) Urim: _____

    (2) Thummim: _____

22. Name the four aspects of the ordination ceremony of the priests in Ex. 29.

    (1) _____ (2) _____

    (3) _____ (4) _____

23. The Book of Exodus reveals the character of God through several redemptive name, such as "Jehovah-Rapha" - God Who Heals (ch. 15) and "Jehovah-Nissi" - God Our (Victory) Banner (ch. 17). In Ex. 31:13, God is revealed as "Jehovah-M'Kaddesh." What does this redemptive name mean?

    _____

24. Contrast law and grace, as seen in Ex. 32:28 and Acts 2:41.

    _____

    _____

25. True or false: God spoke to Moses directly as to a friend, but Moses never actually saw God's face. (Ex. 33) Circle one.

    True   False

26. Ex. 34 speaks of Moses putting a veil over his face when he came down from Mt. Sinai; according to Paul (II Cor. 3), why did Moses hide his face?

    _____

27. What could be the spiritual significance of the wooden objects and furnishings of the tabernacle being overlaid with gold? (Ex. 36)

    _____

28. Name the six furnishings in the tabernacle (Ex. 37-38)

    (1) _____ (2) _____ (3) _____

    (4) _____ (5) _____ (6) _____

29. Just as Moses inspected the construction of the Tabernacle (Ex. 39), even so God someday will inspect and evaluate the quality of our workmanship. God will judge our degree of F_____ and our M_____.

30. The cloud by day and the fiery pillar by night was given to the Israelites for what two main purposes? (Ex. 40)

    (1) _____ (2) _____

31. Name the five sacrifices mentioned in Lev. 1 - 5.

(1) _____ (2) _____ (3) _____

(4) _____ (5) _____

32. Frankincense, part of the offering required in Lev. 2, was one of the gifts brought to Jesus by the Wise Men. What does frankincense signify?

_____

33. What did the requirement in Lev. 3 (that the sacrificial animal must be without blemish) foreshadow in the New Testament?

_____

34. Define "sin of omission" as illustrated in Lev. 5:1 and Jas. 4:17.

_____

_____

35. What does the fire on the altar burning day and night symbolize? (Lev. 6)

_____

_____

36. Why were the priests required to spend seven days and nights within the tabernacle before beginning their ministry? (Lev. 8)

_____

_____

37. In Lev. 9, and three other times in the Bible, the fire of God fell from heaven to consume a man's sacrifice. Name the men involved in these falling-fire events.

(1) _____ (2) _____

(3) _____ (4) _____

38. Name Aaron's two sons who died because they offered "profane fire." (Lev. 10)

(1) _____ (2) _____

39. How do we know that Mary and Joseph were not wealthy? (Lev. 12)

_____

40. Why were persons with leprosy isolated (quarantined)? (Lev. 13)

_____

41. What is the symbolism of the two birds in Lev. 14?

(1) _____

(2) _____

42. What does the sprinkling of blood on the mercy seat teach? (Lev. 16)

    (1) _____

    (2) _____

    (3) _____

43. According to Lev. 17:7, sacrifices which pagans make to false gods are offerings made to

    _____

44. Complete this quotation from Lev. 19:2, "You shall be holy,

    _____

45. List the categories of spiritual crimes that called for the death penalty according to Lev. 20.

    (1) _____   (2) _____

    (3) _____   (4) _____

46. Why were Jewish priests prohibited from any contact with a deceased person, as explained in Lev. 21?

    _____

    _____

47. True worship of God involves these principles (Lev. 22)

    (1) The _____ must be right. (2) The _____ must be right.

    (3) The _____ must be right. (4) The _____ must be right.

48. Most Christians worship on Sunday in fulfillment of the symbolism of what two Jewish festivals? (Lev. 23)

    (1) _____   (2) _____

49. Explain why every day of the year should be celebrated as "Jubilee." (Lev. 25)

    _____

    _____

50. Define the following words found in Lev. 27.

    (1) Consecrate (v. 2) _____

    (2) Vow (v. 2) _____

    (3) Redeem (v. 13) _____

    (4) Devoted (v. 28) _____

COME-REAP Biblical Studies

Numbers-Deuteronomy Examination   Student's Name _____

1. In Israel's first census, the number of men age 20 and above was 603,550. Name the tribe with the largest number of men. (Num. 1)

    _____

2. The tribe of Levi was dedicated to the Lord in place of the firstborn males of all the Israelite families, but there were 273 more firstborn males than Levites. What was done to make up this "shortage" and satisfy God's law? (Num. 3)

    _____

3. Name the three Levitical clans. (Num. 4)

    (1) _____   (2) _____   (3) _____

4. The Nazirite vow (Num. 6) included three aspects; name two of these.

    (1) _____

    (2) _____

5. What was the original minimum and maximum age limits for Levitical service, as written in Num. 8?

    Minimum age: _____   Maximum age: _____

6. When did the pillar of cloud and fire first appear, and when did this miraculous sign of divine guidance disappear? (Num. 9)

    (1) Appeared: _____

    (2) Disappeared: _____

7. During all the wilderness journeys, what was Moses' morning and evening prayer? (Num. 10)

    Morning: "_____, Lord! Let Your enemies be scattered."

    Evening: "_____, O Lord."

8. Who were the "mixed multitude," in Num. 11:4?

    _____

9. What was the sin of Aaron and Miriam in Num. 12?

    _____

10. Name the two men, out of the twelve sent to spy out the land of Canaan, who had faith in God, and list their tribes. (Num. 13)

    (1) _____, tribe of _____   (2) _____, tribe of _____

11. In response to Moses intercession for the rebellious Israelites (Num. 14), two aspects of God's character are revealed. What are they?

    (1) _____

    (2) _____

12. Aaron "stood between the living and the dead," Num. 16:48, foreshadowing what New Testament event?

    _____

13. What did the budding of Aaron's rod confirm? (Num. 17)

    _____

    _____

14. What Old Testament Scripture (in addition to Num. 18:25-32) commanded the Levites to give a tithe from the tithes they received from the other Israelites?

    _____

15. God punished Moses for what two sins he committed? (Num. 20)

    (1) _____

    (2) _____

16. On what occasion did Jesus teach about Moses' lifting up the serpent in the wilderness, as recorded in Num. 21?

    _____

17. In Num. 22, God used a donkey as a "prophet." Name two other occasions in the Bible where God used a donkey.

    (1) _____

    (2) _____

18. Complete the Messianic prophecy in Num. 24:17, "I see Him, but not now; I behold Him, but not near; a _____ shall come out of Jacob; a _____ shall rise out of Israel."

19. Name the priest who was zealous in defending the honor of the Lord from heathen defilement near the tabernacle. (Num. 25)

    _____

20. In Num. 27, Moses chose Joshua to succeed him; what is the primary qualification for spiritual leadership?

_____

21. Name the two kinds of calendars used by the Jews, and the purpose of each one. (Num. 29)

(1) _____

(2) _____

22. Num. 30 gives several regulations concerning making and keeping vows. Discuss briefly the application of these laws as they relate to underage children.

_____

_____

23. When Phinehas led Israel's army to defeat the Midianites (Num. 31), what false prophet was killed?

_____

24. Name the three tribes that stopped short of their destiny, settling on land east of the Jordan River. (Num. 32)

(1) _____   (2) _____   (3) _____

25. Num. 34 describes the borders of the Promised Land, from the wilderness of Zin in the south to Mount Hor in the north. Name the eastern and western borders.

(1) Eastern border (generally): _____

(2) Western border (generally): _____

26. Num. 35 teaches about murder and the death penalty. What is meant by the term, "avenger of blood"?

_____

_____

27. What does the word "Deuteronomy" mean? (Deut. 1)

_____

28. Name two of the three nations who were distantly related to the Israelites, and which they encountered during their 40-years of wilderness wandering. (Deut. 2)

(1) _____   (2) _____

29. Complete this quotation from Deut. 4:29, "You will seek the Lord your God, and you will find Him _____

_____

30. What is "Shema," (Deut. 6)?

_____

_____

31. Why did God drive out the heathen nations "little by little" (Deut. 7:22), rather than all at once?

_____

32. Name God's four purposes for our "wilderness wanderings," Deut. 8.

(1) _____

(2) _____

(3) _____

(4) _____

33. What was the one reason God allowed the Jews to conquer and occupy Canaan? (Deut. 9)

_____

34. Name two of the four divine assignments given to the tribe of Levi . (Deut. 10)

(1) _____

(2) _____

35. From Deut. 12, list two of the four spiritual truths about "the place where the Lord chooses." It was to be a place . . .

(1) _____

(2) _____

36. Spectacular gifts and miraculous powers are not the only test of being a true prophet of God, according to Deut. 13. What else is necessary?

_____

_____

37. What is a "love slave"? (Deut. 15)

_____

38. Name the three annual Jewish feasts. (Deut. 16)

(1) _____

(2) _____

(3) _____

39. What advice did Moses pass along to God's chosen leaders? (Deut. 17:18-19)

(1) _____

(2) _____

(3) _____

(4) _____

40. How can a person know a true prophet from a false prophet? (Deut. 18)

_____

_____

41. Discuss briefly the implications of "eye for eye, tooth for tooth" in Deut. 19.

_____

_____

42. Discuss briefly Paul's purpose of quoting Deut. 21:23 in Gal. 3:13 . . . "He who is hanged is accursed of God."

_____

_____

43. Name the four "Christian" virtues or characteristics mentioned in Deut. 22.

(1) _____   (2) _____

(3) _____   (4) _____

44. What are God's four foundational principles in Deut 24 that should be applied to a Christian's life?

(1) _____

(2) _____

(3) _____

(4) _____

45. Discuss briefly two of the four ways that Israelite law was different from the laws of surrounding nations. (Deut. 25)

(1) _____

(2) _____

46. Name two of the four ideas implied by God's proclamation (Deut 26:18-19) that the Jews were His "special people"? The Jews were . . .

   (1) _____

   (2) _____

47. List the four things or "overtaking blessings" that God has promised His people. (Deut. 28)

   (1) _____   (2) _____

   (3) _____   (4) _____

48. Complete this quotation from Deut. 29:29, "The secret things belong to the Lord our God, but those things which are revealed _____

   _____

49. Complete this quotation from Deut. 33:27, "The eternal God is your refuge, and _____

   _____

50. Why did God bury Moses in an unmarked, unknown grave? (Deut. 34)

   _____

   _____